SYMBOLIC INTERACTION AND NEW SOCIAL MEDIA

STUDIES IN SYMBOLIC INTERACTION

Series Editor: Norman K. Denzin

Recent Volumes:

Volumes 1–35:	Studies in Symbolic Interaction
Volume 36:	Blue Ribbon Papers: Interactionism: The Emerging Landscape
Volume 37:	Studies in Symbolic Interaction
Volume 38:	Blue Ribbon Papers: Behind the Professional Mask: The Self-Revelations of Leading Symbolic Interactionists
Volume 39:	Studies in Symbolic Interaction
Volume 40:	40th Anniversary of Studies in Symbolic Interaction
Volume 41:	Radical Interactionism on the Rise
Volume 42:	Revisiting Symbolic Interaction in Music Studies and New Interpretive Works

STUDIES IN SYMBOLIC INTERACTION VOLUME 43

SYMBOLIC INTERACTION AND NEW SOCIAL MEDIA

EDITED BY

MARK D. JOHNS
Luther College, USA

SHING-LING S. CHEN
University of Northern Iowa, USA

LAURA A. TERLIP
University of Northern Iowa, USA

Emerald

United Kingdom – North America – Japan
India – Malaysia – China

Emerald Group Publishing Limited
Howard House, Wagon Lane, Bingley BD16 1WA, UK

First edition 2014

Reprints and permission service
Contact: permissions@emeraldinsight.com

British Library Cataloguing in Publication Data
A catalogue record for this book is available from the British Library

ISBN: 978-1-78350-933-1
ISSN: 0163-2396 (Series)

Printed and bound by CPI Group (UK) Ltd, Croydon, CR0 4YY

ISOQAR certified Management System, awarded to Emerald for adherence to Environmental standard ISO 14001:2004.

ISOQAR REGISTERED
Certificate Number 1985
ISO 14001

INVESTOR IN PEOPLE

CONTENTS

Dedicated to

Norman K. Denzin
The Father of Qualitative Research

LIST OF CONTRIBUTORS

Shing-Ling S. Chen	University of Northern Iowa, USA
Jeffrey Coons	University of Northern Iowa, USA
Judy Eaton	Wilfrid Laurier University, Canada
Mark D. Johns	Luther College, USA
Michael A. Katovich	Texas Christian University, USA
David Kirschner	Nanyang Technological University, Singapore
Jennifer A. A. Lavoie	Wilfrid Laurier University, Canada
Lara Lengel	Bowling Green State University, USA
Simon Lindgren	Umeå University, Sweden
Annette N. Markham	Aarhus University, Denmark and Loyola University, USA
Justin A. Martin	Southern Illinois University Carbondale, USA
Victoria Ann Newsom	Olympic College, USA
Carrie B. Sanders	Wilfrid Laurier University, Canada
Avi Shoshana	University of Haifa, Israel
Matthew Smith	Wilfrid Laurier University, Canada
Zahirah Suhaimi-Broder	Nanyang Technological University, Singapore
Laura A. Terlip	University of Northern Iowa, USA
J. Patrick Williams	Nanyang Technological University, Singapore

WHEN McLUHAN MET SIMMEL: FORM IS THE CONTENT, MEDIUM IS THE MESSAGE

Shing-Ling S. Chen, Mark D. Johns and Laura A. Terlip

The relationship between form (the structure of a work or medium used) and content (the essence of a work or message conveyed) has garnered much attention from researchers in various fields including sociology, communication, art, film, religion, and philosophy. Among these researchers, Georg Simmel in sociology and Marshall McLuhan in communication provide a resourceful conceptual framework to inform students of communication technologies.

One of Georg Simmel's most notable ideas is how social forms dictate content produced in social interaction (Simmel, 1950, 1972). Social forms such as weddings, funerals, or press conferences with athletic coaches and players, mandate the content of the interaction. In a wedding, the father of the bride, the groom and the best man, all make wedding speeches that are sweet, sentimental, and humorous. In a funeral service, the eulogy delivered is always heartfelt and in praise of the deceased. Dealing with the media, coaches and players all observe the rules to be positive and optimistic, and never air the dirty laundry in public by throwing other coaches and teammates "under the bus." Noticing how social forms informed the content of

Symbolic Interaction and New Social Media
Studies in Symbolic Interaction, Volume 43, 1–5

ISSN: 0163-2396/doi:10.1108/S0163-239620140000043001

interaction (see Fig. 1), Simmel urged researchers to set out to identify forms of social interaction.

Observing how technological formats impacted on human sensory experiences, Marshall McLuhan asserted that effects of media of communication resided in technological features, and not so much in the messages delivered (McLuhan, 1962, 1964). McLuhan noted that the adoption of fixed points of view, made possible by the printing press, contributed to the technique of invention; and the suspension of disbelief, made possible by the electronic media, fostered the enjoyment of audio-visual entertainment. In fact, the best use of any technology requires one to be mindful of the technological features involved. Content thus bears the technological features of the medium used (see Fig. 2). Others concurred with McLuhan's observations that print encouraged reflexive thinking (Eisenstein, 1982), while electronic media rendered human experience fluid and emotional (Couch, 1996). Understanding how technological formats assert their impacts on human sensory experiences, McLuhan urged students of media of communication to centralize technological features in their quest for media effects.

Carl Couch fused together Simmel's discussion of social forms and McLuhan's argument of technological formats, in his examination of not only the relationship between form and content, but more importantly, the relationship between social forms and technological formats (Couch, 1996).

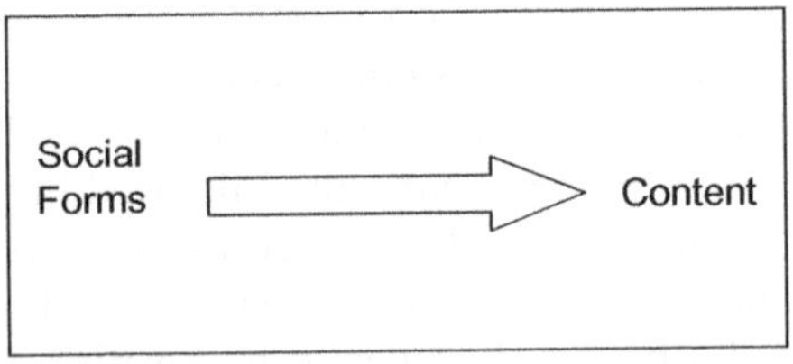

Fig. 1. Simmel's View of Form and Content.

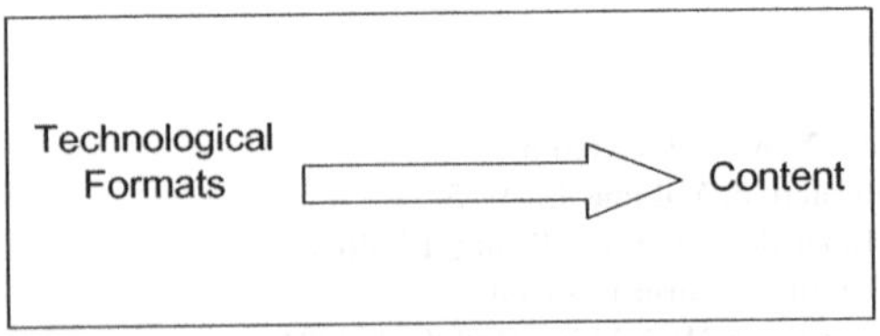

Fig. 2. McLuhan's View of Form and Content.

In his writing, Couch advocated a dialectical view of social forms and technological formats where a multicausal and multidirectional relationship existed (see Fig. 3) between the two. Through the examination of orality, writing systems, printing books and newspapers, as well as the electronic media, Couch articulated a dialectical view where social forms enabled the use of technological innovations, and technological formats, in turn, generated new social forms (Couch, 1996).

In this collection, we witness the dialectical relationship between new social media and social interaction. In "From Object to Flow: Network Sensibility, Symbolic Interactionism, and Social Media," Annette N. Markham and Simon Lindgren recognize the opportunities of social interaction made possible by the new social media, and the complex human relationships generated as a result of it. They advocate the development of network sensitivities in researching social media interactions. They indicate the need to build conceptual and methodological frameworks to better reflect the complexity of mediated communication in social networks.

Jeffrey Coons and Shing-Ling S. Chen in "Social Network Analysis for Facebook: Locating Cliques and Visualizing Sociability," identify the features of the technological format, Facebook, and the presence of the social form, sociability. They propose a research method to articulate the sociability in Facebook, and visualize the relatedness with precision.

In "New Iowa School Redux: *Second Life* as Laboratory," Michael Katovich and Shing-Ling S. Chen extend the utility of New Iowa School laboratory research into the study of human interaction in the online virtual world, *Second Life*. Katovich and Chen juggle between the technological formats, laboratory and *Second Life*, and social forms associated with the two technological contexts. Their argument lays a foundation for the application of New Iowa School laboratory research in the study of social interaction in *Second Life*.

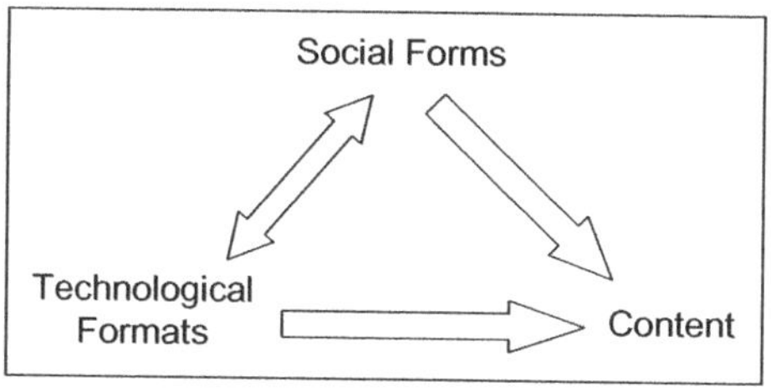

Fig. 3. Couch's View of Social and Technological Forms.

Lara Lengel and Victoria Ann Newsom in "Mutable Selves and Digital Reflexivities: Social Media for Social Change in the Middle East and North America," identify the intricate relationships between social forms and technological formats by highlighting stages of information flow. By examining the role of social media in the "Arab Spring," Newsom and Lengel advance our understanding of the interface between social media and activism.

In "Structural Roles in Massively Multiplayer Online Games: A Case Study of Guild and Raid Leaders in World of Warcraft," J. Patrick Williams, David Kirschner, and Zahirah Suhaimi-Broder articulate the social construction of players' roles in the online gaming environment. By investigating the roles of guild and raid leaders in building and maintaining collaborative group-play online, they highlight the interactive relationship between role construction and online gaming environment.

Justin A. Martin in "(Re)Embodiment of the Digital Self and First Life Body in a New Social Media Environment: Paid Sex Work in *Second Life*," examines paid sex workers in the virtual world of *Second Life*. In his work, we witness how individuals take into account the technological formats offered by *Second Life* to construct both their presentations of selves as well as their interactions with others. Through the action of paid sex workers, we notice that technological formats and social forms amalgamate.

In "Surfing to an Alternative Self: Internet Technology and Sexuality among "Married Straight Homosexual Men"," Avi Shoshana articulates how the technological formats of the Internet enable the construction of sexuality, sexual fantasies, and sexual behavior. Shoshana identifies a form of sexuality that would not have emerged were it not for the Internet. To borrow McLuhan's notion of media as "extensions of man" (1964), the Internet generates the extensions of sexuality.

Whether it is network sensibility, sociability identification, or the New Iowa School laboratory research, advances are made in this volume to adequately research forms of social interaction in the new social media environment. Through raid leaders, paid sex workers, and married straight homosexual men, we witness active construction of symbolic interaction in new social media. The discussion of "Arab Spring" reminds us the dialectic relationship between new social media and symbolic interaction extends beyond the interpersonal level to the macro and global level.

We thank Norman K. Denzin for his guidance and insightful advice in this project. Ten years after the arrival of Web 2.0, it was Denzin's insight to produce a volume to document the progresses made in the research of social media. We are glad to report that researchers, in the course of these ten years, have made significant progress in the investigation of interaction taking place through these rapidly exploding forms of online media. Advancements were made in research methods, as well as in carving out the two leading social media uses: pleasure-seeking/sociability and activism. As we move into the next ten years, we are confident that current research forms a solid foundation for future scholarship.

REFERENCES

Couch, C. (1996). *Information technologies and social orders*. New York, NY: Aldine.

Eisenstein, E. (1982). *The printing press as an agent of change*. Oxford, MA: Oxford University Press.

McLuhan, M. (1962). *The Gutenberg galaxy*. New York, NY: New American Library.

McLuhan, M. (1964). *Understanding media: The extensions of man*. London: Routledge and Kegan-Paul.

Simmel, G. (1950). *The sociology of Georg Simmel*. New York, NY: The Free Press.

Simmel, G. (1972). *Georg Simmel on individuality and social norms*. Chicago, IL: University of Chicago Press.

FROM OBJECT TO FLOW: NETWORK SENSIBILITY, SYMBOLIC INTERACTIONISM, AND SOCIAL MEDIA

Annette N. Markham and Simon Lindgren

ABSTRACT

This article discusses how certain sensibilities and techniques from a network perspective can facilitate different levels of thinking about symbolic interaction in mediated contexts. The concept of network implies emergent structures that shift along with the people whose connections construct these webs of significance. A network sensibility resonates with contemporary social media contexts in that it focuses less on discrete objects and more on the entanglements among elements that may create meaning. From a methodological stance, this involves greater sensitivity to movement and connection, both in the phenomenon and in the researcher's relationship to this flow. The goal is to embody the perspective of moving with and through the data, rather than standing outside it as if it can be observed, captured, isolated, and scrutinized outside the flow. Rather than reducing the scope, the practice of moving through and analyzing various elements of networks generates more data, more

Symbolic Interaction and New Social Media
Studies in Symbolic Interaction, Volume 43, 7–41

ISSN: 0163-2396/doi:10.1108/S0163-239620140000043012

directions, and more layers of meaning. We describe various ways a network sensibility might engender more creative and ethically grounded approaches to studying contemporary cultures of information flow.

Keywords: Network analysis; actor network theory; emergent methods; cultures of flow; qualitative methods; situational mapping

Network analysis, especially as it has been understood in relation to the specific methodological approaches of Social Network Analysis (SNA), is not a tool that is naturally employed by interpretive sociologists, social constructionists, or symbolic interactionists. To state it simply, SNA focuses on the presence of connections between people and the structural dimensions of relations whereas Symbolic Interactionism (SI) focuses on the content or meaning of these relationships as they are enacted and constantly negotiated in everyday communicative interactions. The approaches are seemingly incompatible.

In spite of our issues with the positivist premises and ontological assumptions of standard SNA, we have both been drawn to some of the possibilities offered by a network *sensibility*. On the surface, network maps and visualizations are compelling. They speak to – and make concrete – patterns that we have already started to piece together in our minds. Beneath the surface of their visual impact, we have found that visualizations emerging from network thinking prompt a range of sensibilities not available through analysis of texts. When the tools are separated from the disciplinary parameters for which they were developed, they offer a beguiling method for extending certain approaches, such as grounded theory, SI, or ethnography, and specifying other approaches, such as discourse analysis, actor network theory, or practice theory.

In this essay, we make a case for embracing and critically developing network sensibilities as a way to grapple with the complexity of contemporary social media interactions. Our discussion, mostly focused at the level of method, is intended to contribute to ongoing conversations (e.g., this special issue, as well as Castellani, Castellani, & Spray, 2003; Crossley, 2010; Latour, 2005; Latour, Jensen, Venturini, Grauwin, & Boullier, 2012; Markham, 2012a, 2012b; Salvini, 2010) stressing the need to build conceptual and methodological frameworks that resonate more closely with the complexity of networked, technologically mediated social contexts. Along with the editors of this special issue, we contend that symbolic interactionist concepts remain stymied by ill-fitting but taken-for-granted methods. Most of our methods were designed for and still assume relatively stable, local contexts wherein units of analysis such as individual, speech act, and interaction could be identified and isolated. At least as we write this in early 2012, textbooks still encourage new scholars to draw boundaries around the object of inquiry at very early stages, based on the assumption that the individual and the social are unequivocally linked together as part to whole.

To begin, we clarify the distinction between network analysis and network sensibility. We then discuss three key strengths of using network sensibilities to study the nuances of social media: (1) network practices can generate data and add complexity by producing multiple renderings of potential meaning emerging through social media; (2) the practice of creating and juxtaposing different visualizations and potential explanations of the situation can help shift focus from objects to relations or flow; and (3) through the practice of constantly rebuilding and shifting visual mappings so different elements are highlighted, network analysis can become a catalyst for reflexive and ethical practice.

FROM NETWORK ANALYSIS TO NETWORK SENSIBILITIES

One of the key elements of traditional network analysis is that it maps individuals or other units as points in space by drawing links between them to identify some sort of relationship. The traditional goal of (social) network analysis has been to identify and analyze the structure of relationships in groups. While the approach has been modified and extended somewhat over the years, the unit of analysis remains the pattern of relationships between people, rather than the individuals themselves or the meaning embedded in the individual lines connecting people together.

If we look more closely at the component parts (elements or focal points) of a network analysis approach, we begin to notice sensibilities that resonate strongly with the complexity of computer or internet-mediated, networked cultures. Let us sketch briefly what is implied and invoked in a network approach, which takes us beyond the specific tool or method of SNA.

Even the earliest network studies focused attention on the idea that interaction creates social structures. The premises of network analysis are grounded in general systems theory (e.g., Bertalanffy, 1950), whereby structures – whether biological, organizational, or social – are best understood as the result of ongoing and evolving processes of interrelation among various systems and environmental elements. The concept of a network implies emergent, rather than static, structures that shift along with the people whose connections construct these webs of significance. Capturing an image of a network is rather like taking a snapshot of an ever-moving phenomenon, transforming this flow into a somewhat arbitrary object. This (potentially misleading) aspect of network analysis is not generally highlighted in research reports, because the reader/viewer typically only sees the final capture, not the iterative process of creating it from multiple possibilities. In theory if not practice, network approaches focus on action – the interplay of our dynamic activities with each other, which is the hallmark focus of a symbolic interactionist approach.

This process-oriented view is reflected in the way that a network researcher might create, view, re-center, move, or animate conceptual or analytical maps throughout the course of a study. Although in many cases, the goal is to identify a structure (if not the structure) with some aim of explaining the general context, the process is much more fluid as the method is actualized. When taking apart the practice, the method becomes one that provides information about: the general shape of possible assemblages (in terms of actual or relational size, scope, and range); the position of various nodes (often individual persons); connections among these nodes; the relationships among nodes, to the extent that these can be identified by attributes of a line; and movement (over time or by shifting the focal point of the mapping).[1] Again, there is an underlying temporal component in both the process and product of network analysis, as it is implied that the systems of meaning are always changing.

When separated from the traditional positivistic goals of SNA, a more general network approach includes the inclination toward exploring culture in formation: Humans and/or non-humans interacting and connecting within temporal frameworks to co-construct patterns and structures of meaning, whether ad hoc and temporary or persistent and highly structured over time. Particularly for complex (e.g., Web 2.0) ecologies characterized by convergence, globalization, multiphrenic concepts of identity, and constant shifts in local and global connections, it is necessary to find equally complex tools for thinking. Often this requires disrupting or reconfiguring research methods that are either too rigid or too vague, allowing one to perform, engage, and move with and through data. Network sensibilities are well suited to the symbolic interactionist goal of focusing analytical attention on how identity, meaning, and/or social structures emerge or are negotiated through an ongoing dialogic process.

A network sensibility resonates well with contemporary social media contexts. At one level, the approach involves more visual rendering: Recording and treating as data more of the conceptual and experimental mappings that might otherwise be dismissed as brainstorming. Beyond this, a network sensibility encourages greater sensitivity to movement, connection, and serendipity, both in the phenomenon and in the researcher's relationship to this flow. The goal is to embody the perspective of moving with and through the data, rather than standing outside it as if it can be observed, captured, isolated, and scrutinized outside the flow. Rather than reducing the scope, the practice of moving through and analyzing various elements of networks generates more data, more directions, and more layers of meaning. Indeed, considering the embodied conduct of research, the goal is to acknowledge more senses in the process of sensemaking.

NETWORK SENSIBILITIES AS GENERATIVE TOOL

Most directly, network analysis strategies promote visual mapping of key elements (nodes), connections between them, and the overall structure of the situation, relationship, or system. This type of visualization – which need not look like a typical SNA map – can be used in generative ways throughout a study. By generative, we include the processes of generating data, generating organizational strategies for one's data, generating multiple analytic coding schemes or categories, and generating links between levels such as local/global, relational/structural, and so forth. While the focus may be primarily directed toward the phenomenon, it is equally beneficial to use network sensibilities as a reflexive tool to map one's own conceptual and epistemological standpoints.

Mapping Elements of the Situation

From a traditional cartographic perspective, a fundamental goal of mapping is to identify where one is situated as well as where one has been, in order to direct or guide other travelers unfamiliar with the territory.

When applied to cultural rather than physical terrain, this mapping might produce a visual image of primary or notable landmarks, such as key points of intersection among cultural members, clusters or groupings such as those defined by kinship, age, gender, interests, and key moments, such as rites of passage, rituals, or significant shifts prompted by unusual breaks in patterns. Various images can be used to generate many layers of what might be construed as data, each laid over previous or alternate iterations to illustrate different orientations, generate different objects for analysis, identify different patterns, and demonstrate analytical shifts over time. Clarke (2003, 2005), for example, provides a compelling way to map situations visually, an analytical practice that combines elements of grounded theory, actor network theory, and traditional sociological mapping techniques. The key to this type of "situational analysis" is to use one's field data to generate still more data for analysis. The process is to generate various kinds of maps: Situational maps identify the major human, non-human, discursive, and other elements influencing a situation, as framed by those in the situation as well as the analyst (Clarke, 2003, p. 559). Relational maps take each element in turn as the center of the network, considering the nature of the relationship between this element and other elements that have been specified in the situation. Although tedious, this process of shifting the networks in a meticulous way can trigger important analytical breakthroughs, particularly patterns or elements that are obscure or nonobvious to those in the situation (p. 569). Social worlds/arenas maps, "lay out all the collective actors and the arena(s) of commitment within which they engage" the situation (p. 559). Position maps "lay out the major positions taken and not taken, in the data vis-a-vis particular discursive axes of variation and difference, concern, and controversy" (p. 560).

By creating this range of maps of the situation, the researcher focuses in serial fashion on particular elements of the situation (a person, an issue, an event, a time period, a theme, a technology or medium, etc.) or notable patterns in larger assemblages. Through this process of analysis, more complicated understandings of the situation emerge. This process cannot help but be deeply iterative with each pass through the data.

Adding Complexity

To draw a map is to lay out elements in relation, so as to find or create a pattern that is sensible for a particular purpose or audience. Setting aside the practical aspects of mapping as the process of producing a verisimilitude and simplification of the "landscape" so that others can find their way without getting lost, one can begin to note the more creative aspects of mapping as a process of adding complexity to the situation, generating additional data for research. This might seem to fly in the face of the goal of narrowing one's research scope to a sensible level, but highlights a crucial element of qualitative inquiry: seeking depth and complexity in order to reach thick description. Geertz classically described these multiple layers of meaning "winks upon winks" (1973, p. 9). Playing with different possible mappings can help pull this complexity to the surface, to identify certain general patterns or curiosities that might not otherwise be noticed. This acknowledges the challenge that despite one's goal of identifying a discrete object for inquiry, the object will always be entangled in larger patterns and flows of meaning that operate both at the surface, observable levels and also at less visible, deep structure levels. When adding the premise of swiftly shifting or ad hoc structures, which is an inherent aspect of social media, the utility of situational network mapping becomes more meaningful.

To see how this might work in practice, let's walk through an example of social media following the Japanese earthquake in early 2011. This event had monumental physical consequences and sparked a global series of overlapping and intermingled reactions. As a research phenomenon, it is overwhelming. Still, quelling the urge to describe or explain the entire situation, we can begin with a baseline question of "How did people make sense of the Japanese earthquake through social media?" The frames within which we pose this question are already being formed as we surf interesting data paths and sort various aspects of the situation into our own conceptual frameworks. We are already operating at the structural level, the individual level, and anywhere between. The eventual goal, given our grounding in a symbolic interaction approach, is to focus attention on how meanings emerge or shift through interaction. The initial goal, however, is to track and log those surfing practices that comprise early sensemaking. A fraction of this is illustrated below, to help describe the impact of mapping on the way we might shape research questions and begin to frame the contexts for further study.

We watched the event through our own social media feeds; specifically Twitter and Facebook. Once we realized what was happening, we started following specific hashtags, such as #japan, #tsunami, and #prayforjapan (see Fig. 1).[2] We watched Twitter updates scrolling too fast on our screens for us to decipher individual messages before they disappeared (Fig. 2).

Fig. 1. Author screenshot of a typical Twitter feed for the "Pray for Japan" hashtag.

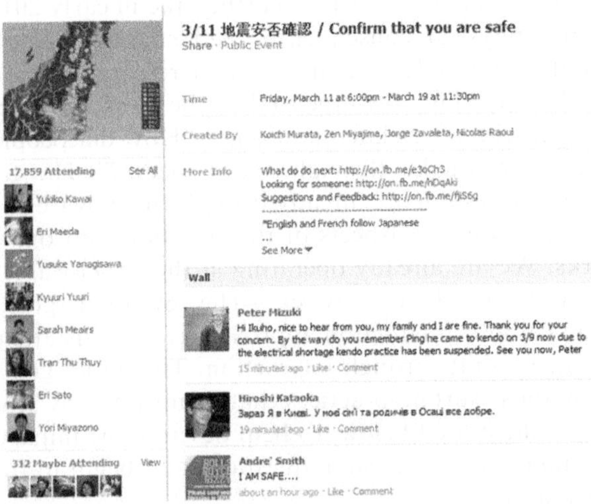

Fig. 2. Author screenshot of Facebook page setup to facilitate contact between people to confirm they are safe.

Stopping the flow and clicking on various links took us to images, videos, and news outlets covering the earthquake. Over the next few days, we framed and reframed the situation, like everyone else paying attention. We processed this event with our friends via social media, meaning emerging and morphing with each piece of information we clicked on (see Figs. 2, 3, and 4).

Fig. 3. Author screenshot of results of search for "Pray for Japan" images.

Fig. 4. Author screenshot of YouTube video of Russia Times televised newscast.

We found it fascinating to watch how various stakeholders or interested observers highlighted distinctive aspects of the situation, whether and how certain visualizations were noticed or passed along, and how the frame of the situation changed over time. Take the number of Tweets and Retweets during the hours following the quake, for example. Creating an animated visualization of the initial response to the disaster by individuals across the globe, as Twitter did (Fig. 5), frames the event in a particular way, focusing our attention on this particular moment, one layer of information among a multitude of possibilities. The visualization is best seen in its animated version, but the screenshot shown here is still compelling.

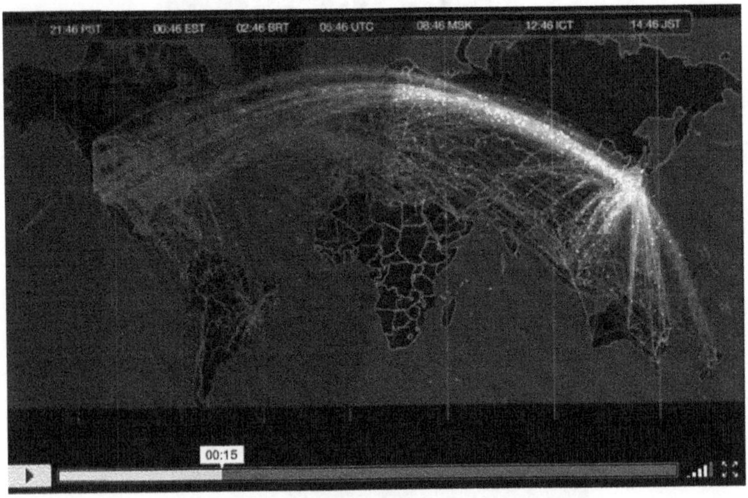

Fig. 5. Screenshot from Twitter's visualization of worldwide retweets of tweets originating in Japan for one hour after the earthquake. In this black/white image, senders' original tweets are brighter, while retweets are darker (Twitter, 2011).

Zooming in on particular messages, one could draw more detailed mappings based on the content of the messages. Alternately, one could zoom in and then follow any unit of information as it moves and morphs (or withers and fades). Take, for example, a YouTube video entitled "Japan," passed around a small network (Figs. 6 and 7).

If the idea of building complexity is taken seriously, this single instance of posting a video on Facebook soon generates data, not necessarily

Figs. 6 and 7. Author screenshot and close-up from YouTube video entitled "Japan," which was posted on a Facebook page shortly after the Japanese earthquake of early 2011 (Aikisystema, 2011).

including the content of the video itself but information about how it functions as part of a larger conversation among a network of individuals. The act of posting the video to Facebook is not just a speech act (and that may not be the best term for it), but adds what Goffman (1974) would call laminations. The video is "up-keyed" in the sense that an additional layer, or lamination, is added between the more literal act that is represented and its potential audience (Goffman, 1974). While the initial video clip on YouTube adds one lamination (this is not the actual event, it's a YouTube page labeled "Japan" that highlights and presents a recording of the event), the recirculation of the same (actually excerpted) content on Facebook by various individuals adds yet another lamination (this is not the actual event, nor is it the YouTube page about the event – it is a video clip about the event embedded in a Facebook status update). Each frame functions rhetorically to impose certain expectations about how the content should be interpreted and responded to. Additional frames are found when we look at the "suggested" videos on the YouTube page, the title of "Japan," on the YouTube page (it turns out this video is not actually Japan or Japanese), and the timing of the posting on Facebook, which follows closely the earthquakes in Japan in March 2011.

These laminations, layers, or mappings are part of our network sensibility. We illustrate two possibilities below: The first map identifies a sketch of certain elements of the situation with the Japan video located as the central node. The second sketches informally how a meme like the Japan video might emerge, among others, as information flows out from the epicenter of the Japanese earthquake (Figs. 8 and 9).

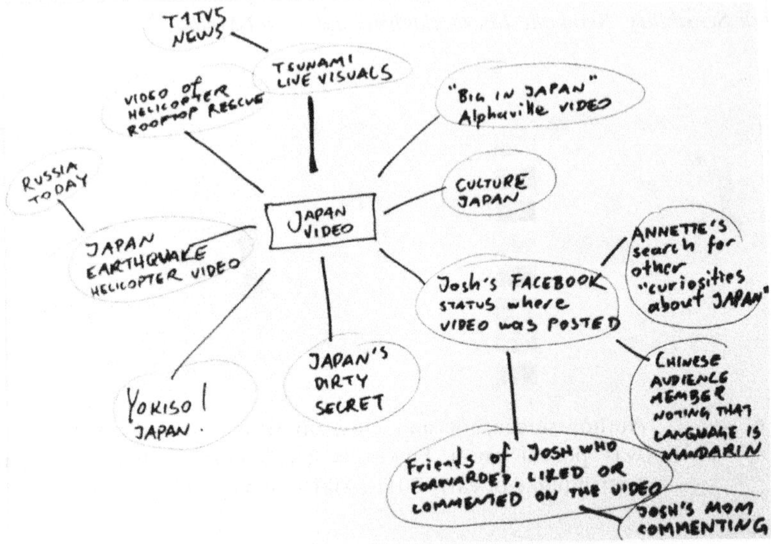

Fig. 8. Rough network map identifying English titled videos recommended alongside the "Japan" video on the date the video was first noticed by Annette, connected to second (later) situational mapping of relevant influences on her understanding of the video in relation to the Japanese earthquakes (Author's research notes).

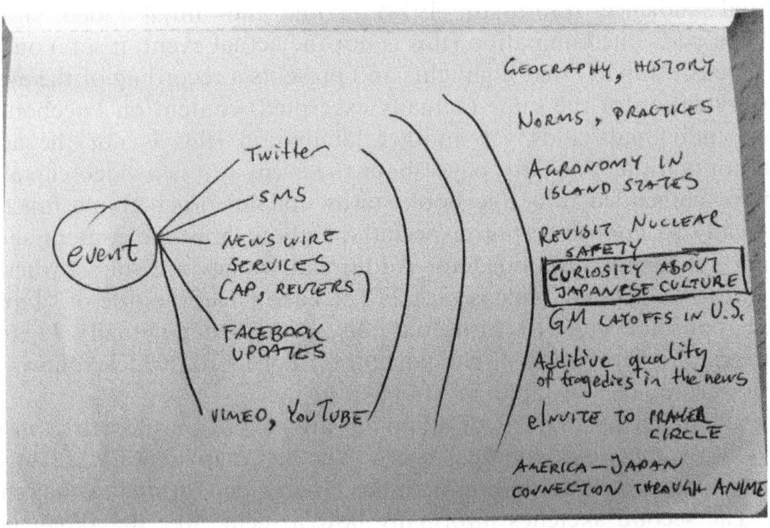

Fig. 9. Generative mapping of actual trends in news about Japan following and possibly caused by the earthquake and the ripple effect of informational waves. Depiction of shift from specific event to cultural memes. The Japan video is in the box on the right side of the image (Author's research notes).

As Clarke notes, it is vital to keep this process of mapping consciously messy, to avoid premature closure (2005, p. 95). This may seem to be just a fancy way of saying that open-ended brainstorming is an important aspect of inquiry, but it goes beyond this. The act of mapping adds complexity that will swiftly engulf the initial thing we thought we wanted to study, thereby removing emphasis from a precise object of analysis. This is identified as a strength, as it then becomes easier to focus on the research question and the data rather than pre-determined theoretical or empirical objects.

Visualizing Layers of Meaning

We most often encounter network maps as the final product of research that focuses on describing large-scale situations. This can be obvious, as in Fig. 10, where the map looks like what we commonly think of as a network map:

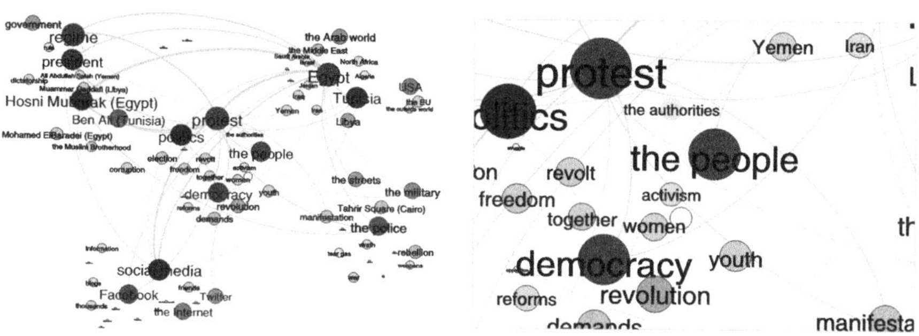

Fig. 10. Network map (and close-up) overviewing news discourse on the events in North Africa and the Middle East during the first half of 2011. Focus on five thematic clusters in five major Swedish newspapers. Image shows initial rough analysis only (Lindgren, 2011a).

They can be subtle or almost invisible, when they don't look like network maps but are based on network thinking, as we see in political commentator Glenn Beck's chalkboard drawings of the Egypt situation in one of his news programs (Fig. 11):

Fig. 11. Author screenshot (and close-up) from online video of the Glenn Beck television program on Fox News, January 31, 2011. Discussion during this part of the program focuses on explanations of what influenced the riots in Egypt. Cartoon faces represent the nature of each country's relationship with the United States (MacNicol, 2011).

They can be animated and seemingly comprehensive, which is increasingly the case with the rising popularity of data visualization and the allure of "big data." This interactive timeline (Fig. 12) produced by *The Guardian*, for example, charts major information streams throughout the Arab Spring, emphasizing times, types, and sources of information.

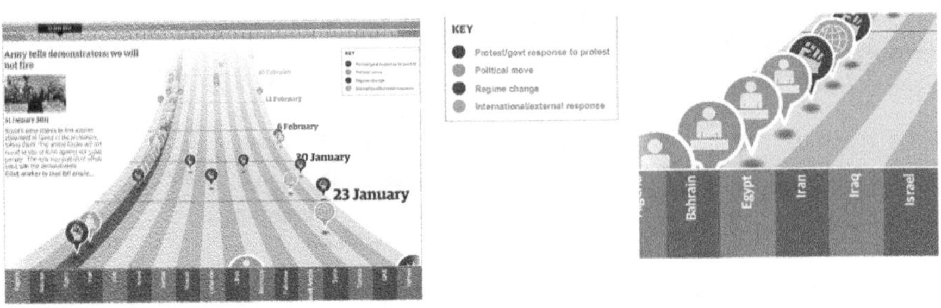

Fig. 12. Author screenshots from "The Path of Protest" interactive timeline developed by *The Guardian* to trace key events surrounding what has become termed "Arab Spring" (Blight, Pulham, & Torpey, 2012).

Fig. 13 illustrates another visually arresting image that strives to make an argument about influence and Tweeting during the early 2011 Egypt protests.

All these examples represent the (somewhat) final product of a process of using network analysis to think about, analyze, and represent a

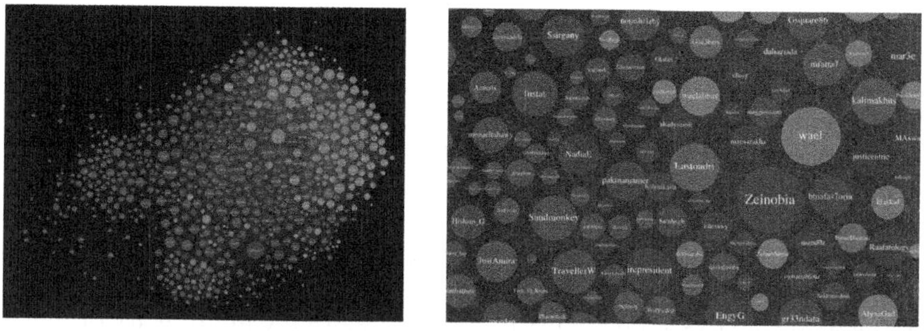

Fig. 13. Author screenshot of Twitter map of pro-democracy movement in Egypt during early 2011. Image intended to illustrate freedom of expression made possible by twitter. Nodes are placed in proximity with those they influence, although no operational definition of "influence" or explanation of methodology is provided by Author (Boguta, 2011).

phenomenon. These final images do not capture how network analysis works in actuality.[3] We can better identify this by doing a bit of meta-analysis, considering the way maps are presented across contexts or over time. Each production will present a different argument about a similar phenomenon. Even a cursory glimpse of the way various stakeholders described or explained the Arab protests shows the complexity of possibilities. Daily, if we were paying attention to the situation, we could see a wide range of visualizations, each presenting a partial depiction, as measured by innumerable variables depending on who is doing the mapping and for what purpose. While some focused on speed and diffusion of information, others focused on relative position and power of individuals and/or key stakeholders. Still others traced the geo-located origins of messages and their subsequent travel, mapping the epicenter or apparent impact of tidal waves of information. This list could go on and on. Taken together and over time, these mappings form networks of meaning of their own, first by virtue of our experience of them while surfing the web or attending to our social network feeds/timelines, and second, in the way these renderings influence other, future renderings or lead to certain premises for how one ought to make sense of a situation. We can see that while the focus is ostensibly on an operationalized version of a phenomenon, the astonishing outcome is that the parts are much more significant and meaningful than the whole,[4] which is not merely elusive but nonexistent and only ever understood through gross oversimplification or generalization.

The generative power of mapping as an iterative layered process of sensemaking might be found using other methods, but visualizations serve at least two functions: First, the activity of producing multiple renderings of the context surrounding a phenomenon destabilizes both the context and the phenomenon, an essential step toward shifting to more complex accounts of contemporary culture. Second, multiple layers of visualizations can provide a systematic trace of one's movement through various analytical categories and interpretations. Whether or not one uses visually oriented methods for thinking, the process, when woven into the findings as well as the analysis, highlights rather than hides the multiplicity of directions possible, offering one's outcomes as a deliberate choice among many for what constitutes the research object or the analytical 'findings.'

SHIFTING FROM OBJECTS TO FLOWS

Consider some of the persistent notions that arise in multiple disciplines over the past few decades: That what we consider an organization is a momentary freezing of flux and transformation (Morgan, 1986), which we can only identify through retrospective sensemaking (Weick, 1969); that space is the crystallization of time (Castells, 2000); that the "individual," far from being a universal concept (e.g., Strathern, 1992), is one that is only understood in terms of relation and interaction (e.g., Blumer, 1969); or that both micro or macro elements of "the social," such as individuals and institutions, respectively, are nothing but networks (Latour, 1997, 2005). All of these ideas call for reconsideration of what is conceptualized and captured as the object of analysis. Pushing this further, decades of epistemological discussions challenge us to consider whether "object of analysis" is the best conceptual frame for engaging in what Rabinow and Marcus call "anthropology of the contemporary" (Rabinow, Marcus, Faubion, & Rees, 2008).

Despite a widespread acknowledgment that phenomena and research situations ought to be considered more fluidly, qualitative methods are historically designed for use in physically situated, local, fairly static contexts. As noted by Rees (Rabinow et al., 2008), "anthropologists are increasingly studying timely phenomena with tools developed to study people out of time" (position 10). It remains easier to focus on the outcomes rather than the processes of interaction. Traditional analytical tools are object oriented – focused on those obdurate qualities of the phenomenon that can be identified, parsed, recorded, displayed for other researchers and scrutinized as discrete units of data. De-fetishizing the object can enable an important shift to what is functioning at the boundaries or movement between objects, which in turn facilitates "working the hyphens," to use an apt phrase by Fine (1994). By deliberately disrupting the act of inscribing objects, it becomes possible to move differently (and more freely) to conduct complex analyses that don't take for granted the dominant categories and frameworks associated with objects and relations among them. Further, the end point of inquiry becomes a discussion point rather than an attempt at an explanation of the whole. Notably, while this stance implies an epistemological shift of sorts, this is not necessarily warranted. The techniques of network analysis may simply be a supplement to other forms of analysis.

From Individuals to Networks

Actor network theorists ask us to consider that contemporary culture requires a shift from actor to network. Individuals are defined by their networks: "An entity is entirely defined by the open-ended lists in the databases" (Latour et al., 2012, p. 3). From this perspective, anything we might call an individual is simply a temporary constitution of attributes. Likewise, what we might call a social structure is an assemblage of common, and possibly persistent, sets of attributes. To make sense of these assemblages, it is not necessary to explain the whole or conduct a holistic study of a bounded field. Rather, it is possible to start anywhere and follow the data – attributes, profiles, persons, memes, or other salient units of information. In some ways, it doesn't matter where one begins because one will always find only parts, as these are much greater than what we might describe as "the whole."

This idea provides a sensible approach in what seem to be more and more complex research situations. As every context is interwoven with and into incomprehensible and ever changing information networks, it can be difficult if not impossible to nail down with any certainty the entities involved in the interaction or the precise objects that might comprise their interactions. In other words, while we might arbitrarily log certain discussion threads, identify Facebook profiles, or analyze a blog post and its comments, these are arbitrary boundaries. In reality, the interactions are much more interconnected in massive social networks we cannot clarify in a way that would have been easy in less electronically mediated times. As we have seen in mathematics and physics, complex systems can be understood by focusing on parts and interactions among elements, starting from almost any point or perspective in the network. Patterns emerge, despite seeming chaos or randomness (Buchanan, 2002). Considering the experience of digital navigation through endless informational pathways, the research challenge is therefore not to consider how to narrow the choices in order to comprehend the whole but to reconsider the notion of "the whole" altogether.

The decision to draw definitional boundaries around the research object prior to its study is rarely random and the rationale is often pragmatic. But what are the underlying epistemological assumptions? Is there something essential about the whole? Is it inevitable that individual elements, put together in some way, will comprise a structure? What if we can no longer take systems theory for granted as the way the world works? What if, as Latour et al. (2012) suggest, the whole is always less than the parts? Again, the difficult shift for us (or anyone steeped in epistemologies that link individuals to structures, who seeks to identify cultural patterns through the systematic analysis of discourse produced among pre-defined groupings of individuals in order to create explanatory or thickly descriptive accounts), is how to radically reconsider and resist the notion of "the whole" at the level of data collection, analysis, and interpretation. If focus on process, association, connection and movement is the goal, it requires shifting from matters of fact to matters of concern (Latour, 2004). The importance lies in the questions that emerge through the research practice of moving, as the individual or the social no longer exists from this perspective and need no longer be used as the unifying or bounding feature of a research project.

Concept mapping is one of many ways to think about this process. As a graphical representation of the relationships among concepts, it enables the researcher to see an overview of a knowledge network, add new concepts or ideas, and focus on the relationships and connections among concepts (Fig. 14).

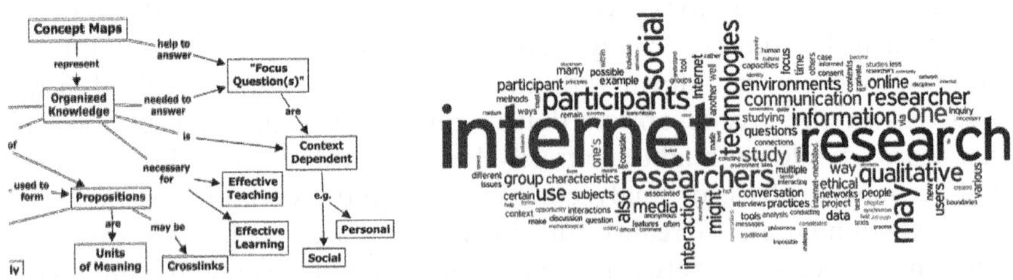

Fig. 14. Two different types of concept maps, the first more traditional (Novak & Cañas, 2008) and the second is a Wordle, generated from the content of one of the Author's articles (Markham, 2009).

Used systematically and iteratively, concept mapping can sponsor less linear or text-centric sensemaking. The practice functions as an organizational tool and might appear to focus on texts or objects [in boxes or circles], but it yields a nonlinear conceptual model that is, by design, emergent and dynamic. The size of various elements, as well as the connections or spaces between them, can be set to highlight certain aspects about the relationships (or lack thereof) between elements.

Such graphs are neither static nor unambiguous representations of any actual circumstances or patterns. Rather, by continuously developing and refining these graphs, one can find a great degree of experimentation, which can actually be seen as an explorative method in its own right. By using various ways of coding the source data, through basing the visualization on different network metrics, and by applying different layout algorithms the researcher may arrive at largely different depictions of the phenomenon. This quite arbitrary and often playful practice has the potential of bringing out new and unexpected insights about data.

Regardless of how the representations are created, the process of looking at visual representations of the complexity of personal connections affords a different sensibility than when we review textual or numeric data. Yet as a tool for data analysis within interpretive social science, it remains sidelined as a precursor to more guided forms of textual analysis. This is an important sensemaking practice to acknowledge and enhance.

From Objects to Connections in Practice: An Example

Let's walk through an example to illustrate how we might apply some of this network sensibility thinking in the context of an actual research project: The study of a Swedish online discussion forum about domestic violence. Here, we focus on only one portion of the study, where we develop different graphical renderings, partly to shift the analytical lens from objects to interactions, partly to make sense of what is happening, and partly to figure out what questions we really ought to be asking about this phenomenon. We have a six-year (2003–2010) sample from a popular Swedish support forum for victims of domestic violence (henceforth DVForum) that includes 16,850 posts from 4,345 participants to 3,304 discussion threads. Note that while this dataset could serve as the basis for its own empirical paper, it is used here merely to exemplify some of the points discussed above.

For the sake of illustration, let us begin with a fairly typical advocacy question about the interaction in social support groups: Is this online forum providing social support in the way we would hope? That is, are people finding the support they need? How does one's understanding of domestic violence possibly shift through engagement in this support group? From a symbolic interaction perspective, we are challenged to figure out how to grapple with a huge, distributed dataset, conduct close level analysis of interactions, and identify how meaning is emerging through ongoing dialogic interactions.

The strategy was to blend various text analysis and network analysis methods in creative and playful combinations. The first map (Fig. 15) is the result of visualizing the most common discussion themes. These themes were identified using Connected Concept Analysis (CCA), (Lindgren, 2012), which uses qualitative constant comparative coding (Glaser, 1965) of a limited part of the data in order to arrive at a conceptual structure to form the basis for further quantitative text processing. In practice, this entails deciding on which key concepts should be measured, and by which words and word combinations these concepts might be measured.[5] Feeding

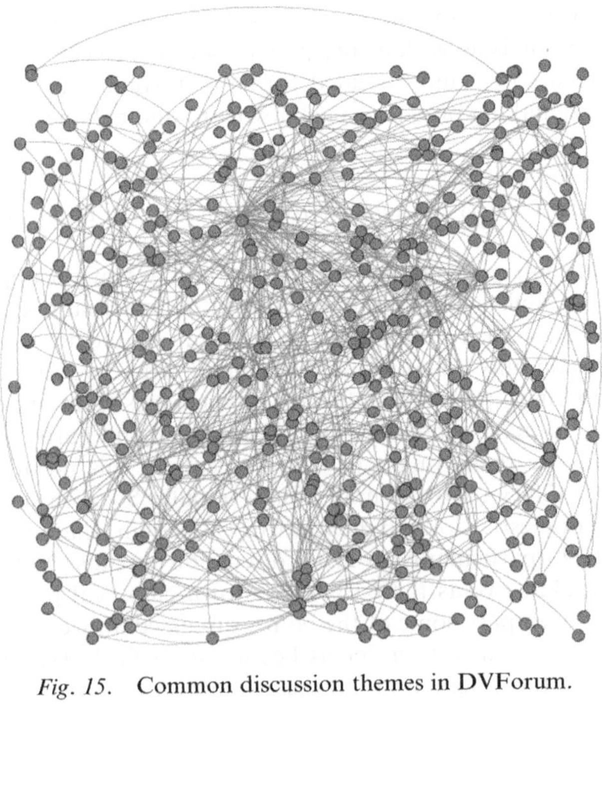

Fig. 15. Common discussion themes in DVForum.

information about the frequency and co-occurrences of these words into Gephi, the first visualization we generated represented a dense and highly interconnected network of concepts. This, in other words, tells us that these discussions happen all over the place.

We don't find this first rough visualization a very satisfying graphic, but it illustrates – along with the images that follow – the way that tracking and logging our own steps can reveal the way we're building our conceptual understanding of the situation as it emerges.

To create a more meaningful map of the topics or relationship between topics, we experimented with various layout algorithms. These are procedures for calculating how relations should be visualized in terms of what variables determine (or should determine) how the elements are placed in relation to each other. In Fig. 16, we changed the visualization of the conceptual network in two ways: First, we set the size of the concept nodes to reflect the number of connections in which each node was involved, highlighting those concepts that appear to be central to the network. Second, we rendered a more circular and uniform graphic by using a force-based algorithm,[6] which aims to draw a graph that is as aesthetically pleasing as possible, with edges of equal length and as few crossing edges as possible.

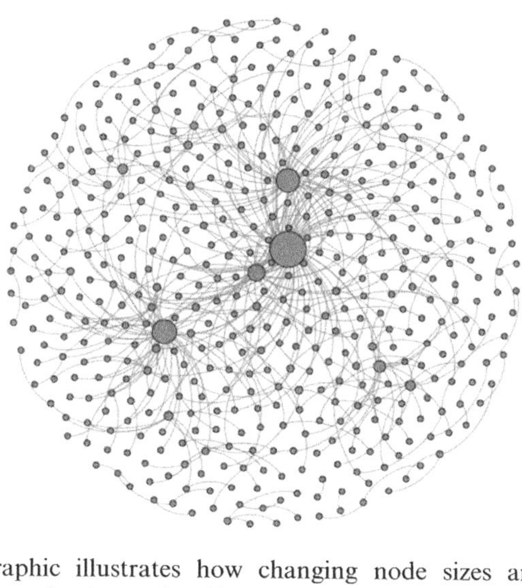

Fig. 16. This graphic illustrates how changing node sizes and using Gephi's capacity to generate circular and uniform displays alters the visualization of data shown originally in Fig. 15.

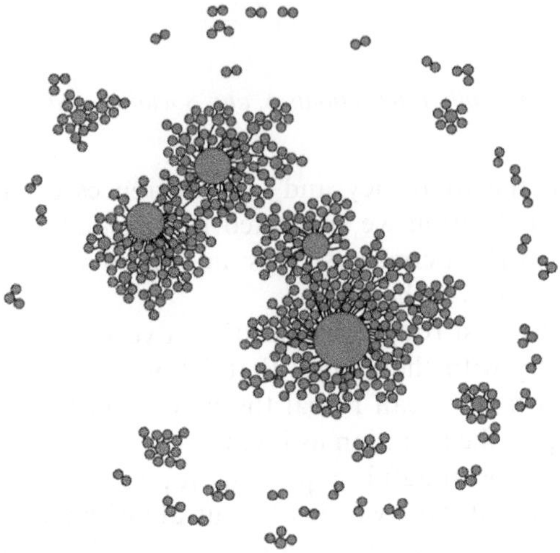

Fig. 17. As with Fig. 16, this graphic illustrates how the use of certain display metrics in the software alters visualization of the same data. This particular algorithm causes the graphic to highlight particular discussion topics that are deemed more authoritative.

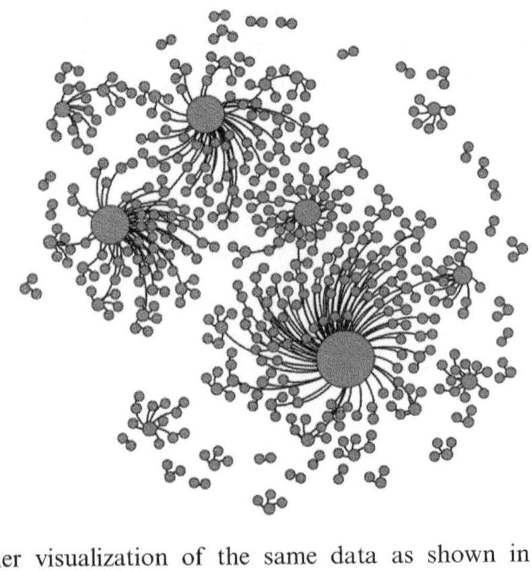

Fig. 18. Another visualization of the same data as shown in Figs. 16 and 17, highlighting supposed 'authoritative' nodes through an attraction distribution metric.

While the graph now gave us a preliminary idea that the forum includes a number of key discussion concepts central to the network, playing around further with network metrics and visualization settings clarified (or altered) the image further (Figs. 17 and 18).

After trying out various layout algorithms, we realized that those algorithms designed to make graphs more compact and readable revealed more interesting information about the conceptual network. The Force Atlas algorithm, a particular feature of the Gephi software, works to make graphs more compact and readable, and provides a way of highlighting authoritative nodes through its "Attraction Distribution" metric. We gradually decided on an increasingly distinct version of the graph showing a set of three to five hubs structuring the discourse in the DVForum. We worked further with the Data Laboratory tools in Gephi, merging, removing and re-coding categories in light of what we had previously found as we conducted partial close readings. Tweaking the graph and adding labels we ended up with what we felt to be a robust analytical visualization of the forum discourse (Fig. 19).

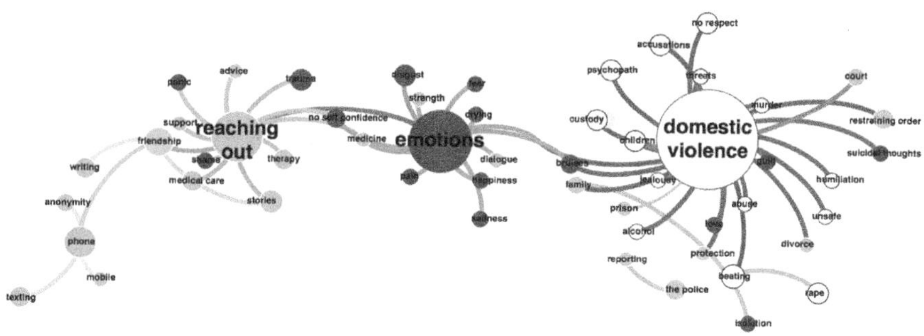

Fig. 19. See text.

The graph in our example shows three general themes. Node sizes reflect the degree of interconnectedness of the respective themes. The shade of the lines (lighter to darker) indicate the strength (weaker to stronger) of co-occurrences between themes in forum posts. An image like this can be used, in relation to this particular illustrative empirical case, to argue that social support is indeed being transmitted or shared in some form in this setting, although we can't read much deeper into this rendering at this point. The theme of domestic violence is addressed and its context is discussed in terms of the violence (beating, rape, humiliation, murder, threats), the surrounding situation (isolation, no respect, children, custody, psychopath, accusations, jealousy, alcohol) and so forth. The participants in the forum discuss this situation in terms of their emotional states (panic, trauma, disgust, shame, sadness, pain, fear, no self-confidence) and their stated longing to find a way out towards happiness. Discussions also revolve around strategies for reaching out and for ending the vicious circle through the help found in the forum. This refers to help with reporting the abuse to the police, getting in touch with medical care, or going to therapy. But to the same extent, the forum addresses the support that comes through friendship, writing and by sharing stories on the forum. The map also shows us aspects of the situation we might not otherwise pay attention to if we are focused too narrowly on the main hubs.

If we were to move further with this particular example, these preliminary interpretations would be augmented and clarified through further close readings of relevant parts of the data. The above steps are presented as an example of this process. We attempt to avoid over-determination, reductionist mapping, or hasty conclusions by adopting a playful or experimental stance to create multiple and iterative renderings of the conceptual network. We can also take any particular element and "deep dive" into it, exploring it more fully and following new paths.

In this particular example, we wanted to look at social network characteristics that influence how the discourse of collective therapy emerges or is structured through social relations. A reasonable next step was therefore to zoom back out, mapping the broad social structure of the forum. How was social support being transmitted? How might we see the social construction of meaning in progress, through the interactions among individuals? To get at this, we decided to start by identifying how participants, rather than the discursive concepts, were related and whether or not their participation was patterned in some way.

To do this, we first isolated post authors, identified the discussions threads in which they were active, and sought co-occurrences, defined as appearances of two given authors in any given thread. We then imported this data into the Map Generator software to produce a sociogram providing a basic graphic depiction of the structure of the network. In order to simplify this map we chose to apply a community detection algorithm to discover the multipartite organization of the DVForum (Rosvall & Bergstrom, 2008). The result of this is shown in Fig. 20. The many isolated nodes do not represent individuals, but instead clusters of 2–30 individuals, grouped together as a consequence of the fact that they interact only in discussion threads with other members of their cluster.

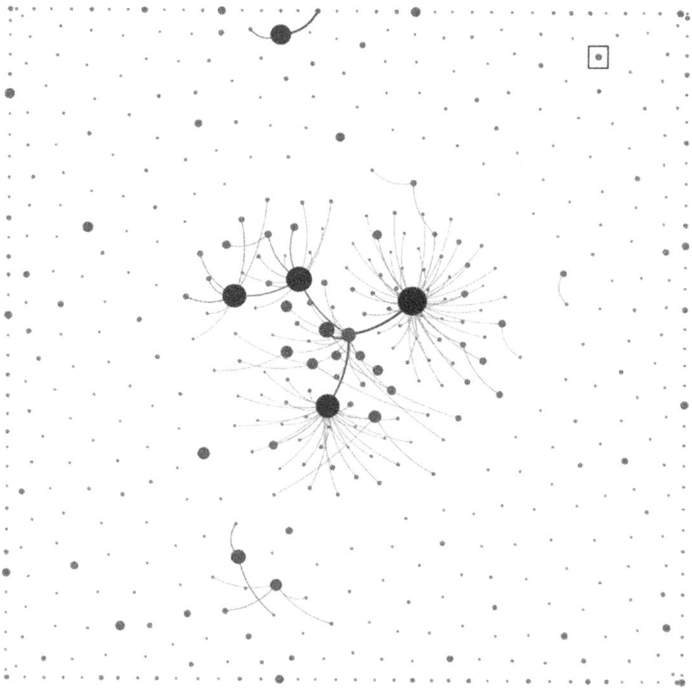

Fig. 20. Multipartite organization of the DVForum.

Before looking closer at the more conspicuous formations at the center of the image, we wanted to consider what might be going on inside such a cluster. We went for a randomly chosen cluster (which has been marked with a square box near the top right corner of the graph). Zooming in, we can see this pattern (Fig. 21).

This particular grouping is constituted by one person in the middle (the participant starting the discussion thread), surrounded by fifteen other people (the participants responding by posting entries in the thread). The exchange doesn't demonstrate much mutual engagement. Although we don't follow up on this analysis, it seems to indicate that clusters like this one comprise an interesting dynamic of what might be ad hoc, temporary moments of social support. It demonstrates a key point in this article, however, in showing how we generate multiple types of data as we conduct these analyses, building complexity. This close-up rendering gives us yet

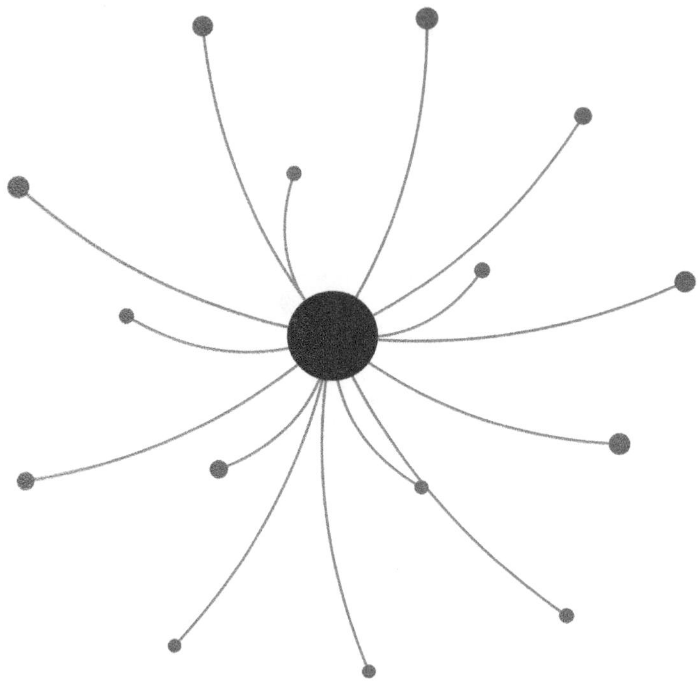

Fig. 21. Zooming in on a randomly chosen cluster from the previous sociogram.

another layer, another web of significance, and a possible conceptual model that could help us later. As described by Soulliere, Britt, and Maines (2001), this process of organizing and tracking multiple sources of data and assumptions is part of a continuing dialogue that "pushes researchers continually to rethink the nature of the dynamics of the situations they are investigating" (p. 255).

Leaving this unexplored territory for another day, we return to focus more closely on the entangled core parts of the network for the rest of the analysis. This meant zooming in on the four core clusters. Fig. 22 visually represents interactions between the 32 participants (1%) through which nearly half (46.4%) of all network flow passes. Ten of these participants correspond to more than a quarter (26.3%) of all flow, meaning that the removal of these nodes would, if not scatter the network completely, fragment it significantly. We marked these 10 key participants with labels (names have been altered). So at this point, we can shift our lens to a more

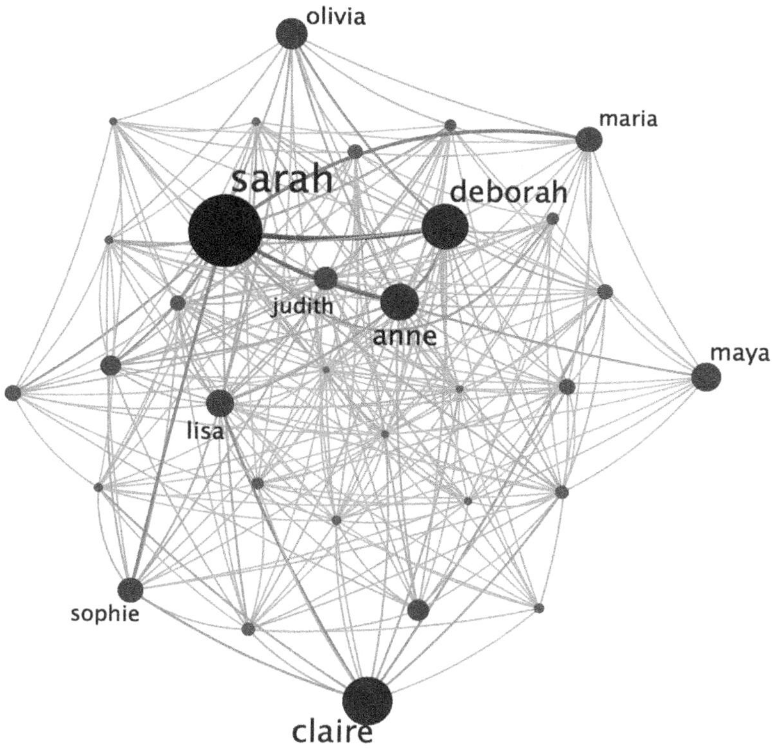

Fig. 22. The core group of the DVForum participants.

object-oriented approach, or look more closely at a subset of individuals. We understood these ten people to be the core group of the DVForum. The degree of mutual connections, in terms of co-occurrences in discussion threads, suggests that these individuals play significant roles in the symbolic construction of potentially shared meaning.

We continued to experiment with different visualizations. We were curious about the characteristics of the discursive contributions of the core participants, which begins to tell us more about the possible role their contributions play in relation to other participants. Fig. 23, for example, shows what sorts of words the core participants used, versus those who participated less. In order to do this, we divided forum participants into groups based on their level of participation. In studies of online communities, users are often defined as belonging to different categories based

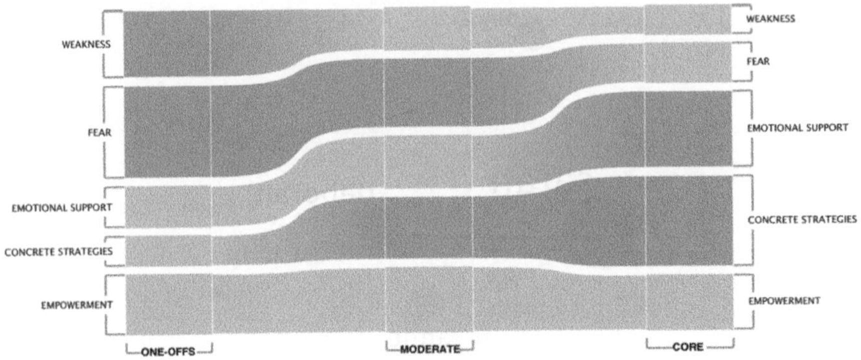

Fig. 23. Words the core participants used, versus words used by those who participated less.

on their level of contribution. Those not actively taking part, but still hanging around the forum, are labeled "lurkers" while the more active ones are called "posters" or "leaders" (Fazeen, Dantu, & Guturu, 2011; Setoyama, Yamazaki, & Namayama, 2011). Social support networks also tend to include the categories of "experts" as well as "seekers" but an interesting observation in relation to these groups is that their borders often are blurred, as these systems make it possible for everyone to contribute as they can (Ackerman, Pipek, & Wulf, 2003). For our example, the 10 key users were labeled as the core, a group of 754 users having posted less than four times to the forum were labeled "one-offs," and the remainder of the forum participants (3,581) were sorted into the broad category of "moderate" users. As for post content, the Bibexcel software was used to filter out everything but the qualitatively coded clusters of words relating to the five discursive categories of Weakness, Fear, Emotional support, Concrete strategies and Empowerment. By sorting types of discourse in relation to types of participants, we were able to generate (with Map Generator's alluvial module) Fig. 23.

In the discursive category of Weakness, we included words relating to the state of helplessness and the inability to act, which is described by many users of the DVForum. Expressions belonging to this category generally refer to a feeling of being isolated and unable to take control of the violent situation. Wordings and formulations of this type are markedly more prominent among the less frequent and occasional participants to the forum, while they are relatively less frequent among the core users.

The same goes for the category of Fear, gathering words relating to anxiety, worry, horror and being afraid used by forum participants. This group of words is the most commonly employed set among one-off posters, while it is the second to smallest in the discourse of core participants. While words describing sisterhood, being strong and standing up to the abuser in the Empowerment category appear to be of similar importance in forum entries from all groups, the categories of Emotional Support and Concrete Strategies are highly prominent in the core and more marginal with less frequent participants. Emotional support refers to affective words relating to an intimacy evoked and felt among like-minded members of the DVForum, and it is in fact quite striking how this theme is the second to smallest among one-offs, but the second to largest among the core. Words referring to concrete strategies for leaving the relationship, and seeking help from social workers, therapists, doctors and lawyers, make up the category of Concrete Strategies which is the least talked about among occasional participants, but the most common among core users.

If we take seriously the premises of social constructionism and symbolic interaction, it is at these moments of action and connection that self, other, and social structures are negotiated. By exploring the complexity of this action through different visual means, we gain a rich, albeit different sense of this negotiation process. In some ways, it feels less comfortable if we consider our inclinations toward thick description and rich, local text-based analysis. Yet these renderings are significant contributions to our understanding of how "the social" might occur on these large scales.

We don't show all the iterations of mappings that eventually led to what you see in this article, but we believe it is crucial to not only take time to draw new renderings but to also keep all earlier drawings, to see the conceptual development. This rigor transforms the informal practice of playing with different visualizations (interpretations) into a more systematic method. We certainly experience the chaos of technological saturation and what Gergen (1991) labels "multiphrenia" at a visceral level. But much of the interpretive stages of social inquiry involve what some might call mind-work, where we sit and think about what's going on. This will inevitably gloss the actual sensemaking process. We are not suggesting that through these processes of mapping we are gaining a more complete picture. It is rather a stronger sense of the complexity as we witness different patterns or connections beyond our own ability to observe. Our comprehension is also more fully realized when we do not erase versions of our interpretive maps, but review the way our conceptualizations have shifted over time. Our example of working with data from the domestic abuse forum describes some of the ways a network sensibility can prompt a methodological and perhaps epistemological approach that better resonates with the study of what is described as cultures of flow. It provides tools for shifting from object to flow, or structure to relation, which can allow the analyst to focus on the intensely relational social actions that create these flows, or on the flows themselves.

FROM MATTERS OF FACT TO MATTERS OF CONCERN: HIGHLIGHTING THE ETHICS OF NETWORK SENSIBILITIES

When operating within a network sensibility, it becomes easier to envision location in relation, or an idea of what it might mean to be "situated." You can see where you are centered, but you can also see how you might stand in relation to other people, elements, situations, or perspectives. At its best, this stance facilitates strong reflexivity. Once we move past the goal of description, mapping becomes a way of highlighting certain aspects of a situation, a process that simultaneously hides or obscures other plausible or actual aspects. Every iteration frames the phenomenon, but also shapes our experience of the phenomenon. So while network maps can provide a way of seeing differently, they are also ways of locking in a particular view. This is only really a problem when the frames become so embedded in everyday ways of seeing that we lose sight of the frame itself. Then, what was once understood as one choice among many is seen only as "the way things are."

Playing with networks can help reveal ways of seeing otherwise. The key to maintaining internal consistency and contextual integrity is to constantly question one's image – and imagination – of the situation, to rebuild and shift the networks so that different elements can be studied and different nodes centered. Of course, this has the benefit of engendering a more robust analysis, but here, the salient point is that it can help identify the way that one's analysis is privileging certain standpoints. This becomes crucial when we approach the final stages of the project, when we draw conclusions about what we've analyzed and build the argument for particular audiences. During this stage, we'll emphasize particular connections, eliminating other options. Interrogating one's own decisions, analyzing conclusions as networks in themselves, provides another level of ethicality.

In a very fundamental way, adopting a network sensibility forces multiple and always-shifting perspectives on any phenomenon. Rather than reducing the scope, the methods of moving through and analyzing various elements of networks generate more data, more directions, and more layers of meaning. If one can embrace the challenge of dealing with such a messy and potentially uncontrollable process, the outcome can yield accounts of social phenomena that are sensitive to irreducible complexity. Because these emerge as a result of a series of decisions, there will always remain multiple possibilities and paths not taken. This may seem unsatisfactory to those of us trained to believe there are no limits to scientific knowledge, but on the flipside, removes the pressure to attempt to provide "the" answer. Weaving an explanation and justification of one's decision-making process into any final report adds transparency and credibility, whereby the researcher can identify and therefore help make the rationale more obvious to readers. It is important to emphasize, as does Grebe (2010), that the political and ethical power of our attitude and practice toward social inquiry "have profound ethical and political implications. ... An epistemological stance that recognises complexity can inform a critical philosophy" (p. 4).

CONCLUSION

A network perspective is not limited to SNA, or quantitative modeling of social networks, or describing visually how things are connected. It is a way of rethinking the sensemaking process, acknowledging that our research practice, like our everyday life, involves a process of mapping, connecting, and recentering the way we see the world around us.

Arguably, social media are changing the way we experience the world. What we consider self, structure, and "the social" are far more temporal and ad hoc than fixed. Whether or not this is the case or anything radically new, social media help us see how our research contexts are not pre-existing milieus but an assemblage of elements "constituted through the connections or articulations among elements" (Balsamo, 2011, p. 15). Guided in many ways by the work of George Marcus (1998), ethnographers have been challenged to move away from extremely localized study. This is not the same as more recent trends toward "big data." Instead, as discourses move more globally, the notion of multiple locations gives way to multiple sites of situated meaning and ongoing processes of what Rodriguez calls "culturing" (2002). We are well situated to reconsider the way we have historically conceptualized individuals, interactions, and social structures, and to focus on methods that can get at the liminal spaces between us, where meaning is formed.

We find play and creativity an essential component of a network sensibility. As Gregory Bateson remarked, "advances in science come from a combination of loose and strict thinking, and this combination is the most precious tool of science" (1972/1987, p. 73). The ability to let loose of some of the strictures of method opens the door to following hunches. Identifying and then systematizing the practices that occur incidentally will only sharpen our disciplinary logics. Mindful engagement of this dualism creates the intellectual space to explore and glean data outside typical research parameters yet provides a mechanism for measuring this freedom against what remains epistemologically sound practice for social research.

A network perspective, loosened from the bounds of its primary disciplinary trajectories, constitutes a range of techniques and approaches that encourage researchers to move into the flow of culture to find meaning. These need not be tied to a particular theoretical position, but can be used as tools to think with, whether it be through drawing more pictures as a part of the systematic process of analysis or by challenging the very foundations of how we have traditionally conceptualized what we consider the research object.

NOTES

1. To note, all of these aspects of a network approach are profoundly enhanced by animation technologies, which may account for the growing popularity of this method; it remains a compelling way to try to encapsulate complex structures of flow in visually stimulating ways. The flipside of this this visual appeal is the extent to which it can simultaneously oversimplify and obscure, an issue that should be considered when thinking about when and how to use network analysis and visualization tools.

2. All screenshots are taken by the authors from publically accessible areas of the web or comprise original works of the authors. Following the best practice ethical principles outlined by the International Communication Association (2010), we determine that our use of these materials falls well within the U.S. doctrine of "Fair Use." Following the ethics guidelines of the Association of Internet Researchers (Markham, Buchanan, & the AOIR Ethics Committee, 2012), we have either

obscured information that might pose any risk to individuals or determined that the information does not pose likely risks from appearance in this context.

3. In fact, although some information is offered to explain the meaning of the size of node, thickness of lines, or placement of information, none of these visualizations describe in any detail the methods used to collect, cull, and analyze the data, or the decision process behind the choice and arrangement of particular elements to the exclusion of others. There is ample room for critique, both regarding the absence of explanation and the hidden or obscured power of algorithms in the knowledge production process, but we do not address it in any depth in this article.
4. This idea is developed further by Latour et al. (2012).
5. See also Lindgren and Lundström (2009, 2011) and Lindgren (2011b).
6. Fruchterman and Reingold (1991).

REFERENCES

Ackerman, M. S., Pipek, V., & Wulf, V. (2003). *Sharing expertise: Beyond knowledge management*. Cambridge, MA: The MIT Press.

Aikisystema. (2011). Japan [Screenshot of YouTube video]. Retrieved from https://www.youtube.com/watch?v=ROaIknIk9LA&feature=player_embedded

Balsamo, A. (2011). *Designing culture: The technological imagination at work*. Durham, NC: Duke University Press.

Bateson, G. (1987). *Steps to an ecology of mind: Collected essays in anthropology, psychiatry, evolution, and epistemology*. Northvale, NJ: Jason Aronson, Inc. (Original work published 1972).

Bertalanffy, L. V. (1950). An outline of general system theory. *British Journal for the Philosophy of Science*, *1*, 134–165.

Blight, G., Pulham, S., & Torpey, P. (2012). Arab spring: An interactive timeline of Middle East Protests [Graphic interactive timeline of Arab Spring]. *The Guardian*. Retrieved from http://www.guardian.co.uk/world/interactive/2011/mar/22/middle-east-protest-interactive-timeline

Blumer, H. (1969). *Symbolic interactionism: Perspective and method*. Englewood Cliffs, NJ: Prentice-Hall.

Boguta, K. (2011). [Network map of Twitter influence]. Retrieved from http://www.kovasboguta.com/1/post/2011/02/first-post.html

Buchanan, M. (2002). *Nexus: Small worlds and the groundbreaking theory of networks*. New York, NY: Norton.

Castellani, B., Castellani, J., & Spray, S. (2003). Grounded neural networking: Modeling complex quantitative data. *Symbolic Interaction*, *26*(4), 577–589.

Castells, M. (2000). *The rise of the network society, the information age: Economy, society and culture* (2nd ed., Vol. 1). Cambridge, MA: Blackwell.

Clarke, A. (2003). Situational analysis: Grounded theory mapping after the postmodern turn. *Symbolic Interaction*, *26*(4), 553–576.

Clarke, A. (2005). *Situational analysis: Grounded theory after the postmodern turn*. Thousand Oaks, CA: Sage.

Crossley, N. (2010). Networks and complexity: Directions for interactionist research? *Symbolic Interaction*, *33*(3), 341–363.

Fazeen, M., Dantu, R., & Guturu, P. (2011). Identification of leaders, lurkers, associates and spammers in a social network: Context-dependent and context-independent approaches. *Social Network Analysis and Mining*, *1*(3), 241–254.

Fine, M. (1994). Working the hyphens: Reinventing self and other in qualitative research. In N. Denzin & Y. Lincoln (Eds.), *Handbook of qualitative research* (pp. 70–82). Thousand Oaks, CA: Sage.

Fruchterman, T. M. J., & Reingold, E. M. (1991). Graph drawing by force-directed placement. *Software: Practice and Experience*, *21*, 1129–1164.

Geertz, C. (1973). *The interpretations of cultures*. New York, NY: Basic Books.

Gergen, K. J. (1991). *The saturated self*. New York, NY: Basic Books.

Glaser, B. G. (1965). The constant comparative method of qualitative analysis. *Social Problems*, *12*, 436–445.

Goffman, E. (1974). *Frame analysis: An essay on the organization of experience*. Cambridge, MA: Harvard University Press.

Grebe, E. (2010). Negativity, difference, and critique: The ethical moment in complexity. In P. Cilliers & R. Preiser (Eds.), *Complexity, difference and identity: An ethical perspective* (pp. 95–111). Dordrecht: Springer. Retrieved from http://www.springerlink.com/index/10.1007/978-90-481-9187-1. Accessed on January 13, 2012.

International Communication Association. (2010). Code of Best Practices in Fair Use for Scholarly Research in Communication. Retrieved from http://centerforsocialmedia.org/fair-use/related-materials/codes/code-best-practices-fair-use-scholarly-research-communication

Latour, B. (1997). On actor network theory: A few clarifications. Retrieved from http://www.nettime.org/Lists-Archives/nettime-l-9801/msg00019.html. Accessed on June 13, 2011.

Latour, B. (2004). From realpolitik to dingpolitik: An introduction to making things public. In B. Latour & P. Weibel (Eds.), *Making things public: Atmospheres of democracy*. Boston, MA: MIT Press. Retrieved from http://bruno-latour.fr/sites/default/files/96-DINGPOLITIK-GB.pdf. Accessed on January 12, 2012.

Latour, B. (2005). *Reassembling the social: An introduction to actor network theory*. Oxford, UK: Oxford University Press.

Latour, B., Jensen, P., Venturini, T., Grauwin, S., & Boullier, D. (2012). The whole is always smaller than its parts: A digital test of Gabriel Tarde's monads. Retrieved from http://www.bruno-latour.fr/sites/default/files/123-WHOLE-PART-FINAL.pdf. Accessed on January 09, 2012.

Lindgren, S. (2011a). Beginning analysis of media discourse on the Arab Spring [Graphic network visualization]. Retrieved from http://www.simonlindgren.com/2011/08/12/beginning-analysis-of-media-discourse-on-the-arab-spring/

Lindgren, S. (2011b). YouTube gunmen? Mapping participatory media discourse on school shooting videos. *Media, Culture & Society*, *33*, 123–136.

Lindgren, S. (2012). *Confronting the challenge of large online texts through connected concept analysis*. Unpublished manuscript.

Lindgren, S., & Lundström, R. (2009). Discursive networks: Visualising media representations of crime victims. In J. Lim (Ed.). *Computer-aided qualitative research 2009* (pp. 68–85). Utrecht: Merlien Institute.

Lindgren, S., & Lundström, R. (2011). Pirate culture and hacktivist mobilization: The cultural and social protocols of# wikileaks on twitter. *New Media & Society*, *13*(6), 999–1018.

MacNicol, G. (2011). Glenn Beck Uses Two Chalkboards to Explain the Crisis in Egypt [Video clip from Glenn Beck show on January 31, 2011]. *Business Insider*. Retrieved from http://articles.businessinsider.com/2011-01-31/entertainment/29986159_1_glenn-beck-dictators-uprising

Marcus, G. (1998). *Ethnography through thick and thin*. Princeton, NJ: Princeton University Press.

Markham, A., Buchanan, E., & The AOIR Ethics Committee. (2012). Ethical decision-making and Internet research 2.0: Recommendations from the AOIR ethics committee. Retrieved from http://www.aoir.org/reports/ethics2.pdf

Markham, A. N. (2009). How can qualitative researchers produce work that is meaningful across time, space, and culture? In N. K. Baym & A. N. Markham (Eds.), *Internet inquiry: Conversations about method* (pp. 131–155). Thousand Oaks, CA: Sage.

Markham, A. N. (2012a). *Moving into the flow: Using a network perspective to explore complexity in Internet contexts*. Center for Internet Research Monograph Series. Aarhus, Denmark: University of Aarhus.

Markham, A. N. (2012b). Fabrication as ethical practice: Qualitative inquiry in ambiguous internet contexts. *Information, Communication and Society*, *15*(3), 343–353.

Morgan, G. (1986). *Images of organization*. Thousand Oaks, CA: Sage.

Novak, J., & Cañas, A. (2008). The Theory Underlying Concept Maps and How to Construct and Use Them. *Technical Report IHMC CmapTools, Florida Institute for Human and Machine Cognition*. Retrieved from http://cmap.ihmc.us/publications/researchpapers/theorycmaps/theoryunderlyingconceptmaps.htm. Accessed on March 25, 2009.

Rabinow, P., Marcus, G., Faubion, J., & Rees, T. (2008). *Designs for an anthropology of the contemporary*. Durham, NC: Duke University Press.

Rodriguez, A. (2002). Culture to culturing. Re-imagining our understanding of intercultural relations. *Journal of Intercultural Communication*, *5*. Retrieved from http://www.immi.se/intercultural/nr5/rodriguez.pdf. Accessed on November 20, 2011.

Rosvall, M., & Bergstrom, C. T. (2008). Maps of random walks on complex networks reveal community structure. *Proceedings of the National Academy of Sciences*, *105*(4), 1118.

Salvini, A. (2010). Symbolic interactionism and social network analysis: An uncertain encounter. *Symbolic Interaction*, *33*(3), 364–388.

Setoyama, Y., Yamazaki, Y., & Namayama, K. (2011). Benefits of peer support in online Japanese breast cancer communities: Differences between lurkers and posters. *Journal of Medical Internet Research*, *13*(4), e122. Retrieved from http://www.jmir.org/2011/4/e122/

Soulliere, D., Britt, D., & Maines, D. (2001). Conceptual modeling as a toolbox for grounded theorists. *The Sociological Quarterly*, *42*(2), 253–269.

Strathern, M. (1992). *After nature: English kinship in the late twentieth century*. Cambridge, MA: Cambridge University Press.

Twitter. (2011). Spread of Information [Screenshot from video clip illustrating Tweets and Retweets following Japanese earthquake]. Retrieved from http://www.flickr.com/photos/twitteroffice/5884626815/in/photostream/

Weick, K. (1969). *The social psychology of organizing*. Boston, MA: Addison-Wesley.

SOCIAL NETWORK ANALYSIS FOR FACEBOOK: LOCATING CLIQUES AND VISUALIZING SOCIABILITY

Jeffrey Coons and Shing-Ling S. Chen

ABSTRACT

Social media such as Facebook thrive with the arrival of Web 2.0. This chapter merges traditional social network analysis (SNA) with symbolic interactionism (SI) to create a hybrid method of SNA to allow researchers to study the sociability found in Facebook. The discussion begins with identifying a common ground of SNA and SI, found in Georg Simmel's work, and then develops methodological procedures to locate cliques in Facebook networks. A visualization technique is also suggested to further single out the social forms found in Facebook.

Keywords: Social network analysis; symbolic interactionism; sociability; cliques; Facebook; sociogram

---

Symbolic Interaction and New Social Media
Studies in Symbolic Interaction, Volume 43, 43–61

ISSN: 0163-2396/doi:10.1108/S0163-239620140000043013

In 2004, a series of changes took place in how the World Wide Web was used. These changes marked the arrival of Web 2.0, as Internet activities entered a new era. The usage of static web pages – one-way communication such as accessing information on web sites or sending e-mail – came to an end. Internet users are now able to interact with each other, engaging in two-way dialogues and reciprocating interactions. Popular Web 2.0 sites include social networking sites such as Facebook and Twitter, video sharing sites such as YouTube, as well as blogs, mashups.

Among the social networking sites, Facebook is the number one social media, with more than one billion users (Fowler, 2012). Facebook is the primary form of communication among college students in the United States (Harris, 2008). In addition, it has become a new hangout for U.S. college students. U.S. college students spent hours a week on Facebook for FOMO, "fear of missing out" (Chang, 2011). The constant fear of missing out has led to an addictive use of Facebook (Ottalini, 2010).

Facebook provides a different form of communication, when compared to e-mail or cell phone. E-mail is generally used by college students for "serious matters," class- or work-related communication, especially ones that require extensive descriptions and/or clear articulations. Cell phone calls or text messages are for brief and immediate communication. Facebook, on the other hand, is used for "non-serious matters," fun or expressive communication, or for staying in touch with others with no specific matters to deal with, nor the need for immediate communication. Sending a "poke" on the Facebook exemplifies an expressive gesture of friendliness with no discursive content, nor does it require immediate response.

With an intent to hang out, to engage in non-task-oriented fun exchanges, Facebook users are engaging in what Georg Simmel termed acts of sociability (Simmel, 1950). Simmel defined sociability as a play-form of association, driven by cordiality. Simmel indicated humans' impulse to merge self with others, to socialize. Out of this impulse to socialize, occasions were formed where individuals gathered, not for any utilitarian purpose, but for the purpose of association. In these occasions – such as a holiday party and an after-church brunch – individuals engaged in free-playing activities to form inter-dependence. In a similar fashion, users blend together in a spirit fun on Facebook.

Facebook users' interest in sociability is demonstrated by engaging in various activities to socialize. To provide status updates, comments, likes, forwards, tags, pokes, and shares are all accomplished with an aim for relationship building and maintenance. To take the profile pictures for instance, although a prime spot to feature oneself, few profile pictures are "selfies" (i.e., pictures taken of oneself while holding the camera at arm's length) or mirror images. Most of the profile pictures show two or more people. Cover photos are nearly all group photos. These photos demonstrate the most essential aspect of the user: the relationships that one engages in. Thus, it is more important for users to feature their relationships, rather than themselves, in their profile or cover photos. Photos found in albums are mostly group photos as well. Showcasing one's social relationships is a major purpose of using Facebook.

Due to the sociable and relational nature of Facebook use, researchers interested in studying Facebook activities quickly found that survey or content analysis are not suitable for mining the relational aspect of Facebook activities. Both survey and content analysis can only scratch the surface of Facebook activities with descriptions of the attributes of users or the characteristics of the posts. Both are unsuitable tools to investigate the relationships embedded in Facebook activities. To mine the relationships embedded in Facebook activities, one would have to use qualitative analysis.

However, traditional qualitative analysis which provides an excellent tool for field researchers to study social relationships is, in fact, rather inadequate for Facebook analysis. First of all, the large number of posts on Facebook makes observation an overwhelming task. Secondly, the relationships presented by Facebook posts are simply too complex to be fully recognizable. It is clear that researchers need methodological tools to help manage data and delineate relationships for qualitative analysis. The purpose of this report is to present a hybrid form of social network analysis (SNA) technique to assist qualitative researchers to perform Facebook analysis.

The reason why Facebook activities are unmanageable and the relationships presented are unrecognizable by naked eye observation stems from the fact that social media allow users to publish and broadcast themselves. Unlike mass media, print or broadcasting, which are uni-directional and two-dimensional communication, best illustrated by David Berlo's source–message–channel–receiver model (Berlo, 1960), social media are multi-directional and three-dimensional (3D) communication. With mass media, users, readers or audience, for the most part are passive consumers. With social media, users are no longer passive, as they now author, send, receive, forward, share, and broadcast, all at the same time.

Facing such complex activities, Facebook researchers need a research tool to help organize data and delineate relationships for analysis. To organize data and delineate relationships in social networks, SNA (Scott, 2009) provides a natural solution for researchers. SNA is derived from Graph Theory, with applications mainly in mathematics and computer science.

Although a quantitative approach, SNA, in fact, shares a common intellectual root with symbolic interactionism (SI) (Couch, 1989; Mead, 1934). Both SNA and SI researchers share the common goal of locating geometric forms in social relationships. The common goal of SNA and SI can be traced back to their common intellectual root in Georg Simmel. The common ground between SNA and SI stems from Georg Simmel's work in metropolis (Wellman, 1988). Simmel's work on forms of social relationships, and how forms determine the content of relational communication, influenced researchers interested in structural analysis as well as those interested in SI. Researchers from both SNA and SI derived their interest from Simmel's work to study how the forms of social relationships post constrains on social behaviors. Simmel's work became the precursor for both SNA and SI. Operating from a common intellectual root, SNA provides SI researchers a natural tool to manage data in their search of the social forms embedded in Facebook.

RELATIONAL DATA

SNA is a set of methods for the analysis of the relational aspects of social structures. The use of SNA depends on the availability of relational data (Scott, 2009). Relational data are data that show connections among users (i.e., agents) or activities.

The first step of SNA is to transform raw data into relational data (Scott, 2009). Raw data, as seen on a user's Facebook wall, need to be recorded and organized into data matrices. Data matrices are tables of figures with rows and columns. The first data matrix to be created is Agent-by-Activity matrix (Scott, 2009), where agents occupy the first column, and activities are the first row (see Table 1). To create this matrix, researchers first record activities on the first row. Agents who participate in activities, appear on the first column and have a "1" in the corresponding cell of the matrix, designating the activities in which the agent participated. Non-participation in an activity is shown by a "0" entry in the corresponding cell. Agent-by-Activity matrix shows direct and indirect connections among agents and activities (Scott, 2009).

In the classroom exercise of this method, students were asked to prepare the relational data of their own Facebook wall for a month using the

Table 1. Agent by Activity.

	Paul S./Wall Post – his wall/ 3-1-12	Paul S./Wall Post – his wall/3-2-12/8:06 a.m.	Joey G./Wall Post – his wall/ 3-2-12	Paul S./Wall Post – his wall/3-2-12/12:24 p.m.	Me/Cover Photo/3-3-12	Paul S./Wall Post – his wall/ 3-5-12
Me	1	1	1	1	1	1
Paul S.	1	1	0	1	0	1
Gary F.	0	1	0	0	0	0
Eric Q.	0	1	0	0	0	1
Joey G.	0	0	1	0	0	0
Tom B.	0	0	0	0	0	0
Marisa D.	0	0	0	0	1	0
Abby K.	0	0	0	0	1	0
Jason M.	0	0	0	0	0	0
Macon V.	0	0	0	0	0	0
Tanner J.	0	0	0	0	0	0
Steve F.	0	0	0	0	0	0
Tony K.	0	0	0	0	0	0
Deb K.	0	0	0	0	0	0
Gary K.	0	0	0	0	0	0
Thomas H.	0	0	0	0	0	0
Karen K. E.	0	0	0	0	0	0
Seth B.	0	0	0	0	0	0
Spencer F.	0	0	0	0	0	0
Mike B.	0	0	0	0	0	0
David K.	0	0	0	0	0	0
Travis T.	0	0	0	0	0	0
Seth C.	0	0	0	0	0	0
Peter A.	0	0	0	0	0	0
Rocky G.	0	0	0	0	0	0

Agent-by-Activity matrix. The reason why the Facebook wall was selected for the analysis of one's Facebook activities was due to the fact that the wall provided a log of a user's activities, as well as those of others sent to the user. Students were asked to record any dyadic activity, including posting, commenting, liking, sharing, poking, confirming friendship, or tagging, by placing these onto the Agent-by-Activity matrix, with each activity occupying a different column, and agents who participated in the activity received a "1" in their respective cells.

Activities to be recorded are dyadic interactions between two users. Posts that received responses were activities to be recorded – such as a photo post that received a like, or a status update that received a comment or a share. A post that received no response of any kind, "comment, like, or share," is not considered as an activity to be recorded, as it was not a dyadic interaction. Nor is a poke or a friend request that received no response.

The purpose of an Agent-by-Activity matrix is to render the raw data on the Facebook wall manageable. After an Agent-by-Activity matrix is created, another matrix needs to be created, based on the data recorded on the Agent-by-Activity matrix. The second matrix that needs to be created is Agent-by-Agent matrix (Scott, 2009) where agents are shown in both the first column and the first row (see Table 2). That is, each agent is listed twice, once in a row, and once in a column. Each individual cells show whether particular pairs of agents are connected by common activities which both participated in. The presence of a common activity between two agents is represented by a "1" entry in the appropriate cell of the matrix. The absence of a connection is represented by a "0" entry. If there is more than one common activity, a number would reflect the number of common activities that a pair of agents have in common. The strength of a relation can be seen by the number of activities that the pair of agents have in common.

The top and bottom halves of the data in an Agent-by-Agent matrix are identical as they show the same pairs of agents. Since the top and the bottom halves are redundant, the convention is to construct only the bottom half of the matrix (Scott, 2009). That is, SNA only requires the bottom half of the Agent-by-Agent matrix, not the full matrix.

By going through all the activities listed on the Agent-by-Activity matrix, the Agent-by-Agent matrix shows direct relations among agents, a feature not readily apparent in the Agent-by-Activity matrix (Scott, 2009). Constructing an Agent-by-Agent matrix allows researchers to identify all the agents of a particular group, and to trace their various connections

Table 2. Agent by Agent.

Jason M.	Macon V.	Tanner J.	Steve F.	Tony K.	Deb K.	Gary K.	Thomas H.	Karen E.	Seth B.	Spencer F.	Mike B.	David K.	Travis T.	Seth C.	Peter A.	Rocky G.
■																
1	■															
1	1	■														
0	0	0	■													
0	0	0	0	■												
0	0	0	0	0	■											
0	0	0	0	0	0	■										
0	0	0	0	0	0	0	■									
0	0	0	0	0	0	0	0	■								
0	0	0	0	0	0	0	0	0	■							
0	0	0	0	0	0	0	0	0	1	■						
0	0	0	0	0	0	0	0	0	0	0	■					
0	0	0	0	0	0	0	0	0	0	0	0	■				
0	0	0	0	0	0	0	0	0	1	1	0	0	■			
0	0	0	0	0	0	0	0	0	0	0	0	0	0	■		
0	0	0	0	0	0	0	0	0	1	1	0	0	1	0	■	
0	0	0	0	0	0	0	0	0	1	1	0	0	1	0	1	■

with one another. Thus, the purpose of the Agent-by-Agent matrix is to delineate the relatedness among agents.

Once constructed, the Agent-by-Agent matrix is ready to be used for network analysis. While there are computer programs available for network analysis, in the classroom exercise, students are required to use the old fashioned paper-and-pencil method to perform the analysis. The intent to forgo the computer program and adopt manual analysis is rooted in a fundamental belief of qualitative research, that of building a familiarity with the data over time. SNA seeks to locate the networks, SI seeks not only to locate the networks but also to describe the nature of relatedness. To describe the nature of relatedness, a sound understanding of the agents and the activities that connect them is needed. Such a sound understanding could only be gained via working with the data intimately.

SOCIOGRAM AND VISUALIZATION

To perform a network analysis, the Agent-by-Agent matrix is to be converted into a graph of points (agents), connected by lines (activities or relations), to create the visualization of social structures embedded in the group (Scott, 2009). To avoid an unrecognizable thicket of lines, arranging points on a circle shape is recommended. The graph constructed, is called sociogram, or social network diagram. The sociogram is a technique for visualizing social networks. Initial configuration is seen as a trial configuration, as redrafting may be required to produce a clear and satisfactory layout.

The purpose of the sociogram is to reveal the patterns of connections among points (Scott, 2009). Using the sociogram, the properties of points and lines in a graph can be revealed or visualized. To visualize the formal properties of points and lines, looking for the patterns of the connections is the key, the actual positioning of points on the network is not important. That is, it is the mere presence or absence of a link that is of importance, not where a point is shown on a graph. The unit of analysis is a relationship, a link, not an agent, a point on sociogram (Scott, 2009).

In the classroom exercise, to facilitate the construction of sociograms, a 3D modeling computer application, SketchUp (http://www.sketchup.com/intl/en/download/gsu.html) was used. SketchUp was selected due to its user friendly interface. SketchUp, commonly used for architecture, interior design, and engineering, is free for download and unlimited use. An advantage of using SketchUp to provide graphic visualization for SNA is that the sociogram constructed can be modeled in (3D). Relations are represented by 3D points and lines. Users have the ability rotate and change perspectives, which makes drafting and redrafting easily achievable. The 3D view of the sociogram allows a comprehensive view of the structural aspect of a network.

In the classroom exercise, since the data collected stem from one's Facebook wall, students were instructed to construct ego-centric sociograms by placing themselves as the center, and other agents in a circle surrounding the center, as well as making lines connecting the center and other agents. The rationale of arranging agents in a circle surrounding the center is to reduce as many crisscrossed lines as possible, to render the network surrounding the center more recognizable (see Fig. 1). The sociograms reflect the relationships indicated in the Agent-by-Agent matrix.

Cliques

Constructing sociograms allows researchers to locate the social structures – that is, the patterns of social relationships – embedded in a

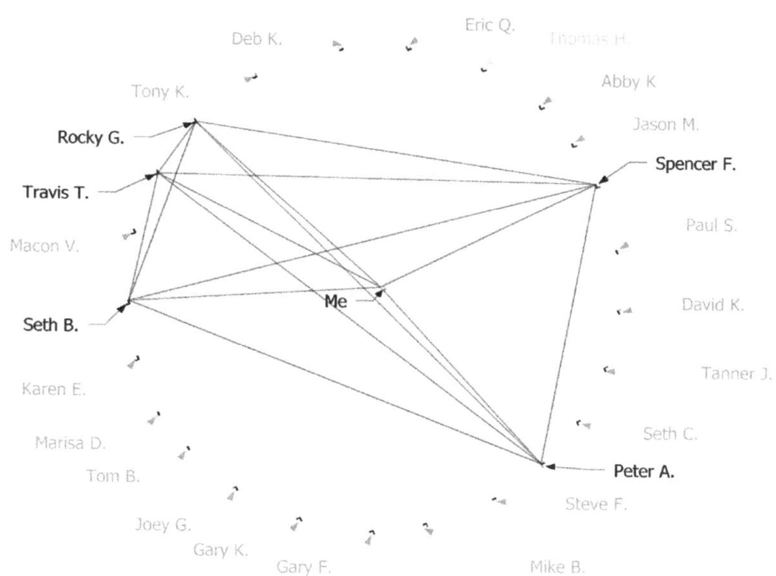

Fig. 1. Cliques.

group. The patterns of social relationships to be located are termed cliques in SNA. The sociogram generally has the form of a star, with the center having radiating lines connecting with agents, as well as other agents having lines connecting among themselves. A clique is a sub-group in a network, presented by a sub-graph in a sociogram. The sub-graph is a set of points which are (1) connected, (2) maximal, and (3) existing in a cycle. The diamond-shaped clique represents the over stacking of several smaller triangular cliques. Smaller cliques may include a clique of high school friends, a clique of co-workers, a clique of family, and a clique of current college friends. The main clique usually contains active individuals from the small cliques. Most main cliques usually have the size of 6–8 agents.

Connected

In any given group or network, people's informal social relations tie them into cohesive sub-groups. A clique is a cohesive sub-group that is important to a person's identity, social support, and sense of belonging. A clique has its own norms, values, and orientations, demonstrating the common saying, "Birds of a feather flock together." Cliques are naturally existing in any given groups or networks (Scott, 2009).

A clique is represented by a sub-graph in the sociogram. A sub-graph is a group of mutually connected points. Sub-graphs are visible as pockets of high density in a sociogram. Points that constitute a sub-graph are lined with one another through paths. Points of a sub-graph can "reach" one another through continuous chains of connections. The study of cliques is, thus, the study of sub-graphs (Scott, 2009).

Maximal

Aside from having points that are connected, a clique is also a sub-graph that is maximal. Being maximal means having the largest amount of points that exhibits a certain defining characteristic of the whole graph (Scott, 2009). In other words, a clique is the largest sub-group that possesses a particular defining characteristic of the whole group. A clique is maximal when it is the largest sub-graph that can be found, without the defining characteristic disappearing. When a sub-graph is maximal, it is impossible to add any new member without diluting the defining characteristic. That is why, in order to preserve the strength of the defining characteristic, a clique has to be exclusive. Although there may be several cliques present in a network, a clique is maximal when it is not contained in any other clique.

Cycle

A clique is the strongest when it exists in a cycle, a path that returns to its starting point (Scott, 2009). Taken from the geometric concept that the circle is the strongest shape, a cycle provides the needed social attentiveness and reciprocal responsiveness to build a strong sub-group in a network. The attentiveness and responsiveness allow individuals in a clique to continuously share and provide feedback to one another regarding a defining characteristic, critical to the clique.

In the classroom exercise, to locate the maximal clique, students used a tracing method. This tracing starts from the center and returns to the center, with an attempt to include as many connections as possible. Students started with the center, then, looked for any point that was connected to this staring point, and then looked for any point that was connected to this additional point. The Agent-by-Agent matrix can provide clues about potential points that one point is connected to. Students were encouraged to reference their Agent-by-Agent matrices to look for points of connections. Students were encouraged to zoom in and out, a feature of SketchUp, to explore connectedness. The tracing procedure is repeated until no further connections can be found, that is, when the tracing comes to a halt. To create a cycle, students then connected the last agent in the tracing with the center. The boundary of a clique, a connected and maximal cycle, is thus discovered. Once the clique is discovered, students were asked to color the boundaries of the clique to bring out the formal properties of the clique. Color helps visualize the clique identified (see Fig. 2).

The purpose of clique analysis is to find one or more cliques, and isolated agents. However, most of the students were active Facebook users,

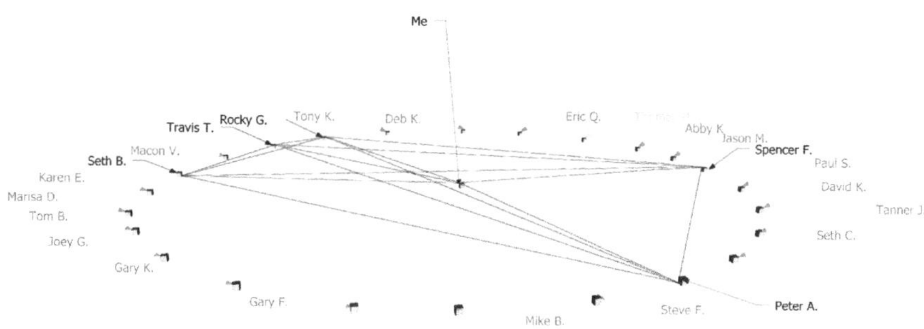

Fig. 2. Enhanced Clique View.

thus, their sociograms were dense graphs. Dense graphs are likely to show the dominance of a single large clique.

SOCIABILITY ON FACEBOOK

In the classroom exercise, upon locating the cliques, students were asked to describe the forms of communication found among members of the cliques. Most clique activities are reported to be expressive communication in nature, meaningless discursive communication, containing inside jokes or expressing shared sentiments. Status updates by the host or wall posts by other agents are mainly used to express one's emotional states. Expressive communication was the dominant form of communication on Facebook, with an intent to generate sociability.

Expressive communication is conducted and sociability is constructed on Facebook mainly using photos and descriptions. Both photos and descriptions create shared foci for users, thus, allow users to communicate even though they are separated by time and space. Photos are expressive in nature, communicating emotions. Descriptions, although as a form of discursive communication with a bias favoring referential communication (Couch, 1996), are used, in fact, in Facebook, as a form of expressive communication. Statements are used mostly to describe emotions and sentiments, and specify the meaning of the photos posted. Thus, Facebook, the technological format, predicated the communication content, expressive and emotive in nature, and fostered the social relationship constructed, sociability.

Reports show forms of expressive communication contribute to the construction of sociability on Facebook. Expressive communication manifests itself in the forms of 3E – Engagement, Empathy, and Entertainment.

Engagement

Facebook activities are essentially social activities. A user working on his Facebook in the privacy of his own home, half-naked perhaps, is in fact participating in social activities in a public forum on Facebook. Posting on Facebook, users project a future of getting a response in the form of a like, share, or comment. Not getting a response may be experienced as a disappointment. Disappointed Facebook users can promote their posts, with a small fee paid to Facebook, to enhance the visibility and priority of their posts, with the hope of obtaining responses. Thus, posting, although it is a one-way communication, is in fact, intended as a delayed two-way communication. Receiving a response, that is, attention, is the ultimate reward. The value of a post and the skills of a user are illustrated by the number of responses, the amount of attention a post received. Facebook accounts, although mostly belong to individuals, are not at all individualistic. In fact, they are totally social. Facebook users have an exhibitionist mentality, yearning to be noticed.

To initiate an engagement is to self-disclose. Users sacrifice parts of their selves which serve as a shared focus of attention, in attempts to engage others. Forms of self-disclosures range from a simple hello, indicating one's availability and desire to engage, to intimate display of what is on one's mind.

Forms of intent to engage include sending greetings, such as, "How everybody doing today?" or "Happy Friday Everybody!!!!!! Have a Blessed Weekend!!!!!!" Posting invitations shows an intent to engage, with statements such as "Who all wants to hangout????? Hit me up," "Anyone wanna go to iron man 3 today at 4 or 445?" or "whose moving to Florida with me?!!" Intent to engage also includes posting updates about oneself to keep others informed. Updates include one's deeds such as "Just declared a major," and "Safe Haven soundtrack on repeat :)" and one's emotional states such as "getting my first tattoo this week! def nervous ..., " and "Live in fear, final exams." With a shared focus, provided by Facebook, posting inquiries is another form of engagement such as "Got the trees off my iPad but can't get the rest off ... HELP!" or "Anybody know of any places hiring?" Venting is also an intent to engage, with posts such as "I cannot stand a liar!!" or "My car would get fucking broken into. There's $1,000 or more to fixing my car I don't have. Seriously fuck today."

Empathy

Responses to posts on the Facebook are mostly, if not entirely, empathetic. Since users are "friends" with one another, that is, they share sentiments and interest on at least one issue, they are expected to exhibit a sense of solidarity by replying to posts with empathetic responses. Empathy exudes in responses that show compliments or encouragement to posts. Complementary responses are expected to posts, mostly photos, that show happy or successful events, with statements such as "You are so beautiful!" "AWWWWW!!!!" "Great pics!" or "Congrats for winning! Awesome!!" Responses to those with posts of adversaries, exhibit understanding and support such as: "I am with you, man," or "Hang in there!" Responses to posts of upcoming conquests show encouragement such as "Go get it!! Have a great game!!"

Entertainment

While a status update may sometimes serve to inform friends of a life event, Facebook is less of an information source and more often an entertainment center. Users gather at Facebook to entertain and to be entertained. It is a taken-for-granted understanding that one should do one's best to promote the entertaining value of Facebook to fulfill the leisure purpose of the forum. Posts are often humorous, fun or sarcastic statements or photos of comic acts. Posts are also affectionate with photos or videos of cute babies, couples, or pets. Posts also contain bizarre photos of unusual acts or scenes. Relaxing photos of beautiful or serene scenes are common posts as well.

Epitomizing the entertaining value of Facebook is the posting of memes. A meme is a statement, picture, or video that spreads from person to person via the Internet. A meme encompasses all the characteristics mentioned above, humorous, affectionate, bizarre or relaxing. A meme may be a picture of Willy Wonka with a caption of "So tattoos will look ugly when I'm old? Tell me more about how beautiful you'll be in 60 years." (http://cdn.themetapicture.com/media/funny-Wonka-meme-chocolate-factory.jpg) or a video of a walrus doing sit-ups to "Eye of the Tiger" theme (http://www.youtube.com/watch?v=QNRiml9s_OE), or the video of Lydia Callis, the animated sign-language interpreter for New York Mayor Michael Bloomberg (http://www.youtube.com/watch?v=jTGsj7Srl-U). Memes like these allow Facebook users to chuckle together. Successful memes are liked, shared, and commented upon by many. Seeking and enjoying memes is one of the reasons why Facebook use is addictive.

SI AND SNA

With technological formats that emphasize the construction and maintenance of relationships, and with the activities of users essentially socially oriented, Facebook lends itself to be studied most effectively by researchers who adopt SI where social relationships are the prime focus of study. However, in order to render the thickets of relations manageable, and to delineate the relatedness among users, symbolic interactionists need to adopt SNA for assistance. SNA helps with the preparation of relational data matrices to delineate the relatedness among users. In addition, with SNA, symbolic interactionists are able to locate the cliques existing in the networks. The sociogram further aids researchers to visualize the cliques. Visualizing the clique helps provide a fine grain view of the forms of sociability in Facebook. Analyzing the features of communication among members of the cliques gives flesh to the bone structure of the cliques.

There are computer software programs available for network analysis, such as UCINET Software, and for visualizing the network, such as Netdraw. However, it is the authors' contention that a qualitative approach, analyzing and visualizing the networks by hand, is a more adequate method when studying sociability, a non-instrumental and non-utilitarian relationship. Analyzing the network by hand – creating relational data matrices, drawing the sociogram, and tracing the clique by hand – provides a familiarity with the data which is crucial when analyzing the features of communication later on.

Conventional SNA relies on UCINET and Netdraw to analyze and visualize networks. However, SNA is typically used to study networks developed in bureaucracy, namely, boards of directors in organizations. Top officials of large corporations often serve on each other's boards. SNA set out to analyze the interlocking ties among top officials, with an aim to illustrate that a small group of people hold much of the decision-making power across many organizations. In this type of study, the mere connection established between boards of different organizations – having the same members serving on different boards – automatically implicates the shared interest, financial and political, between the organizations. There is an understanding that when the same board members are found in different organizations, these board members would naturally make decisions reflecting the interests of the organizations that they serve. Thus, locating the networks of various boards in many organizations is key to SNA studies, examining the features of communication of these boards members is not a focus of attention.

Facebook is not an instrumental organization such as a board of directors, nor is sociability a utilitarian form of relationship. Facebook is entertaining and frivolous, and sociability is about sentiment and humor. No economic or political decisions are made on Facebook, where users are engaging in non-serious activities. Thus, when studying sociability on Facebook, merely locating the connections among users does not reveal much about the nature of sociability. Detailed analyses of the communication taking place among clique members are needed in order to reveal the formal features of sociability. To conduct a detailed analysis of communication in cliques requires a thorough understanding of the communication taking place in the network. A thorough understanding of the data can be achieved when researchers forgo software programs and conduct analyses by hand.

When visualizing networks, the authors highly recommend the use of a 3D-drawing software, such as SketchUp. 3D drawings are more useful than the conventional 2D drawings. With 3D drawing, it does not matter where one places the agents when drawing the sociogram, the 3D features allow researchers to examine the forms of sociograms from various angles, which allows users to detect similarity in shapes of various sociograms (see Fig. 3). Methodologically, 3D can better capture the broadcasting ability of Facebook users, with broadcasting meaning distributing messages to dispersed audience in all directions.

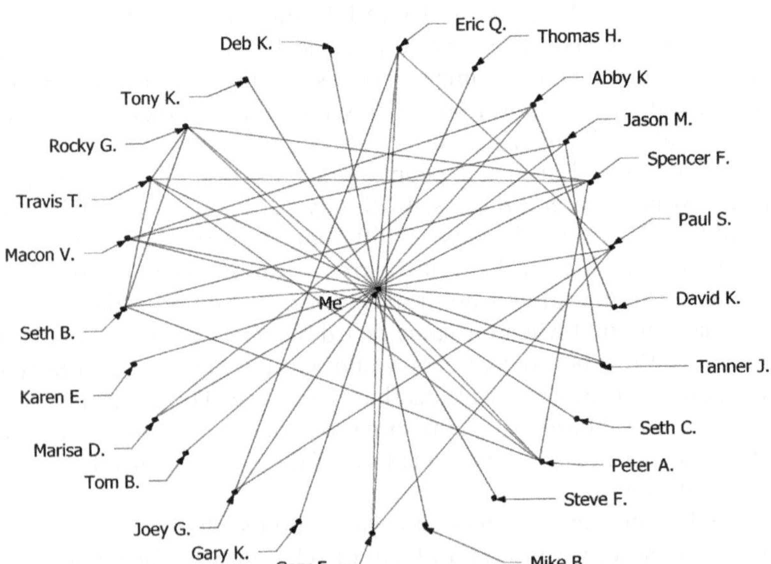

Fig. 3. Sociogram.

In addition, using 3D drawing software, researchers are able to compare and contrast the networks with presumable structural similarities. Networks with structural similarities can be found in organizations such as colleges and universities, churches, supermarkets, sororities and fraternities, and single parent households. For example, structural comparisons and contrasts of the networks of several single-father households yields insights into the role of the father, and the form of relationships fostered in the family (Scott, 2009).

Researchers can examine different networks that share structural similarities, they can also identify a network of interest and compare and contrast the changes taking place in the network over time. In the classroom exercise, the cliques identified when network analyses were conducted in March (that involved the spring break) had different forms and features of communication as compared to the cliques identified in October (that did not involve the spring break). Cliques in March reflect spring break activities, while cliques in October are tied to usual college life. Thus with the network analysis, researchers can conduct cross sectional studies or examinations over time.

REFERENCES

Berlo, D. K. (1960). *The process of communication*. New York, NY: Holt, Rinehart, & Winston.

Chang, P. (2011, May 20). FOMO: The unintended effects of social media addition. Retrieved from http://www.nbcnewyork.com/news/local/Social-Media-Is-Causing-Anxiety-and-Depression-122260279.html

Couch, C. J. (1989). *Social processes and relationships*. New York, NY: General Hall.

Couch, C. J. (1996). *Information technologies and social orders*. New York, NY: Aldine.

Fowler, G. A. (2012, October 4). Facebook: One billion and counting. Retrieved from http://online.wsj.com/article/SB10000872396390443635404578036164027386112.html

Harris, K. (2008). Using social networking sites as student engagement tools. *Diverse Issues in Higher Education*, *25*, 18.

Mead, G. H. (1934). *Mind, self, and society*. Chicago, IL: University of Chicago Press.

Ottalini, D. (2010, April 21). Students addicted to social media – New UM study. Retrieved from http://www.newsdesk.umd.edu/sociss/release.cfm?ArticleID=2144

Scott, J. G. (2009). *Social network analysis: A handbook*. New York, NY: Sage.

Simmel, G. (1950). In K. Wolff (Ed.), *The sociology of Georg Simmel*. New York, NY: Nabu Press.

Wellman, B. (1988). Structural analysis: From method and metaphor to theory and substance. In B. Wellman & S. D. Berkowitz (Eds.), *Social structures: A network approach* (pp. 19–61). Vancouver: Empirical Press.

APPENDIX: ESSENTIAL SNA CONCEPTS (SCOTT, 2009)

Adjacency – two points, connected by a line, are adjacent to each other

Betweenness – an agent that is between the various other agents in the graph, serving as a gatekeeper or a broker

Bridge – a central point that connects two or more peaks

Bridgers – points that are connected to two or more cycles, but are not members of neither one of them

Centrality – a structural center of a graph

Cluster – all the direct contacts of a peak

Cycle – a path that returns to its own starting point

Degree – the total number of points in an agent's neighborhood is her degree

Density – the number of lines present

Ego-Centric Network Analysis – an analysis of links surrounding a participate agent

Geodesic – the shortest path between two points

Global Centrality – an agent that has a strategically important position in the overall structure of the network

Hangers – points that are connected to a member of a cycle, but are not members of a cycle

Isolated Trees – points that are connected with one another, are not connected to any cycle

Local Centrality – an agent that has a large number of connections in her immediate environment, that is, a large neighborhood of direct connections

Neighborhood – points to which a particular point is adjacent, are called as its neighborhood

Path – a walk where each point and each line are distinct

Peak – a point that is more central than any other point

Peripheral Points – agents with low centrality, who are loosely connected to the network

Socio-Centric Network Analysis – an analysis of patterns of connection in the network as a whole

Walk – a sequence of lines in a graph

NEW IOWA SCHOOL REDUX: *SECOND LIFE* AS LABORATORY

Michael A. Katovich and Shing-Ling S. Chen

ABSTRACT

This paper provides a general comparison between the ethos, methodological mission, and theoretical standpoint of the New Iowa School, established by Carl Couch and his students and Second Life, *a three dimensional virtual world that invites particular forms of sociation. Despite differences in orientation and purpose, as well as biases in communication, we propose that the methodological and conceptual emphasis underlying the research generated from New Iowa School experimental studies can provide a useful framework for research into the virtual worlds created in* Second Life. *In the course of citing similarities and differences between the New Iowa School and* Second Life, *we also note that contrived worlds in laboratories and virtual worlds in user domains not only have relevant analogical processes to outside, in situ social worlds, but consist of social stages for performances that have application to the various social stages constructed by actors in the real world. In conclusion, we suggest that the New Iowa School and* Second Life *represent different but compatible realities in their own right, that the conceptual depth associated with the New Iowa School can inform research into* Second Life *interactions, and that each offer insights into*

Symbolic Interaction and New Social Media
Studies in Symbolic Interaction, Volume 43, 63–84

ISSN: 0163-2396/doi:10.1108/S0163-239620140000043014

the external worlds inhabited by real actors who navigate across time and space in their everyday lives.

Keywords: New Iowa School; *Second Life*; virtual worlds; laboratory

Serious discourse between scholars, thinkers, artists, and technicians has revolved around dramatic changes in technologies and the concomitant impact of such changes. The advent of electronic technologies, made famous to students of communication and others in the intellectual community by McLuhan's (1964) daring assertions and predictions, contributed to a long line of criticism and elaboration, directed at, among other things, the acceleration of such communication and its consequences (see Kurzweil, 2005). One does not have to buy into all of the ominous or fantastic predictions offered by the above, or any other students of internet technologies, to realize that the transmission of communication has not only altered expectations regarding the timing, rhythm, tempo, and duration of such information, but has also reoriented those who wish to study the social places or dynamic physical worlds in which communication and the construction of social information takes place.

In the field of social psychology, extending into communication studies of conversation analysis, researchers have employed electronic technologies for varieties of studies and methods of documentation (see Heath, Hindmarsh, & Luff, 2010). In one of the symbolic interactionist traditions, emanating from the University of Iowa, Asch's (1951) photographed study of conformity and Milgram's (1974) provocative video-taped examinations of the authoritarian presence, provided "new Iowa School research" with the impetus and tools to create "provocative stages" in which subjects, acting as agents, would improvise roles for the purpose of performing with improvisational others in the context of controlled environments (Katovich, 1984). Such studies provided the groundwork upon which researchers could utilize varieties of information technologies, heretofore acknowledged, generally, as internet technologies, in order to study the dynamics and intervals of social life in controlled settings.

Later, the emergence of internet technologies enabled researchers to extend, literally and figuratively, the laboratory contexts through the creation of simulated environments. As with the controlled laboratory studies, technologies derived from internet worlds allowed researchers to observe, systematically, real and consequential performances by subjects. Despite criticism of such simulations as unnatural, and in particular, antithetical to the interactionist ethos to examine social life in situ (Denzin, 1970; Lofland, 1976), the possibilities of not only examining enacted performances on a simulated and controlled stage began to inspire some to look into how powerful social media could involve human interactions in what has become known as virtual time and place. At the risk of oversimplification, such interactions take place in worlds created by humans online. The imagined processes that emerge from such a creation provide narratives and identities that participants define as real in their consequences (Thomas, 1923).

For instance, Philip Rosedale (who goes by the avatar name of Philip Linden) and associates of Linden Lab have gained widespread notoriety through their construction of simulated performances in a virtual online world, *Second Life* (Boellstorff, 2008). *Second Life* enables users, called residents, to interact with one another through avatars. The users engage, collectively, in a wide range of social activities from exploring their world (known as the grid), meeting others and socializing, participating in group activities, to creating and trading virtual properties and services using the virtual currency, the Linden dollar (L$). *Second Life* is a viable site for social research as individuals assuming avatars, and coordinating their navigation through virtual reality, form relationships, construct romance, establish systems of economic transactions, and build communal solidarity – in short, the participants create human culture (Boellstorff, 2008).

However, the wide range of activities found in *Second Life* makes it difficult to clearly understand its ongoing and enlivened patterns (or, loosely, its structure) whether focusing on the broader online community, a more specific role-playing game, or an ephemeral online chat. The diffused and dispersed activities make it difficult for researchers who are interested in investigating *Second Life* to detect systematic arrangements and key markings that make up the virtual world. Amid such complexities, Boellstorff (2008) utilized ethnographic research to investigate *Second Life*. Although he provided insightful research, he also noted the challenge of filtering though large amounts of data – "ten thousand pages of fieldnotes from participant observation, interviewing, and focus groups, plus approximately ten thousand additional pages of blogs, newsletters, and other websites" (Boellstorff, 2008, p. 75)

Borrowing from Boellstorff we advocate an effective and efficient research method for *Second Life*, which we term the New Iowa School of laboratory research. We argue that such research can extend the generic concepts that Iowa School researchers developed while employing video-taped technologies in controlled laboratory settings. In order to make such arguments clear, we first demonstrate the striking structural similarities between the New Iowa School laboratory, and *Second Life*. Based on the similarities noted, we assert the validity of applying New Iowa School laboratory research to the study of *Second Life*. Second, we wish to offer a program of research that can extend future research in virtual worlds, allowing for varieties of possibilities that acknowledge the enormous popularity and attention paid to virtual games, avatars, and the social construction of narratives that accompanies the creation of such games and the correlation between identifying one's self as a person and as an avatar embedded into the virtual games.

NEW IOWA SCHOOL LABORATORY AND WEB 1.0

The New Iowa School laboratory was designed by Carl Couch and associates (Couch, Katovich, & Buban, 1994; Couch, Saxton, & Katovich, 1986; Saxton & Couch, 1975), as an approach in the tradition of symbolic interaction and in particular, as an extension of Mead's (1932, 1934, 1938) discourse on temporality, the social self, and the social act. Couch and associates advocated a dynamic epistemological framework that allowed for knowing the world as it is, a moving, dynamic, and transforming entity in process, and establishing the methodological recipes (making use of extant video technologies) that would allow researching social processes and relationships as they occurred in the controlled environment of the laboratory. The New Iowa School laboratory is different from traditional laboratory research where participants were only allowed to react to stimuli. In the New Iowa School laboratory, participants were treated as intelligent individuals who interacted with one another. Couch and associates advised the researchers to establish a context in the laboratory, assign participants with identities tied to the context, and provide a social objective for participants to engage in interaction in the laboratory. The social interaction in the laboratory was then video recorded. The video recording and playback allow researchers to conduct a thorough analysis of the elements and processes of relationship construction.

Previous work comparing the New Iowa School world of the laboratory to other socially constructed worlds has advocated two comparable analogies. First, New Iowa School researchers have argued that studying social acts and social relationships in the laboratory abides by the same principles advocated by researchers in naturalistic settings (Katovich, 1984; Katovich, Saxton, & Powell, 1986; Molseed, 1994). Second, the generic concepts generated in laboratory and naturalistic settings apply to the social life constructed in online environments (Chen & Johns, 2002). Accordingly, the manner of investigation that emphasizes detecting empirical patterns and generating generic concepts that describe such patterns serves as a link between varieties of social worlds, ranging from the durable and naturalistic, to the staged and temporally bounded. Specifically, the New Iowa School laboratory, a controlled setting, eliminates the interference of unrelated factors as it "magnifies selected features of social life" (Katovich, 1984, p. 55). Cyberspace, an equally controlled setting, also offers a "filtered online environment (willfully) constructed among (online) users" (Chen & Johns, 2002, p. 32) who focus their attention on certain topics.

As the principle investigator of the New Iowa School, Couch (1987, pp. 3–5) instructed laboratory researchers to establish a context, assign identities, and provide a social objective for participants in the laboratory. The context established is artificial in that the researcher creates it purposively, to elicit an explicit and specific social relationship that he/she has targeted, theoretically, for investigation. While artificial in the literal sense of the term, the researcher establishes a cooperative relationship (rather than a deceptive relationship) with participants who interact with one another by accepting the laboratory context as authentic, or as defined by an open, rather than a suspicious awareness context (Glaser & Strauss, 1964). Similarly, Internet users willfully and openly accept the online environment as an authentic arena in which to conduct their activities, whether placing an online order or posting a response to an online discussion list. Internet users also suspend their disbelief when interacting with other users online, accessing the information on websites for work or pleasure.

Couch emphasized that New Iowa School laboratory participants are given the opportunities not only to accept the laboratory setting as real, but also to anticipate future events, access each other's intentions, and act purposively, engaging in minded behavior (Mead, 1934). Similar to laboratory participants, online users project cooperative behaviors beyond the here and now (and, while suspending disbelief, imagine such futures as existing in real worlds), imagine, simultaneously, the intentions of the other and how such intentions fit with those of the self, and create an intersubjective reality that participants regard as substantial enough to maintain interest over time.

In effect, as Couch (1987, p. 8) offered, the copresence established in the laboratory (and we argue, that is established online) provides for tangible activities that the researcher can analyze within the ethos of documenting those done in real life (RL) situations and in real time. As a result, the interaction in the New Iowa School laboratory, although technically an artificial environment, exhibits genuine emotions and substantive experiences. In the similar fashion, users of the Internet, although a virtual environment, also experience real joy or agony.

In the New Iowa School laboratory, Couch instructed researchers to assign participants identities, pertaining to the social relationship studied. Couch also advised that the assignment of identities had some congruence with the participants' everyday understandings of their worlds and that the activities associated with such identities correlated, in part, with how participants behaved in their ordinary, taken-for-granted routines. In effect, the assigned identities and accompanying activities did not create the emergent doubt that occurred in the more dramatic experiments (conducted by Asch and Milgram, for example), but remained in the world of "restorable reach" as Schutz and Luckmann (1973, pp. 36–38) put it. Similarly, in the online environment, users willingly construct identities for themselves and incorporate their methods of being into a practical process of announcing, validating, and affirming such identities in relation to others (see Stone, 1962, pp. 89–92). In effect, participants in laboratory and online studies become situated, as they do in everyday life, and "organize their exchanges with others based on their understanding of the identities and the context where they were situated" (Chen & Johns, 2002, p. 34).

The above comparisons between the New Iowa School laboratory and internet activities were made based on the use of Web 1.0, an early stage of the World Wide Web, characterized by one-way textual communication. In the context of Web 1.0, users adopted identities that rendered them, more or less, as passive consumers of online information. They browsed webpages but did not (and could not) contribute to the content, which the researchers restricted, thereby denying the opportunities for external editing. Instead of restructuring the environment then, participants confined their activities to that which maintained the extant boundaries as created by the researchers. Such activity consisted of sending e-mails, visiting websites, and placing online orders.

With the arrival of Web 2.0 in 2004, users' activities expanded to include two-way communication as well as the use of graphics. Users could transcend the boundaries imposed regarding online information and adopt emerging identities that contributed to a transformation from passive to active contributors regarding the website content. In accord with Mead (1934, p. 135), users' identities (or selves within the confines of the online world) did not necessarily exist in full prior to their activities, but developed as they became more active in adapting to and creating new boundaries in regard to their participation. The content of behavior in Web 2.0 became open for external editing and allowing for user-generated and unscripted activities. With user-generated content came emergent social media, or on-the-spot websites created for social interaction and relationships building. In everyday life, Facebook and Twitter provide notable examples of social media. In the online environment of *Second Life*, a highly interactive online platform, specific place-based community interaction came about as users actively manipulated content. In this way, *Second Life*, although artificial in that it is confined to a specifically created environment, takes on the appearance of "large-scale social contexts with visual and interactive components, somewhat like 'environment' and 'space'" (Boellstorff, 2008, p. 17).

NEW IOWA SCHOOL LABORATORY AND WEB 2.0

With features of social interaction and relationships building, *Second Life* is even more strikingly similar to the New Iowa School laboratory than its Web 1.0 predecessor. After all, generating and analyzing social relationships are the ethos of New Iowa School laboratory research. With the expansion from Web 1.0 to Web 2.0, *Second Life* embodies not only all the similarities noted above between Web 1.0 sites and the New Iowa School laboratory, but also new features that provide more noticeable similarities with the New Iowa School laboratory. Enhanced similarities include the emphases on constructed context, suspension of disbelief, role-playing, and agency. Features, unique to *Second Life*, with marked similarities to the New Iowa School laboratory, include having tangible places, overt time activities, and the emphasis on social interaction and relationships.

Constructed Context

In the New Iowa School laboratory, the general social contexts of interaction are constructed by the researcher and communicated to the participants. The contexts vary considerably and could resemble, say, a living room for the tenant-land lord negotiation or an office for labor-management negotiation. To facilitate the interaction, researchers may decorate the context with furniture or props to create a familiar ambience for subjects, but also one that avoids an air-tight atmosphere that might intimidate or create dis-ease on the part of participants.

In *Second Life*, the social context is constructed by residents. With the visualization tools provided by Web 2.0, residents may construct or purchase items to decorate their homes, storefronts (such as bookstores or night clubs) or buildings. Unlike the pre-fabricated physical worlds of the laboratory, Web 2.0 residents engage in a more fanciful contextualization, sometimes going to great lengths to decorate the environment and attract other residents to visit and engage in social interaction. While different in regard to initial constructions, both the laboratory and online environments have a malleable character that, again, encourages emergent reconstructions of place, identities, and even intentions as interaction proceeds.

Suspension of Disbelief

Researchers create the general premises for participant gathering in both the New Iowa School laboratory and *Second Life*. This creation of initiation of contact among participants lends an artificial appearance to the environments. None of the participants would gather together at the specific places in the specific intervals of time spontaneously or in the course of being in everyday life. Owing to such implied artificiality, researchers invite participants to imagine that their gathering occurred as if it appears as an everyday extension of their ordinary navigation through time and space. In effect, researchers ask participants in the New Iowa School and *Second Life* research contexts to see the laboratory or online environment as an ordinary context for social interaction that emerges according to a taken-for-granted logic. Such imagination does not call for a dramatic alteration of perception. Rather, as with introducing a new game, participants can recognize that minor suspensions of disbelief, remedial cooperation, and slight changes in the physical environment "complex social structures can be created within a single room laboratory" (Couch, 1987, p. 17).

As Couch discovered in his New Iowa School research, *Second Life* residents actually have fun suspending their disbelief and interacting with one another in the contexts created. Owing to the aforementioned fanciful nature of *Second Life* environments, participants can imagine themselves as traveling long distances, flying (by pressing the "F" key), or even teleporting themselves to novel places. In *Second Life*, although structures created by residents mostly adhere to the laws of physics, participants can build environments that allow for shared ignorance of specific constraints, as if playing with physical laws while adhering to them at the same time (Boellstorff, 2008).

The New Iowa School laboratory calls for ordinary human activity (e.g., bargaining and negotiation) in pretend environments (that, through suspension become seen as real) whereas *Second Life* online activity does allow for the human to transcend obdurate boundaries. One of the more extraordinary human abilities that *Second Life* residents realize occurs as they carry on two coherent and practical conversations at once. When a resident chats with others in a group, he/she can also carry on an instant-message conversation with another individual. While such activity may appear as ordinary multi-tasking on the surface, residents find it remarkable that they can engage in such simultaneity as if they engaged only in one task, making it appear "like being able to talk and whisper at the same time" (Boellstorff, 2008, p. 13).

Role-Playing

As mentioned, the researcher in the New Iowa School laboratory assigns identities to participants and asks the participants to take them seriously enough to engage in purposeful behavior with another. The identities assumed by participants have familiar anchor-points and allow for the construction of interaction through conversation, which the researcher can analyze. Assigning identities that participants are familiar with allows participants to have the understanding of the standpoints or concerns, as well as the vocabularies of the identities assigned. In the interaction, participants role play the perceived behavior of the identities assigned (Couch, 1987).

In *Second Life*, residents freely take on identities of their own choice. Identities assumed usually are ones that residents have familiarized themselves with outside of the *Second Life*, or ones that residents aspire to. During the interaction, residents role play the perceived behavior of the chosen identities. The differences between the role-playing and identity creation in New Iowa School laboratory and those in *Second Life* reside in the types of identities role-played. In the New Iowa School laboratory, participants are asked to role play categorical identities, or those based on hypothetical social relationships such as landlords and tenants, clerks and customers, managers and employees, parents and children. In *Second Life*, residents also assume categorical identities, but will often redefine such identities through the use of fantastic elaborations which are fictional, magical and supernatural.

Despite the allowance of differences in *Second Life*, which does not restrict participants to remain grounded in the hypothetical gravitational reality of the categorical identity, research of interactions in the context of *Second Life* resembles the research generated in the New Iowa School. The *Second Life* and New Iowa School goals resemble each other in that despite difference regarding remaining grounded or allowing flight from the impositions of categorical identities, the key focus on conversational analysis links the two approaches. In effect, while the content of identities can differ immensely, the form of interaction designed for analysis remains congruent.

Agency and Construction

Whether confined to role-playing grounded categorical identities or allowing for fantastic flight from such grounded identities, both the New Iowa School laboratory and *Second Life* emphasize the notion of agency in participants and residents. On the surface the New Iowa School laboratory and the *Second Life* online environment (Linden Lab) have strict boundaries, controlled by researchers. Both New Iowa School laboratory researchers and Linden Lab construct the details of the laboratories and request that such details be taken into account by the participants, who did not participate in the planning or the enactment of their surroundings. However, instead of treating the authoritarian position as static and confined to permanent closed awareness contexts (Glaser & Strauss, 1964), the researchers in the New Iowa School and *Second Life* encourage user-generated interaction and the exercise of generating new content within the pre-constructed confines. An analogy occurs in theater, as the actors, who did not participate in writing the script or creating the scenic stage, nevertheless practice their art through interpretation in between the lines and the scenery through which they navigate.

The analogy with acting becomes all the more apparent when considering agency in laboratory participants, Carl Couch and his students insisted that New Iowa School researchers needed to treat participants as intelligent individuals who were able to assess others' intentions, anticipate upcoming events, and organize their action as a response (Couch et al., 1986). In effect New Iowa School research allows for a leap of faith in regard to participants; they may alter the universe which the researchers have constructed, but such alterations will maintain in the spirit of the construction as well as generate relevant data for the researchers to analyze. Similarly, *Second Life* provides a looser environment that encourages imaginative and creative alterations by its residents. Although looser in its structure (and allowing for more alterations), the SL (*Second Life*) researchers demonstrate a leap of faith that the participants will act in ways that allow researchers to examine the "ability of humans to craft themselves" (Boellstorff, 2008, p. 57). As Boellsdorf notes:

> Linden Lab maintains the basic platform for *Second Life*: a landscape with land, water, trees, and sky; a set of building tools, a means to control, modify, and communicate between avatars. Nearly everything else is the result of persons or groups of people spending millions of hours every month in acts of creation. (Boellstorff, 2008, pp. 11–12)

One of the creative activities that residents lavish time and money on is to create avatars. Allowance for such a creation provides the researcher with opportunities to record and analyze intentionality in the making and to research "the ... multiple embodiments (of the self), often across gender, race, even species (for instance, a handsome man, a wolf, and a robot)" (Boellstorff, 2008, p. 129). Again, while New Iowa School laboratory participants assume identities that have concrete referential significance, and carry out interactions that are utilitarian in nature, *Second Life* residents assume identities that are fantastic, and participate in exchanges that are expressive in nature. Even so, despite such differences, the opportunities to analyze, systematically, how participants create micro-interactional worlds within the broader pre-constructed worlds drives both New Iowa School and *Second Life* research.

Tangible Places

A New Iowa School lab consists of a suite of interlocking rooms segregated from ordinary places. Researchers design the rooms to exclude extraneous factors that interfere with the generation and observation of uncluttered specimens of social processes and relationships. The design of New Iowa School laboratory research includes sound proof and window-less rooms to minimize auditory and visual distractions (Couch, 1987). The lab, then, allows for the observation of what otherwise is not or might not be observable. Excluding extraneous noise and sight, however, magnifies the sounds and sights within the laboratory, making for "a provocative stage that elicits vibrant social processes" (Couch, 1987, p. 4).

A signature feature of *Second Life* also involves the notion of place, made possible by the visualization tools of Web 2.0. It is noted that a specified "place," while not as structurally intact as a laboratory, provides sharply defined markers that define the key parameters of *Second Life* (Boellstorff, 2008). Unlike Facebook or Twitter users, who roam in the cyberspace and interact with accounts, *Second Life* users reside in a place that provides tangible boundaries; they interact with others in a location imagined as enduring over time. The metaphorical power of place in *Second Life* becomes a defining characteristic of users' imagined location as "even the term 'resident' underscores how 'a sense of place' is fundamental to *Second Life*" (Boellstorff, 2008, p. 91).

Whereas the New Iowa School participant navigates within a visibly pre-constructed environment, a *Second Life* user can build his/her domain in *Second Life* by using "prims," or primitive shapes that the user can transform into social objects to suit specific purposes as defined by the tasks in *Second Life*. Before doing that, however, he/she would have to pay a virtual real estate agent for a piece of land where his/her house sits; and for the right to own land, he/she has to pay Linden Lab a monthly "land use fee." Other than personal homes, businesses are built as well in *Second Life* – dance clubs, furniture stores, boutiques, and the like. Whether it is a personal home or a business, the place is built and decorated to express oneself as well as to serve as a tangible locale for social interactions.

The tangible interaction platform in *Second Life* bears a visual resemblance and a close reference to the obdurate external world. In *Second Life*, one can find parts of New Orleans's French Quarter in the wake of Hurricane Katrina, buildings ranging from a spaceflight museum to an Iraqi War Memorial, and the recreation of the Twin Towers destroyed in the 9/11 attacks (Boellstorff, 2008). Similar to the way researchers design the New Iowa School laboratory to generate a specific process of social interaction, so do researchers encourage users to explore and build places in *Second Life* to create social worlds that the users can share for mutual and common interests.

Over Time Activities

The New Iowa School laboratory and the *Second Life* online environment create compelling spatial-temporal worlds in which participants find (and in some cases create and re-create) themselves. Participants assume identities at the onset of the experiments and endeavors, but in the process of engagement, develop and maintain functional identities that become linked to such engagement over time and distinct to the places they navigate. The identities not only define individual engagement, but become congruent with others; each of the participants comes to a realization of their connection to specific others, allowing them to establish a social understanding of their participation as it exists across space and time (Miller, Hintz, & Couch, 1975).

Couch and his students paid a great deal of attention to the across time and across space nature of human involvement (Couch et al., 1994). One of the primary rationales for creating the New Iowa School as distinct from the earlier version of the Iowa School, founded by Couch's mentor, Manford Kuhn, rested on the utilization of audio-video-tape technology that could account for how humans situated conduct by using social pasts to project desired futures (Katovich & Couch, 1992). Documenting how participants used the projected future to guide present behavior (and create novel pasts from which to draw) became one of the primary foci of the New Iowa School studies. In the same fashion, *Second Life* online participation also occurs across time and across space. The emergence of the fantastic, for instance, or places and times that become virtually created by the participants, make sense in the context of what the online participants recognize in conjunction with the onset (the past present) of the endeavor.

In addition, in the course of laboratory interaction, Couch indicated that individuals attempt to determine each other's intentions when they establish copresence (Couch, 1987). Couch and his students maintained that individuals possessed the ability to not only assess intentionality, but to provide public announcements, so that what might be considered individual motivation becomes shared in accordance with the congruent functional identities that emerged in the laboratory over time (Miller et al., 1975). For instance, when hearing a cry for help by a distal other, copresent individuals representing a two person group (dyad) assess the meaning of such a cry and agree to engage in joint action in the attempt to resolve the perceived problem (cf. Blumer, 1969, p. 3). New Iowa School laboratory researchers have used this dyadic feature of interaction as their root metaphor of human coordination. The process beginning with the mutual impulse to act and culminating in the consummation of shared futures regarding such action (and mirroring, in part, Mead's (1938) perception of the social act) occurs in a laboratory that researchers set up that allows participants the opportunity to assess each other's intentions in regard to this act.

Allowing for actors to provide substance within broadly defined frameworks further allows researchers to avoid the pitfall of traditional laboratory studies that stress an endpoint of reacting, momentarily, to stimuli, thereby constraining participants and denying them the opportunity to anticipate future events or to assess the intention of others. Couch, in particular, stressed an alternate use of the laboratory that provided a broad enough context and a flexibility in regard to assigned identities in order "to elicit the generation of anticipation and intention from the participants, not to eradicate them" (Couch, 1987, p. 27).

In a similar vein, activities constructed by participants within the context of *Second Life* anticipated the activities of others over time. When a user logs on with his/her avatar name and password, he/she has chosen to spend time in *Second Life* and interact with others in the virtual worlds. Entering *Second Life* is an intentional act, as is any subsequent activity chosen. Residents generally anticipate a pleasurable future when entering *Second Life*; after all, *Second Life* provides a motto to provide opportunities to "experience endless surprises and unexpected delights in a world imagined and created by people like you" (Linden Labs). While encountering other avatars in *Second Life*, residents are able to assess each other's intention with the context provided.

SL residents' abilities to anticipate the future, act with intentionality, and assess each other's intention underscore all the activities found in *Second Life*. One hosts a gathering in one's home with roomful of guests discussing philosophical issues. Or, one gets dressed to attend a wedding in a church on a virtual mountain, and attends the reception in a club afterwards. As one leaves the activities and logs off, "*Second Life* disappears from your computer screen, but as you go to your kitchen to chop vegetables, you think about all those people still dancing away in a club with a bride and groom, watching a virtual sun set over a virtual sea" (Boellstorff, 2008, p. 16).

Social Interaction and Relationships

Couch iterated that the goal of New Iowa School laboratory research, to examine social processes, necessitated recording the precise processes and intervals that revealed how people acted with, toward, for, and against each other (Couch, 1987). To achieve this goal, Couch believed that researchers committed to a sociological imagination (Mills, 1959) should make the actions of dyads, rather than collections of individuals, the target of observation. He separated, explicitly, New Iowa School laboratory research from other extant types of laboratory research in social psychology that made the activity of the individuals, or the activity of aggregates of individuals, the object of investigation. Couch argued that a true sociological approach in the laboratory keyed on social activities, that observers could detect by watching for indications of reciprocally acknowledged attention and explicit sharing of foci (Miller et al., 1975). Following the lead of Simmel (1950, 1971) in particular, New Iowa School laboratory research established the minimum unit of observation as consisting of two or more persons acting with each other to achieve social objectives. Importantly, a still camera pointed at the area of interaction comprised by three-to-five individuals kept all members of the group, in sizes of two, three, or five, in the camera angle at all times.

As one of the various contemporary social media, *Second Life* is also designed for social interaction and relationships building. Boellstorff (2008, p. 180) noted that "what makes virtual worlds 'worlds' is that they are places (that represent) sites of culture" in which people interact. Such places and cultural sites include the most significant connections established by human beings, most notably, long-standing friendships. Although asynchronic interaction is possible, the majority of social interaction in *Second Life* took place between residents who shared the same world at the same time. Interactions included residents gathered for a performance of live music, a fashion show, religious meeting, a game, or a contest (Boellstorff, 2008). Even when participating in a game or contest, where one may act independently, the goal is mainly affiliation. People who gathered for a game of Tringo, for instance, were gathered more for relating to others than for winning a game. Tringo "is not just a game; it is a place to meet people" (Boellstorff, 2008, p. 182).

Perhaps even more intensely than in New Iowa School research, which relied, primarily, on strangers (in order to assess how two or more people, without shared histories, constructed social action in deliberate, step-by-step processes), social interaction and relationship building are key to the stability of one's identity in *Second Life*. Even in cases in which one may have multiple avatars, individuals will typically interact with specific others consistently, resulting in establishing a tight and secure dyadic relationship. Such a relationship requires consistency in presenting one main avatar to another, who reciprocates with his/her avatar over time. This perceived requirement for consistency is indicated by one resident's experience:

> when I first started I alternated between two main avatars, and was planning on making more, but since I started actually meeting and hanging out with the same people I haven't really changed my basic look ... I started having static relationships, and wanted to remain a single entity. (Boellstorff, 2008, pp. 129–130)

While a *Second Life* resident usually has a main avatar/account with which he/she operates, alternate accounts (or "alts") created and controlled by a single person become commonly accepted practices. In the event that an individual will use more than one avatar, an expected change of identity becomes associated with the change of social interaction and relationships. This expectation appears similar to changes in performances and preparation documented most famously by Goffman (1956, 1959) in his explorations of frontstage and backstage behaviors, deference, and demeanor. Usually residents would not log off of one avatar's account and then immediately reenter *Second Life* as another avatar; a lag time is needed to prepare for the reentry as another persona. Consider the following statement made by a resident:

> I take a breath and prepare myself into whatever "mode" I'm logging in as, because both alts are very real – my second alt is very much a part of me, the part I choose not to express here on my main account. (Boellstorff, 2008, p. 149)

With tangible places, over time activities, and social interaction and relationships, *Second Life* exhibits even greater structural similarities with the New Iowa School laboratory than its predecessors, the Web 1.0 sites. These similarities provide *Second Life* researchers a solid foundation to employ the New Iowa School laboratory methodological guidelines when investigating *Second Life*. After all, both the New Iowa School laboratory and *Second Life* are virtual environments that produce real social interactions.

VIRTUAL, NOT ACTUAL, BUT REAL

For years, students of human communication have reminded us that technologies, especially relevant in regard to procedures for recording and disseminating information, create virtual worlds. Writing was the first such technology, creating a manufactured world (McLuhan, 1962; Ong, 1982). However, oral or printed accounts offer virtual reality, with far less fidelity, when compared with audio/video recording and broadcasting systems (Couch, 1996). The New Iowa School laboratory and *Second Life* utilize distinct technologies to provide virtual reality. Researchers involved in both worlds made efforts to achieve a greater fidelity, making the suspension of disbelief appear more seamless in its enactment. In a New Iowa School laboratory, an established context, with decoration, other engaging participants, as well as an urgent social objective to accomplish, enticed participants to get in the act to produce a researchable form of social interaction. Couch noted the importance of creating a meaningful social objective to entice the production of social interaction in a recorded laboratory session. While acknowledging that initially "the participants on occasion 'played to the camera,' in most instances they quickly lost interest in the camera when they turned to their assigned task" (Couch, 1987, p. 14). Similarly, *Second Life* activities and relationships do not exist in a "cyberspatial vacuum" (Boellstorff, 2008, p. 24). *Second Life* is an online virtual world that resembles the actual world in RL with a landscape, residents, mountains, buildings, and water. Users "imported and reconfigured everyday aspects of the actual world, from gravity and sunlight to embodiment and language" (Boellstorff, 2008, p. 63). Almost as soon as the residents began participating, the imagined world that seemed evident was transformed into a real world associated with fungible resources that residents took seriously.

Real social interaction and human experiences emerge in the "contrived" New Iowa School laboratories and *Second Life* domains. Researchers report on the visible and researchable human experiences and their consequences not only in the virtual environments. In effect, the reality created by participants in the New Iowa School and *Second Life* worlds become intense enough that transitions back into the "real world" require re-preparation. In the New Iowa School laboratory, for instance, debriefings occurred after each recording session. After completing tasks, researchers informed the participants to "shed their sociological identities and reenter the real world" (Couch, 1987, p. 63). Unlike the earlier social psychology experiments that relied on deception and false identities, resentment among participants after the experiments not only became minimized, but several participants reported that they learned something about themselves, a goal of the early pragmatists who advocated experimentation that would allow for minded behavior (Katovich, 1984).

SL interactions and relationships also have consequences that individuals experience in their actual, non-virtual worlds. In a sequence entitled, "*Second Life* Affair Ends in Divorce" (CNN.com/europe, 2008), a newscast reported that a British couple who married in a lavish *Second Life* wedding ceremony broke off their marriage after one of them had an alleged "affair" in the online world. Another piece of evidence regarding the ramifications of virtual world activities in regard to the actual world involved acts of altruism. Activities held within *Second Life* to raise awareness and money for actual-world nonprofit activities, such as cancer research or natural disaster relief, resulted in the accumulation of monies in accounts outside of the *Second Life* (Boellstorff, 2008). While the possibility of consequences in *Second Life* and New Iowa School research can involve various interpretations, the activities conducted in seemingly "artificial worlds" can become obdurate blue prints that have impacts on actual-world activities and realities (Couch, 1987). The New Iowa School laboratory, for instance, provides researchers the ability to identify with precision the critical elements needed in the construction of a relationship, and the processes of how elements fit together. The goal is to transfer the generic descriptions learned in the laboratory into applications for analysis of actual-world settings. In effect, the designed simplification of the laboratory experience provides refined tools to deal with the complexity of worlds outside of the laboratory, filled with extraneous factors.

The study of *Second Life* may also be used to understand the actual world. However, given the sociability of *Second Life*, it seems to be more important to study *Second Life* as *Second Life*, in and of itself, not as a blueprint for the actual world. After all, New Iowa School laboratory participants come and go. *Second Life* residents stay. Such duration creates a novel reason for treating *Second Life* as a world, sui generis. *Second Life* residents suspend their disbelief and commit themselves readily to a specific bias of communication, sociability. The sociability of *Second Life* is developed on its own terms, although it may reference the actual world, but it is not formed from it. Events and identities in *Second Life* may reference ideas from the actual world (from landscape to gender) and may index actual-world issues (from economics to political campaigns), but this referencing and indexing takes place within *Second Life* (Boellstorff, 2008).

THE BIAS OF COMMUNICATION

While we have identified a key difference between a particular application regarding communication bias between the New Iowa School laboratory and *Second Life*, this same bias reveals some striking similarities. The difference between the two centers on the fact that the laboratory serves a utilitarian purpose, while *Second Life* is created for fantasizing pleasure. However, Innis (1951) has noted how various real or imagined features of a communication technology invite significant social ramifications. The bias of communication of *Second Life*, sociability (pleasure seeking and relationship building) may differ from the more utilitarian and purposeful problem solving tasks in the laboratory, but the eventual solidary alignment, however defined, can reveal a comparable social bond in both worlds.

The first experience of surprises and delights in *Second Life* is in the creation of an avatar. A user creates an avatar or avatars for him/herself, which serve, loosely, as alter ego(s). As an alter ego distinct from a person's normal or original personality, the creation can take on various shapes and forms, mainly expressive in nature. Avatars with horns, wings, or tails are common examples. In this light, residents in *Second Life* employ avatars for personal and recreational use. The pleasure of building experienced by residents represents a form of play, or a joy in and of itself. However, while building an avatar is an expression of one's selfhood, building a home provides the pride of engaging in purposeful achievement. Boellstorff cites one user's experience as follows: "… when making money was not directly at issue … like many I found great pleasure in building my home, using the well-named 'create' command and the same assumption about place and presence that undergirded building for profit" (2008, p. 210).

Whether engaged in play for the sake of play or for purposeful achievement, users engaged in *Second Life* interaction expect abidance by an ethic of anonymity. As one participant noted, "I make my living in *Second Life* as an escort. This is NOT the sort of thing I wish to have associated with my real self" (Boellstorff, 2008, p. 131). To preserve the anonymity, residents objected to the plan to add voice to *Second Life* as tone and cadence become vulnerable indicators of the person's being outside of *Second Life*.

Similarly, New Iowa School participants expect that their behaviors and consequences will only reveal themselves via anonymous references, indicated by the functional/categorical identities enacted or assumed in the lab. Each of the participants has personal names, but their renditions, statements, and behaviors become linked to the impersonal designations of numbers (e.g., "subject 3") or identities themselves (e.g., "Representative A," "Constituent C"). Just as the sociability in *Second Life* becomes a persona restricted to the specific domain of *Second Life*, so do the identities of participants in New Iowa School studies. The biases of communication (sociability, utilitarian cooperation) may differ in content, but each bias takes on the same anonymous character linked to impersonal designations, rather to specified personalities.

Although we have provided a very broad analogy between *Second Life* and the New Iowa School, we have also identified some key correlations that hopefully, can inspire more specific investigation. All generalities considered, based on the striking similarities of *Second Life* and the New Iowa

School laboratory, it is advisable to study *Second Life* utilizing the New Iowa School laboratory approach. We especially recommend that *Second Life* utilize recordings, done responsibly and with sensitivity to issues of anonymity, to enable research into the activities of *Second Life* residents. Third party software (such as Jing Project, Camtasia, Fraps, and others) is available for audio-video recording of interaction in *Second Life*. Recording not only provides a complete set of data for analysis, but the playback feature also allows researchers to research, or study the sequence of interaction iteratively, in order to attain precise interactional descriptions. In addition, *Second Life* automatically saves local chat and instant-message conversations to log files on the hard drive, relieving researchers the chore of transcribing the interaction.

The differences between the New Iowa School laboratory and *Second Life* caution researchers to study *Second Life* in its own right, as a world of play. Such a world does reveal significant differences between the utilitarian tasks in the New Iowa School laboratory, which become defined in accord with a strict, self-contained narrative of a beginning, middle, and end. Nevertheless, the world of play, even in itself, generates patterns of activity, however fanciful, that creates its own narrative. Such a narrative may not reveal the more precise confines as evidenced in the New Iowa School lab, but its distinct bias can reveal a more complex and perhaps, non-linear narrative that can inform researchers of novel patterns associated with "doing social life" in controlled environments. In any event, despite acknowledged differences in content, the form of analysis employed by the New Iowa School can allow those who study *Second Life* to develop and create generic concepts in order to make the significance of residential behavior of *Second Life* participants available for sociological and social psychological analysis.

REFERENCES

Asch, S. (1951). Effects of group pressure upon the modification and distortion of judgments. In H. Guetzdow (Ed.), *Groups, leadership, and men* (pp. 177–190). New York, NY: Carnegie Press.

Blumer, H. (1969). *Symbolic interactionism: Perspective and method.* Englewood Cliffs, NJ: Prentice-Hall.

Boellstorff, T. (2008). *Coming of age in second life: An anthropologist explores the virtually human.* Princeton, NJ: Princeton University Press.

Chen, S.-L., & Johns, M. D. (2002). Empiricism in cyberspace: The New Iowa School goes online. In Norman K. Denzin (Ed.), *Studies in symbolic interaction* (Vol. 25, pp. 25–43). Bingley, UK: Emerald Group Publishing Limited.

CNN.com/europe. (2008, November 14). *Second Life* affair ends in divorce. Retrieved from http://www.cnn.com/2008/WORLD/europe/11/14/second.life.divorce/index.html?iref=topnews

Couch, C. J. (1987). *Researching social processes in the laboratory*. Greenwich, CT: JAI Press.

Couch, C. J. (1996). *Information technologies and social orders*. New York, NJ: Aldine.

Couch, C. J., Katovich, M. A., & Buban, S. L. (1994). Beyond Blumer and Kuhn: Researching and studying across-time data through the use of point-in-space laboratory procedures. In L. Reynolds & B. Herrman (Eds.), *Symbolic interaction: An introduction to social psychology* (pp. 121–140). New York, NY: General Hall Press.

Couch, C. J., Saxton, S. L., & Katovich, M. A. (1986). Introduction. In C. J. Couch, S. L. Saxton, & M. A. Katovich (Eds.), *Studies in symbolic interaction: The Iowa school* (pp. vvii–xxv). Greenwich, CT: JAI Press.

Denzin, N. (1970). *The research act: A theoretical introduction to sociological methods*. Chicago, IL: Aldine.

Glaser, B., & Strauss, A. (1964). Awareness contexts and social interaction. *American Sociological Review*, *29*, 669–679.

Goffman, E. (1956). The nature of deference and demeanor. *American Anthropologist*, *58*, 473–502.

Goffman, E. (1959). *The presentation of self in everyday life*. Garden City, NY: Doubleday.

Heath, C., Hindmarsh, J., & Luff, P. (2010). *Video in qualitative research*. Thousand Oaks, CA: Sage.

Innis, H. (1951). *The bias of communication*. Toronto: University of Toronto Press.

Katovich, M. A. (1984). The laboratory as a provocative stage. *Studies in Symbolic Interaction*, *5*, 49–67.

Katovich, M. A., & Couch, C. J. (1992). The nature of social pasts and their use as foundations for situated action. *Symbolic Interaction*, *15*, 25–47.

Katovich, M. A., Saxton, S. L., & Powell, J. (1986). Naturalism in the laboratory. In C. J. Couch, S. L. Saxton, & M. A. Katovich (Eds.), *Studies in symbolic interaction: The Iowa school* (pp. 79–88) Greenwich, CT: JAI Press.

Kurzweil, R. (2005). *The singularity is near*. New York, NY: Penguin Group.

Lofland, J. (1976). *Doing social life: The qualitative study of human interaction in natural settings*. New York, NY: Wiley.

McLuhan, M. (1962). *The Gutenberg galaxy*. New York, NY: New American Library.

McLuhan, M. (1964). *Understanding media*. London: Routledge and Kegan-Paul.

Mead, G. H. (1932). *The philosophy of the present*. Chicago, IL: University of Chicago Press.

Mead, G. H. (1934). *Mind, self, and society*. Chicago, IL: University of Chicago Press.

Mead, G. H. (1938). *The philosophy of the act*. Chicago, IL: University of Chicago Press.

Milgram, S. (1974). *Obedience to authority*. New York, NY: Harper & Row.

Miller, D. E., Hintz, R. A., & Couch, C. J. (1975). The elements and structure of openings. *The Sociological Quarterly*, *16*, 479–499.

Mills, C. W. (1959). *The sociological imagination*. New York, NY: Anchor.

Molseed, M. (1994). Naturalistic observation in the laboratory. *Symbolic Interaction*, *17*, 239–251.

Ong, W. (1982). *Orality and literacy*. London, UK: Methuen.

Saxton, S. L., & Couch, C. J. (1975). Recording social interaction. In C. J. Couch & R. A. Hintz (Eds.), *Constructing social life* (pp. 255–262). Champaign, IL: Stipes.

Schutz, A., & Luckmann, T. (1973). *The structures of the life world*. Evanston, IL: Northwestern University Press.

Simmel, G. (1950). In D. Levine (Ed.), *The sociology of Georg Simmel*. New York, NY: The Free Press.

Simmel, G. (1971). In D. Levine (Ed.), *On individuality and social forms*. Chicago, IL: University of Chicago Press.

Stone, G. (1962). Appearance and the Self. In A. Rose (Ed.), *Human behavior and social processes* (pp. 86–118). Boston, MA: Houghton-Mifflin.

Thomas, W. I. (1923). *The unadjusted girl*. Boston, MA: Little-Brown.

MUTABLE SELVES AND DIGITAL REFLEXIVITIES: SOCIAL MEDIA FOR SOCIAL CHANGE IN THE MIDDLE EAST AND NORTH AFRICA

Lara Lengel and Victoria Ann Newsom

ABSTRACT

To examine how social media restrict and recreate messages within current interactionist scripts in the Middle East and North Africa (MENA), this study applies a framework of digital reflexivity highlighting stages of information flow. It applies the symbolic interaction concept of emotional events to analyze the self-immolation of Mohamed Bouazizi and the role of social media in disseminating Bouazizi's act as one catalyst of the MENA citizen uprisings. The role of social media in the "Arab Spring" merits investigation because social media provide opportunities to examine shifting identities, interactions, and actions of citizen activists in the MENA uprisings. This study is important and timely because little symbolic interactionist scholarship exists on MENA identities and social movements, or on crowd interaction and activism outside

Symbolic Interaction and New Social Media
Studies in Symbolic Interaction, Volume 43, 85–119

ISSN: 0163-2396/doi:10.1108/S0163-239620140000043015

the West. The nuanced nature of MENA political activism and complex processes of the development of activists' "mutable" selves (Zurcher, 1977) are fluid and resistant to symbolically defined social roles, interactionist scripts and reflexivity, and public communication practices in a MENA under political and social transition.

Keywords: Activism; online social networks; Tunisia; Egypt; revolution, 2010–2011; protest movements

The story begins with struggle and sorrow. A father, unable to adequately support his family in the provincial town of Sidi Bouzid, Tunisia, in a region marked by high unemployment, corruption, and economic strife, finds work in construction in neighboring Libya. A son, age three, cannot fully grasp what a fatal heart attack is. All he knows is *abbi* [my daddy] is never coming home.

In the years following his father's untimely death, the son, Tarek al-Tayeb Mohamed Bouazizi, has gained a greater understanding of the pain of losing a father he loved and of the challenges his mother experienced raising a large family. Although his mother remarried her brother-in-law sometime after her husband's death, her second spouse was unable to find consistent work due to ill health.

By age 10, the young Mohamed realizes that it will be up to him to support his family. He commits to being the sole provider for his mother, stepfather, and five younger siblings, by selling fresh produce in the local *souk* [market] from a small wheeled cart.

He is respected and admired by members of the community. He was known to give fruit and vegetables to families more poor than his own.

Others in the community, however – those in bureaucratic and leadership positions, positions that afforded opportunities to seize teeny bits of power in an otherwise disempowered town and region – did not bestow respect and admiration on Mohamed Bouazizi. From age 10, when he first took on the role of sole provider for his family, the story continues for sixteen years of irksome bureaucracies, petty bullying, and ongoing performances of power inequities. Nearly each day, local police officers aggressively targeted the young boy, who often brought back to his mother less than $3 for a day's work. The harassment continued as Bouazizi matured to a young man. Officers repeatedly confiscated his scales and the produce he attempted to sell from his humble market cart because he lacked what they claimed was a necessary permit. He refused to participate in necessary bribery of city officials for said permit and lacked the funds necessary to pay a recent city fine of 400 dinars (US$280; equivalent to two months of his wages).

The "real" story begins on December 17, 2010, with an alleged slap to Bouazizi's face and a curse to his late father by a local policewoman; an act of public humiliation and demoralization had reached a peak. The 26-year-old Bouazizi, accompanied by his uncle and stepfather, went to the Sidi Bouzid municipality building to register a complaint, and was turned away. Perhaps sensing he had no other options to support his family in dignity, he returned to the municipality building, doused himself with a can of paint thinner, and lit himself on fire in an act of public, non-violent protest. Witnesses used the camera function of their mobile phone devices to capture Bouazizi's act and share the story and video via Facebook. And a revolution began.

Note the characteristic tone of this narrative, compiled from a variety of online sources.[1] This narrative could be paired with stories of oppression and resistance familiar to many Westerners, including the story of Rodney King or the more recent story of Trayvon Martin. Bouazizi's story is one that would be told time and time again as voices in various areas across the Middle East and North Africa (MENA) region were raised in protest of totalitarian regimes, wealthy dictators, and gross inequities (Worth, 2011). And this narrative would become the center of, and inspiration for, many of the following uprisings we have come to identify as part of what is widely known as the Arab Spring. This story would also remain at the center of international political consciousness because it was reiterated time and time again through social media. As stated in the BBC documentary, *How Facebook Changed the World*, the story became as much about the framing process used to transmit the story through social media as it was a story of Bouazizi's actions and the protests that followed. Now citizens could tell their stories and get them heard on a global stage. "But something of worldwide importance was about to happen. Disenfranchised people everywhere were about to discover that the internet revolution had tipped the balance of power in their favour" (Pollack & Husain, 2011). Notably, this story now resonates as a success story for a tool that can be used to promote oppositional voices and social change around the world. But is this the complete story? Are the voices of citizens from around the world clearly reaching a global stage, intact, and is the message remaining steady? And is a major part of the original message being lost or hidden behind a more powerful narrative of technological success?

Because of this event and those following, social media are widely cited as fueling citizen uprisings in the MENA. However, MENA social movements scholarship critiques such "instant" and incomplete analyses, arguing for "processural, dynamic, and historicized" approaches to understand complexities of social change (Beinin & Vairel, 2011, p. ix). Nevertheless, the role of social media in the Arab Spring merits investigation because social media provide opportunities to examine shifting identities, interactions, and actions of MENA citizen activists. While social media and the unprofessional witness accounts therein are clearly powerful tools for motivating change, we need to examine how those tools are used by existent power structures to translate and edit the organic messages as they reach the global stage.

This study is important and timely because little symbolic interactionist scholarship exists on MENA identities[2] and social movements, or on crowd interaction and activism outside the West. It takes a "processural" approach to explore historical contexts of social interaction and social change in the MENA, the nuanced nature of MENA political activism, and the complex processes of the development of activists' "mutable" selves (Zurcher, 1977), fluid and resistant to symbolically defined social roles (Goffman, 1959, 1974), interactionist scripts and reflexivity (Garfinkle, 1967), and public communication practices in a MENA under political and social transition.

CRITICAL EMOTIONAL EVENTS

Symbolic Interaction (SI) research on citizen-lead public protests is rare, however what does exist draws upon the SI work on the centrality of emotion as central to phenomena under analysis (Denzin, 1980, 1983a, 1983b, 1984, 1985; Jasper, 1998, 2011; Mattley, 2002; Shott, 1979; Yang, 2000; Zurcher, 1982). Sewell (1996) analyzed the capacity for emotional events to fuel activism.

Critical emotional events have been contextualized by Sewell (1996) as "(1) a ramified sequence of occurrences that (2) is recognized as notable by contemporaries, and that (3) results in a durable transformation of structures" (p. 844). Building on Sewell's effort, Yang (2005) defines a critical emotional event in the context of collective action as "a ramified sequence of emotional occurrences that results in the transformation of the dynamics of collective action" (p. 80). Yang (2005) argues, "just as critical historical events may transform historical structures, so critical emotional events may transform the dynamics of collective action. They do so by dramatizing the relationships among movement activists, publics, and opponents. Such relationships compel action" (p. 80).

To date, no SI scholarship on the MENA exists. The self-immolation of Mohammed Bouazizi, the event often cited for paving the way for the Arab Spring, is such a key critical emotional event. Media reinforced this, evidenced by article titles such as "In town at center of Tunisia uprising, 23 years of repressed emotions burst forth" (Chick, 2011). Yet, how was the message of this emotional event framed and sent to the world stage? How did this message become a catalyst for the Western understanding of the Arab Spring? How did social media recreate the message that Bouazizi's act of resistance started the "Democratic Revolution in the Middle East"?

To examine how social media restrict and recreate messages within current interactionist scripts, we (2011) apply a framework of digital reflexivity that highlights stages of information flow. This is complicated by traditional structures of government-controlled communicative networks, enacting a convergence toward "ever more complex relations between top-down" media and "bottom-up participatory culture" (Jenkins, 2006, p. 243). Activities such as government-sponsored internet service interruptions, seizing of Facebook account passwords, and other top-down controlling practices motivate activists to re-claim their lives by reworking pre-existent corporate, or government media forms, calling others to action, and sharing their own lived experiences to a global audience.

Social media such as Facebook and Twitter are, by nature, intertextual, narrative, and self-reflexive; they refer to and cite each other and themselves constantly. The resulting structure is a form of narrative architecture (Jenkins, 2004), that redefines norms for digital message consumption. When users script their lives on Facebook they are following the narrative structures prescribed by the architecture of that social network. The resulting personalized space functions as a type of performative digital reflexivity, structuring and making sense of identity through the understood social script utilized within the narrative architecture.

Our framework of digital reflexivity allows us to examine how the narratives of the Arab Spring reflect a greater metanarrative of "democratic process" and "progress" narrated through a Western lens; structured through multiple presentations within social media. While stories are told as organic and evolved solely within MENA local knowledge, ultimately they function to locate MENA voices within Westernized cultural scripts. The narrative architecture of social media thus serves as a digitally reflexive frame wherein individuals inside of the MENA recognize a way of getting themselves heard, while simultaneously Western media frames and reframes the messages so that what emerges fits its own lens.

LOCATING ONLINE ACTIVISM

In order to better understand how digital activism functions within the Arab Spring, we must first examine the mechanism for delivering these activist messages. While media choices for consumers are far more vast than in the past, and the ability for individual consumers to act as producers and provide news materials and alternative entertainments, institutional controls and demands remain active in mediating what ultimately reaches a general public. The narrative structures of the media forms, the limits of access, and even the advertising-based functions of search engines such as Google play a role in how easily accessible information actually is for individual users. Similarly, narrative precedents influence how information is spread, as Facebook pages, tweets, viral videos, and news stories are passed from user to user through established patterns of symbolic convergence and meaning-making. These patterns include "authorities" noted for expertise in particular topic areas, regardless of offline-understandings of expertise; or popular celebrities including figures like Hollywood celebrities George Takei (Huffington Post, 2012) and Ben Affleck (Cohn, 2012), or political celebrities such as Nelson Mandela or the Dalai Lama, who are viewed as leaders on topic of social interest.

Nevertheless, users are sources of information online as social media have partially disrupted the traditional structures of the media industry itself. Henry Jenkins (2006) describes this phenomenon as "media convergence":

> [Convergence] represents a paradigm shift – a move from medium-specific content toward content that flows across multiple media channels, toward the increased interdependence of communications systems, toward multiple ways of accessing media content, and toward ever more complex relations between top-down corporate media and bottom-up participatory culture. (p. 243)

Jenkins' convergence describes how the technologies themselves, including media consumer practices, are being manipulated and re-conceived by both the industry and the consumer. This process of convergence opens the doorway for consumers to reshape their realities: consumers utilize that process to re-claim their own lives from industry-based timelines and restrictions by sharing their own opinions, reworking pre-existent or corporate media forms, and presenting original materials to a growing public audience. This audience counters the perceived audience of corporate media structures, and in some senses threatens the traditionally understood means of media control.

SYMBOLIC CONVERGENCE/MEDIA CONVERGENCE

Media convergence is also reflective of symbolic convergence. There is a specific knowledge base required for tweeting – including an understanding of the limitations of the format itself. In a sense, learning how to use Twitter is like learning local dialects and experiencing in local knowledge and requires an ability to "read" specific symbols and styles. Digital symbols and language therefore must be accounted for because they act as modes of translation between offline realities, hence a need for digital literacies. Add to this the literal translations required for local knowledge to reach a different locality, such as translations from Arabic to English, whether this is done online or by the speaker or "tweeter" themselves, and one starts to understand why images, videos, and symbols are a prominent form of message transmission through social media. These symbols are converging in multiple forms of media, and are taking on characteristics allowing them to act as universal modes of communication. However, colloquialisms and local ideologies may still lose significance as the messages continue to travel through the multiple media forms.

What results from this form of symbolic and media convergence is a complex layering of real and perceived media control and monitoring. Yes, consumers can pick and choose their media preferences in ways that far supersede traditional controls. This does not, however, mean that corporate and institutional structures are no longer in place and acting as gatekeepers for digital media flow. Recent debates over proposed U.S. laws such as PIPA and SOPA illustrate that new industries have risen to challenge older, more established media conglomerates, and those new industries are themselves selectively marketing alternatives to the consumer public.

Because social media spaces are virtual, and because within social media contexts the rules surrounding ownership, asset use, and production itself are perceived as fluid, the ability for constant re-interpretation of control of intellectual properties, how they can be managed, and by whom, is constantly changing. Further complicating the changing patterns of media product controls due to new communication technologies, digital media are, by nature, intertextual; they refer to and cite each other and themselves constantly. For example, viral videos, pictures, blogs, and stories are constantly reposted and refer to themselves and each other; then, on Facebook and other social media sites as these media are reposted they may be reiterated or altered by each new person posting. And media forms are not limited to one particular form of media, and often are created based on the success of another media product. Therefore, as news programs, entertainments, and other media forms bleed into each other, understandings of where one set of controls ceases to exist so another can begin are vague and uncertain.

The structure of the multiple layers of convergent media becomes a narrative architecture (Jenkins, 2004). In studying video game spaces, Jenkins (2004) illustrates how video games reflect standard narrative structures while allowing individual interaction that suggests player have control over story flow. The narrative architecture of digital social media echoes Garfinkle's (1967) *reflexivity*, wherein individual identity is constructed within understood social scripts and defined by constant verbal and symbolic expectations. Within Garfinkle's discussion, the world is only stable because of mutual and shared expectations rooted in a shared social narrative. Within what we identify as the *digital reflexivity* of social media, stability comes from shared symbolic constructions and narratives, whether or not those symbols are appropriated from multiple offline localities. As the users of social media pick and choose the performance of self they create online, ultimately they are choosing a role in their normalized script of choice, and remain constrained by the digital tools which are simultaneously their method of free communication. Thus, echoing McLuhan (1964), the media form itself dictates a part of the reality for the self-performance.

Thus, the narratives of the Arab Spring reflect democratic metanarratives and stories of perceived progress as narrated by Western voices. The processes of translation, through the digital language structures and digital storytelling format, reinforce the Western metanarratives. In this way, the original voices are heard, but in a translated language dictated by traditional media structures and performed for Western audiences. And while, as in game spaces, native and organic users of local knowledges do have the ability to frame themselves (Newsom, Lengel, & Cassara, 2011) and, in gamer terminology, "choose their own adventures," the boundaries of the narrative remain the purview of the accepted media powers.

PRESENTATION OF THE ACTIVIST SELF

While the literature on identity, interaction, and social media is growing, Langlois, Elmer, McKelvey, and Devereaux (2009) argue more research needs to be conducted to "further understand the networking of publics and their issues by considering how online platforms provide the material, communicational, and social means for a public to exist and therefore define the parameters for assembling issues and publics and circumscribe a horizon of political agency" (p. 415). Research and scholarly efforts looking at efforts for freedoms, democracy, and peace in the MENA is historically focused activism, and that focus is now shifting toward online efforts for social change (Bennett & Segerberg, 2011; Dahlgren, 2009; Eltantawy & Wies, 2011; Faris, 2008a, 2008b; Gladwell & Shirky, 2011; Hermida, Lewis, & Zamith, 2014; Juris, 2004; Pearce & Kendzior, 2012; Valenzuela, Arriagada, & Scherman, 2012) and activisms utilizing social media in the MENA (Gaworecki, 2011; Jansen, 2010; Lotan et al., 2011; Newsom et al., 2011; Suárez, 2011; Wheeler, 2009; Wilson & Dunn, 2011).

SI is reflected in many aspects of social media and activist goals utilizing social media. Goffman's (1959) focus on symbolically defined social roles, and individual's strategic choices of which roles to inhabit, reveals nuances of identity construction and choices within social media. For Goffman the self is a product of culture; within digital media the self is a product of multiple scripted layers. Again echoing Goffman (1974), people then fit events and ideas into this scripted framework, and generally ignore or protest what is not clearly situated within the frame. Thus the symbolic frame becomes more important than the message, echoing in McLuhan's (1964) analysis of mediated messages.

Add to this Garfinkle's (1967) discussion of indexicality, or how we make sense of the self in culture; the expanded range of frames of interaction offered by online communication (see Miller, 1995); and reflexivity, how we reconstruct reality to suit the story of self we decided to tell. The symbolic frames inherent with the architecture of digital media encourage meaning-making through symbolic processes as we symbolically illustrate a chosen version of self and then find ways to make that self understood within a larger online narrative or structure. Social media encourage visual and textual symbolic data as parts of a larger social script, reinforced and framed by the social network itself.

At this point, the traditions of symbolic interactionism provide another step as we investigate how the symbols within these frames function. Drawing on Bormann's (1972) Symbolic Convergence Theory, we come to understand how meaning is collectively defined and reified through shared cultural symbols. Symbols created within mediated spaces function in this same manner, as the symbols become catalysts for shared fantasies and meaning-making. In a sense, social media emulate Vico's (1744/1968) process of *fantasia* as users create myths and stories to create a sense of reality within the media structure. The process happens through narrative stylings, as news stories, blogs, and tweets become part of a larger narrative script. As noted above, online social media have been widely cited in Western popular and political presses as fueling the citizen uprisings in Tunisia and Egypt. Yet, these "moments" of social media do not exist independent of the greater stories being told online, and must be framed within a larger narrative so that full sense-making and reflexivity apply.[4]

The stories told through social media, like the story of Mohamed Bouazizi's self-immolation, become the legends of fantasia and metanarratives. The characters in these stories, such as Bouazizi himself, become heroes emulated by others seeking to generate similar stories, in this case stories repudiating real or imagined oppressions. Illustrating the power of this heroic-martyr styling, Bouazizi has been compared in news stories and blogs to Martin Luther King, Ghandi, Malcom X, and even Nelson Mandela who, at the time of submitting this study for review, was still alive (Ikhide, 2011; Janmohamed, 2011; Luca, 2011). Yet this illustrates how the internet and social media can also incorporate false stories and false heroes, and storytellers will borrow the legend to reinforce their own stories. Following the heroism of Bouazizi as depicted in social media, other stories were created and linked to that narrative, some of them based in errors, incomplete or misinformation and rumors that can easily be treated as fact in digital media narratives. Examples of this include false reports in 2011 of the deaths (via Twitter) of Nelson Mandela (Parker, 2011; Sinclair, 2011) and Hugo Chavez (Blood, 2011; Lalate, 2012; Octavio, 2011).

The connective ties do not even have to be as clear as in these cases. News stories connect Bouazizi's actions, the subsequent revolutions, and the power of Facebook and social media to spark revolutions to the economic turmoil occurring in Europe (Lister, 2011) and the Occupy Wall Street movements in the United States (Estes, 2011; Lewis, 2011). Complicating matters further, fake news stories and even fake news sites such as *The Onion* or Christwire.org are mistaken for real sources. And even governments can interfere in media processes based on a rumor; rumors of a coup d'état in China forced the closure of a Twitter-like service. This was presumably done, by the Chinese government, to avoid any potential revolutions in the manner sparked by Bouazizi's martyrdom (Fallows, 2011; Jade, 2012; Lewis, 2011).

Nevertheless, the role social media play in the events in the MENA are still worthy of interrogation, most notably as social media provide opportunities to examine the individual voices being raised through social media. One must note, however, that to function in the created narratives, the voices become a part of the story, and the actors take on the roles provided through the storytelling process. Therefore, the voices of the activists speaking from the MENA reflect selves that must adapt to the scripts of each media space. Thus, the activist self is a fluid one. The "mutable" self, as posited by Zurcher (1977), is a changing, fluid "(self as process)," that is particularly appropriate for analysis of the vast recent citizen actions in the MENA.

In her work on SI in the digital age, Robinson argues, "the symbolic interactionist framework is crucial to understanding the cyberself-ing process because the cyberself is formed and negotiated in the same manner as the offline self" (2007, p. 94). Within online activisms, the cyberself is a mutable and changing self that can reflect multiple aspects of identity and be used as a characterization to reach out to multiple audiences. If activists create a relatable, mutable self, such as the "everyman" hero characterization of Bouazizi, as the heroic figure in a social change metanarrative, they can draw in support from a larger portion of potential protestors and supporters.

However, these communication and digital media tools and selves are more restricted and limited than popular opinion assumes. While social media in this respect have been used to aid the efforts of campaigners, political organizers, and protestors, some activist efforts have been aimed at reaching Western audiences to encourage a variety of levels of support and aid in reaching social reform goals. Examining the Arab Spring from a Western gaze, messages of hope are designed to appeal to global audiences.

APPLYING A FRAMEWORK OF *DIGITAL REFLEXIVITY* IN COMMUNICATION FLOW

In our graduate and undergraduate classes, each of us has asked students to explain what they understand about the "Arab Spring." We have been struck by the responses from students that fixate on the freedoms represented, not by the social movement goals, but by the media technology used to generate the messages. So while students recognize and understand that it is the voices of citizens from oppressed regions that are being represented by Arab Spring and communicated to the world, their focus remains on how the social media form itself is making this possible, rather than reflecting on the words within the messages coming from the MENA. Thus, the local messages from within those nations impacted by Arab Spring have taken on a global nature wherein the medium has become the point of the message.

To better understand how these "glocal" messages function, we utilize a schema of information devised to analyze "citizen journalism" in the Arab Spring (Newsom et al., 2011). We use this framework to analyze the negotiation of communication messages by various agents through multiple stages of transmission and dissemination, a process we call *digital reflexivity*. We look at the ideal of local knowledge as it is transformed into global knowledge, and how the messages are open to manipulation and bias through the various stages of mediation and gatekeeping cited in the framework. Through the application of this framework, we can see how messages are constructed, essentialized, reconstructed, and ultimately made invisible by the media's narrative architecture.

The Framework functions around a series of digitally reflexive steps. First, individuals speak out. Then resistance leaders reframe individual voices to suit their needs. Resistance rhetoric is disseminated into the local area. Regional activists share resistance rhetoric to stimulate awareness and further action. Governmental regimes and others in positions of power get hold of rhetoric, reframing or erasing to serve their needs. Reframed rhetoric is disseminated on a larger scale. Then the West receives the rhetoric and reframes it to suit itself. This framework was designed to determine the movement of information through digital and social media, and how the messages must be negotiated and manipulated at each stage. At each stage, we investigate how the message is restructured within the digital narrative architecture, and then monitored and reframed by the gatekeepers at each level. This reveals the process wherein local messages from citizens and activists become retold as messages of social media activism. By revealing the process through which digital reflexivity functions, we hope to illustrate ways wherein local messages can themselves reach past gatekeeping mechanisms to a wider audience.

DIGITALLY REFLEXIVE MUTABLE SELVES

The narrative of Mohammed Bouazizi is a narrative of resistance, and works within the metanarratives of social reform familiar to Western audiences. A metanarrative of this nature situates the self – both the selves of the participants in the uprisings and the self-created to act as surrogate for the audience member – as heroes. Bouazizi's story, the imagery of him burning, the location of his suicide in front of the Governor's office, and the crowds of protesters that started forming there to mark the "sacrifice" all spread through Tunisia, and then through Al Jazeera television throughout the MENA (Pollack & Husain, 2011). As the story progressed through the stages illustrated in our framework, these symbols became an iconography used to spur further resistance, and generate a means of moving the message beyond the borders of a culture that recognizes the historical significance of the emotional space.

In analyzing the digital reflexivity of this incident, note how the original images from Sidi Bouzid travelled to reach a Western audience, and the message changed from Bouazizi's personal complaint against the architecture of power, constructed by a repressive bureaucracy and arbitrated by bullying local officials, and became one-of-many messages about generating revolutions through social media. The messages take on new characteristics at each stage of the process, culminating in the metanarrative of technology-based revolution.[5]

Individuals Speak Out

The process begins with Bouazizi's actions in setting himself on fire as a means of vocalizing his concerns on December 17, 2010. Citizens who happened to be within view of Bouazizi's self-immolation bear witness. Some capture the act on camera phone (Cassara & Lengel, 2013). These citizens share their stories and images with others, locally and globally. Local protests begin within hours of Bouazizi's self-immolation (Thorne, 2011). A few days later, another unemployed young man in Lahseen Naji, climbs an electrical pole in Sidi Bouzid, shouted "No for misery, no for unemployment," then electrocutes himself in protest against joblessness and a lack of food and other necessities (Andoni, 2010; Whitaker, 2010). Almost a month of protests continue from this point, until Tunisian President Zine El Abidine Ben Ali flees the country on January 14, 2011 (Spencer, 2011).

This process is the beginning of the martyr-hero identity of Bouazizi. His actions reputedly the inspiration for Naji and numerous others to follow in his wake, Bouazizi's identity is now the focal point of a revolution. His actions and his story become noted in Sidi Bouzid, and word of the event then travels, via shared cell phone images and Facebook, to other parts of Tunisia. As the story travels, it builds a momentum and a following that will attract the attention of both activist leaders and political forces in the MENA.

Resistance Leaders Reframe Individual Voices to Suit Their Needs

Bouazizi's identity as a martyr-hero became a rallying point for local revolutionaries. As residents of Sidi Bouzid rose up against local and regional authorities, other local revolutionaries seized the opportunity to promote the narratives of Bouazizi and Naji. Using social media to promote and organize protests, trade union activists from The Tunisian Federation of Labour Unions led more than 1,000 citizens expressing solidarity with Sidi Bouzid against the Governorate leadership in the capital city Tunis capital on December 27, 2010 (Bhatnagar, 2010). This protest clashed with government security forces, leading to new aspects of the story to add to the social media narration. Trade unionists then organized another rally in Gafsa on the following day with similar results, while lawyers held a rally at the governor's palace (Randeree, 2010b).

Among the changes promoted were legal protests against Tunisian censorship, which ironically was not actively applied to social media (Ryan, 2011b). Therefore, not only did the physical protests occur, social media-driven and organized; the use of social media to spread the word of what was happening became, in itself, a form of protest. This became heightened as Anonymous, a loosely knit group of Web-activists, picked up on the protests and disseminated them further.

Of serious consideration is the role that social media played for protestors and insurgent leadership, especially seen in contrast to how governmental leaders handled the situation. One of the often cited "mistakes" of the Tunisian story is the action taken by former President Ben Ali in response to the protests. Ben Ali, rather than trying to defuse the situation, enflamed the protestors by promising to punish them "severely" on December 29, 2011, after news of the protests had spread to the capitol in Tunis (Borger, 2010). By this point it was too late to defuse the situation or remove it from a broader political view. The lack of social media restriction, and the fact that Ben Ali and others saw it as a social tool only rather than a form of media or the press, clearly limited their recognition and response.

Resistance Rhetoric is Disseminated Throughout the Region, Stimulating Awareness and Further Action

Bouazizi's emotional act and the town of Sidi Bouzid itself would soon become icons for progressive social change in the greater MENA region. The protests in Sidi Bouzid, and the way they were repeated throughout southern Tunisia became a pattern for protest that could be emulated in other parts of the Arab world. With the successful overthrow of Ben Ali and the advent of new, democratic elections, Bouazizi became a hero-figure who could be upheld as a sign of democratic victory. Resistance leaders in Egypt and Yemen were among the first to reiterate the story and recreate the protests in their own nations (Sterling, 2011).

As these and other protests began to be framed in international media as "The Arab Spring," literally indicating progress that can be read in Western terms, direct appeals to Western ideologies and support mechanisms also became evident in the way that demonstrators and insurgent leaders promoted what was happening in the region.

The narratives and images of the critical emotional events and location of these events were used to appeal beyond the stage of the MENA itself. For example, the space of Sidi Bouzid, like the story of Bouazizi itself, became a reference point as similar stories arose in other Tunisian provincial towns, in the capital, Tunis, in Cairo, and in other demonstration sites. Now new uprisings were intentionally echoing the protests in Sidi Bouzid, referencing those initial protests, and referencing the power of the media tool that made those protests reach a larger audience.[3]

In his work on interactions of public space and social media and "emerging logics of aggregation," Juris (2012) notes, "Space is important, first, on a microlevel" (p. 259) as protestors contest "the sovereign power of the state to regulate and control the distribution of bodies in space ... in part, by appropriating and resignifying particular urban spaces such as public parks and squares as arenas for public assembly and democratic expression" (2012, p. 259 – see also Feldman, 1991; Fernandez, 2008; Foucault, 1979; Schradie, 2011; Sewell, 2001; Tilly, 2000; Zajko & Béland, 2008). Such public spaces of protest are "terrains of resistance" (Routledge, 1994) and, as Juris notes, "physical sites of contention involving myriad embodied spatial struggles with the police and symbolic sites of contention over the meaning of space" (2012, p. 259). Sidi Bouzid became a terrain of resistance for the Arab Spring, emulated and resurrected, whether physically or in metaphor, as new protests continued to develop. Thus the digitally reflexive value of Sidi Bouzid became a symbol of regional change.

In Egypt similar demonstrations began forming, with similar images and narratives promoted through social media. Again, these demonstrations were focused on removing government officials and promoting the stories of the oppressions being suffered by Egyptian citizens. Stories about individual citizens injured or killed during the protests, coupled with images illustrating the sheer numbers of protestors became strong statements of how powerful this resistance movement was becoming. And again, protestors and demonstration leaders used social media to both organize and reach out for outside support.

But it is Tahrir Square that remains the most important physical space of the Arab Spring protests. Analyzing the material significance of Tiananmen Square in the 1989 protests in China, Yang argues, "places have symbolic meanings" (2005, p. 83). She notes, "movement organizers often choose to stage actions in places rich in symbolic meaning and emotional overtones in order to build the proper kind of emotions among participants and the public" (pp. 84–85). Before January 2011, Tahrir Square meant many things to many people. However, as Mohamed Elshahed, a researcher of mid-20th century architecture and urban planning in Egypt, argues:

> Commentators in the West have been quick to credit online social networking with empowering the protests. But the revolution that started in January 2011 in Cairo has provided powerful evidence that the virtual is not enough: in the course of several historic days in Tahrir Square it became decisively clear that the occupation of physical urban space was, and continues to be, crucial to the success and continuity of the revolution. (2011, para. 4)

Elshahed, a doctoral candidate in the Middle East Studies Department at New York University, moved from Brooklyn back to Cairo for what he "anticipated would be a quiet year of research" (para. 1) on his dissertation. Upon his return to his native city, Elshahed witnessed the transformation of a policed space. The physical limitations of Tahrir Square, prior to January 2011:

> were the result of political design, of policies that not only discouraged but also prohibited public assembly. Under emergency law – established from the moment Mubarak took office in 1981 and yet to be lifted – a gathering of even a few adults in a public square would constitute cause for arrest. Like all autocracies, the Mubarak government

> understood the power of a true public square, of a place where citizens meet, mingle, promenade, gather, protest, perform and share ideas; it understood that a true midan – Arabic for public square – is a physical manifestation of democracy. (2011, para. 5)

The historical knowledge and lived experience of an autocracy's annihilation of what could, and should be a truly *public* space, inform the meaning that Elshahed, and his country men and women now ascribe to Tahrir Square. In the West, however, the lack of knowledge and experience of citizenship under autocratic rule could lead to a less nuanced understanding of the importance of the offline protests.

Regimes Appropriation of Resistance Rhetoric

After President Ben Ali fled Tunisia, political activists within other areas of the MENA picked up on the story of Mohamed Bouazizi and used it as a critical emotional event to fuel protests in their own localities. As Bouazizi's story and the stories of others speaking out against oppressive government regimes spread, more and more protests began forming.

Regional activists in neighboring nations used Bouazizi's immolation as a challenge to citizens threatening protest. One notable example occurred on January 12, 2011, in Boukhadra, a northeastern Algerian mining town situated close to the Algerian-Tunisian border. Twenty-two young un- or underemployed Algerians protested lack of employment opportunities and affordable housing in front of the town hall. According to testimony collected by the reporters at the Algerian regional news organization, *El Watan*, the mayor of Boukhadra yelled, "*Illa andek courage, Dir kima Bouaziz, Chaal rouhek!*" [If you have courage, do like Bouazizi, immolate yourself!]. One of the protestors, Mohsen Bouterfif, a 37-year-old unemployed mason and father of two, did just that. Since the incident the mayor was relieved of his duties by the *wali* [governor] of the Tébessa province where Boukhadra is situated (Benslimane & Badaoui, 2011; Siddiqi, 2011).

Not only are the self-immolations of Bouazizi and Bouterfif critical emotional events, the images of these events are crucial in the digital metanarratives of protest, matrydom, and revolution. One particularly powerful image of Tarek al-Tayeb Mohamed Bouazizi's self-immolation in front of the Sidi Bouzid town hall can be found reposted in *The Telegraph* (UK) article (2011, October 21), "Arab Spring: Timeline of the African and Middle East rebellions." At the time we were completing this article, the image, which depicts Bouazizi in a standing or running posture as flames engulf his entire body, could also found in *The Telegraph* (UK) multimedia archives (n.d.). It is important to note, however, that the image, highly likely taken with a camera phone by a witness at the site, has been removed from its original posting; the image's history has been silenced by Western media.

Bouazizi's self-immolation image has also been used in photo montages by digital artists such as one known as "MaraZie2011." The montage includes the body in flames in the background juxtaposed with a portrait of Bouazizi in the lower right foreground. A similar image, depicting a person on his hands and knees as he becomes more overwhelmed by the flames, was incorporated into an article, "What Anonymous could do to promote human rights" by Pascual Strømsnæs (2011). This piece draws upon Bouazizi's act as a call to action for the activists known as Anonymous to turn their attention to China where, Strømsnæs argues, "the aftermaths of what many have coined the 'Facebook revolution' things have taken a serious turn for the worse for those working to improve human rights." Strømsnæs noted on March 24, 2011, just eleven weeks after Bouazizi's succumbed to his burns on January 4, 2011, "At the same time the organization Chinese Human Rights Defenders reports that the toughest crackdown against Chinese activists in many years is taking place at the moment as a number of human rights lawyers and other activists have disappeared within the last few days. With all this in mind, it is fairly obvious that the chinese [*sic*] regime have been fearfully watching the events unfold in North Africa and in the Middle East. One could hope that some electronic spark is lit within China that would snowball into the likes of what we have seen in Tunisia and in Egypt" (Strømsnæs, 2011, para. 5).

The mutable activist self shifts identities from context to context. For example, Strømsnæs may have incorrectly attributed the image to Bouazizi as it is also seen in news reports of the self-immolation of Mohsen Bouterfif in Boukhadra, Algeria in blogs including *Solidarité Maroc* (2011) and by news media such as *Bulawayo24News* (2011) in Bulawayo, Zimbabwe. Similarly, an image of Mohsen Bouterfif is incorrectly identified as Bouazizi by afrik-news.com published by media including the *Salem-News* in Salem, Oregon under two headlines, "The Butterfly Effect," by Paul Balles (2012), and "Bouazizi was followed by self immolation of Mohsen Bouterfif in Algeria, Yacoub Ould Dahoud in Mautritania" with a tag line from Manama, Bahrain.

Regimes Reframe or Erase Resistance Rhetoric

Images and examples from these protests were then captured and spread through social media elsewhere in the broader MENA region

(Carpenter & Schenker, 2011). On January 26, 2011, Hasan Ali Akleh enacted a self-immolation on the main street of the small Syrian town of al-Hasakah, as a form of protest against the Syrian government. Similar to that of Bouazizi, Ali Akleh's act has been situated as the start of the Syrian uprisings (Williams, 2012). Local resistance leaders promoted this story and spread word of Akleh's self-sacrifice through social media. As word began to spread, government officials banned potential protests and demonstrations, seeking to avoid a repeat of what had occurred in Tunisia – yet word of the government blocking protests was also promoted by resistance leaders. It took six weeks in the face of government obstruction for a large-scale protests to break out in Syria, first in the town of Jisr al-Shughour coinciding with the funeral of a slain activist held there (Swami, 2012) and, later, throughout the nation.

Perhaps the best-executed enactment of a regime reframing protest rhetoric to meet its own objectives is the Syrian-government "produced" pro-government rally in Damascus. To audiences lacking expertise in geophysical and socio-political nuances of the region, images of the rally in Damascus' central bank square on March 29, 2011, widely available through Wiki Commons (see Figs. 1–3), appear similar to those of the

Fig. 1. Demonstrators in Tahrir Square, Cairo, February 9, 2011. *Source*: Photo Credit, Wikimedia Commons.

Figs. 2 and 3. "Protestors" in a Pro-Regime Rally in Damascus. *Source*: Photo Credit, Wikimedia Commons.

anti-government demonstrations that previous occurred in Tunisia and Egypt. Not only is the pro-government rally in Damascus barely mentioned by Western media, images and video footage of this and other pro-regime events were mistaken for mass anti-government protests by global media organizations.

Reframed Rhetoric is Disseminated on a Larger Scale

Activists in Egypt, building on the momentum of the Tunisian reforms, reframed the story for their own needs and also to reach out to another group of protesters, this time in the United States. Egyptian protesters encouraged activists participating in the Occupy movement in the United States to protest outside of the Pennsylvania firm, Combined Systems, the company known for supplying tear gas canisters to the Egyptian military that was used against the citizens in Tahrir Square and elsewhere in the nation. Activists from organizations including the Students for Justice in Palestine from the University of Pittsburg, the Youngstown, Ohio-based Arab-American Community Center, and the Coalition for Peace in the Middle East engaged in peaceful protests on the 2012 Martin Luther King, Jr. Day outside Combined Systems and the Egyptian Consulate in New York City in solidarity with Egyptian citizens (Barrows-Freedman, 2012). Commenting on the event, Occupy activist Matthew Cappiello argued Egyptian activists "understand the value that international communication can bring" (cited in Estes, 2011).

Other ways Bouazizi's story was reframed was through offline alternative media forms. One notable example is the graffiti art mural honoring Bouazizi (see Fig. 4).Created by artist Daniel Doherty, the mural is a part of the Clarion Alley Mural Project (CAMP) situated in Clarion Alley, between Mission and Valencia streets in the Mission District of San Francisco. CAMP was founded by a collective of six Mission District community artist/activists who realized the impact of the community art mural cluster in nearby Balmy Alley which focused on socio-political struggle in Central America. Since the organization's birth in October 1992, CAMP has supported the work of local and global artists who have created more than 100 murals on a diverse themes surrounding justice and social inclusiveness (Aaron, 2009). Doughtery's mural articulates the narrative of Bouazizi's story and features a portrait of Bouazizi, a representation of a fruit and vegetable cart and a map of North Africa situated over flora, harkening to Tunisia's nickname, *Tunis el-hadra* [Tunisia, the green].

Anna Lekas Miller, independent journalist and activist, argues Bouzazi's act can be situated as a step in a counter-colonizing process on the west by the Arab World:

> I love this.
>
> I love this for a lot of reasons—I love this because it is Mohamed Bouazizi, the too often forgotten martyr that put the Arab Spring in motion. I love this because the text

Fig. 4. Community Mural Tribute to Mohamed Bouazizi. *Source*: Photo credit, Anna Lekas Miller (2012) (used with permission).

> tells a story that begins tragically yet ends hopefully. I love this because of the Arabic words that don't come up in the photo. I love this because it was a history that we longed for in our own country, but didn't realize we could have—until we did.
>
> I love this because in a way, the Arab World is "colonizing" the western world as we study the tactics of resistance that cascades into revolution, imitating it to reclaim our collective right to sovereign justice, rather than imposing notions of democracy on one another. I hope that this is the future—testing and sharing tactics, showing solidarity and support, and reclaiming our countries and cultures as ours as exchange colonialism for a collective victory towards liberation and self-determination. (Lekas Miller, 2012)

The flows of news, images, and personal stories about the unrest in the MENA (see, for instance, Beaumont, 2011; Borger, 2010; Chick, 2011; Fallows, 2011; Ikhide, 2011; Luca, 2011; Randeree, 2010a; Sadiki, 2011; Spencer, 2011; Thorne, 2011; Villa-Vicencio, 2012; Worth, 2011) through both "traditional" and social media provided opportunities to examine the individual voices, narratives, and contexts. One must note, however, that to function in the reframed rhetoric, the voices become a part of the story, and the actors take on the roles provided through the storytelling process. As analyzed earlier, the voices of MENA activists reflect selves that must adapt to the scripts of each media space. Thus, the activist self is a fluid, "mutable" self (Zurcher, 1977), whose actions, however locally constituted, speak to larger issues of injustice and inspire other activist engagement against oppression in other communities and nations.

The West Receives the Rhetoric and Reframes It to Suit Itself

Online activism at its ideal best is a tool to generate an increase of knowledge about social reform topics, and to engender a positive response toward the reform goals by an increasing audience. However, local knowledge presented as online activism is self-containing if an awareness of a social reform need is a prerequisite to exposure. To break this cycle, local voices must reach an audience outside of their normal range. The "citizen journalism" and other related efforts evident in Arab Spring activism have been reconstructed and re-created by Western global institutions and power brokers that act as gatekeepers of information flow so that the message can reach a wide audience. The Western media's framing of the "Arab Spring," literally indicating progress that can be read in Western terms, appealed to Western ideologies and support mechanisms. The framing also became evident in the way that demonstrators and insurgent leaders promoted what was happening in the region. The narratives and images were used to appeal beyond the stage of the MENA itself, and comparisons to other global situations began to surface.

In their work "Networking Democracy," Loader and Mercea (2011) argue "the influence of social media upon democratic politics reveal a complex picture that should lead us to be wary about celebratory accounts. It is clearly necessary to avoid the utopian optimism of the earlier experiments in digital democracy. Yet, they do also point to the potential of disruptive moments and actions which open the possibilities for some co-construction of networks and platforms where the formation, maintenance and [defense] of political positions may be played out" (p. 5).

Such utopian optimism is articulated in the metanarratives. For example, U.S. Vice President, Joe Biden announced, "What is at stake in Egypt and across the Middle East is not just about Egypt alone." The BBC documentary *How Facebook Changed the Word: The Arab Spring* begins with the story of Bouazizi's "sacrifice" and progresses through the multiple revolutions throughout the region (Pollack & Husain, 2011).

Bouazizi's effort has thus become a moment within the digitally reflexive process wherein "Facebook Changed the World." Crowning the process of re-creating the incident for a global audience, this new rhetoric, focused on Facebook, has even been compared to European unrest and new political voices protesting economic concerns (Lister, 2011). As indicated above, and as reported in such media as *The Atlantic Wire*, the Occupy Wall Street movements had a direct influence on the Arab Spring, "and vice versa" (Estes, 2011, p. 1).

Protestors in regions outside of the Arab World began promoting Arab Spring activism as both a means of enhancing the development of the Arab World and promoting the need for activism and protests in other regions. Consider, for example, an image (see Fig. 5) from an demonstration to encourage Ohio voters to support worker rights through a veto referendum to block Ohio Senate Bill 5 which would drastically limit public employees' collective bargaining provisions. While the specific contexts of this protest differ from those in North Africa, the similarities between citizens' concerns of economic justice and worker rights in North Africa and in U.S. Midwest are evident in the protest poster linking the Tunisian and Egyptian citizen protests earlier that year with the October 2011 demonstration in northwest

Fig. 5. Demonstrating for Workers Rights and Economic Justice. *Source*: Photo credit, Lara Lengel (used with permission).

Ohio: "Tunis √ Cairo √ Toledo ?" Note in the image the flag carried by one of the demonstrators. The Corporate America Flag, which substitutes stars with corporate logos, is an activist tool created by Adbusters a "global network of culture jammers and creatives working to change the way information flows, the way corporations wield power, and the way meaning is produced in our society" (Adbusters Media Foundation, n.d.). The Corporate America Flag has been widely used by activists in the Occupy Movement. Western media (see, for instance, Apps, 2011; Mak, 2011; Slaughter, 2011; Solnit, 2011) have drawn numerous connections between the Arab Spring movements to that of Occupy Wall Street and the broader Occupy movement. Such connections are best accompanied by an explication on the comparative seriousness for MENA citizen activists, who often take their lives in their hands when engaging in public protest in the face of many of the authoritarian regimes in the MENA, versus activists protesting in the U.S. For example, in her article, "Occupy Wall Street and the Arab Spring" in *The Atlantic*, Anne Marie Slaughter reminds readers:

> There is a big difference between young men and women willing to face bullets to change their government and those who are gathering under far less dangerous and indeed often fun circumstances. But I stand by my fundamental point, which is that the drivers of all these movements is a deep sense of both injustice and invisibility, and that the only way to meet their demands is through meaningful political change. (2011, para. 6)

While noting the relative dangers of public protest in the MENA, the connection between those who are seeking ways to fight economic and social injustice is unambiguous, as performed in the narratives and images of those fighting for similar goals.

Reporters outside the west also noted the broader contextual connections between Occupy and the Arab Spring. In her blog, "The Big Picture" for Pakistan's *Express, Tribune*, Heba Islam (2011) argues:

> Is there a connection between these protests and does that connection mean something, are questions worth exploring. The large scale level on which these protests are taking place is not the only factor that indicates this might be a 'history-changing' event. Here are some others. The Arab Spring refers to several uprisings, linking them together. Similarly, one can assume there is a connection between the Arab Spring and Occupy Wall Street – as much as the media (undeniably fettered by corporate interests) scoffs at Occupy Wall Street and would consider a connection between the protests in New York and those in Damascus ludicrous, they have one characteristic in common – they are criticising a system. In some cases, this paradigm was political dictatorship. In others, it is economic dictatorship.

The image that accompanies Islam's article, "The significance of Occupy Wall Street and the Arab Spring," from which the above passage is taken, focuses on a man, probably in his twenties, holding a piece of slightly creased cardboard, what appears to be cut from a box. The simple sign asks the powerful question:

IF NOT US

WHO?

Created with red paint, letters drip like blood, most visibly under the words "NOT" and "WHO." Credited to Reuters, the photo caption reads, "People aren't protesting against a bill or a person – they want relief from political and economic dictatorship" (Islam, 2011).

Perhaps what is most compelling is the wide visual and textual narrative the image represents. The protester is an exceptional example of the 'mutable self,' precisely because he is *unexceptional*. His dark hair and thin frame, which is adorned by a sport jacket and backpack, could be any young man, anywhere. He stands in front of what appears to be a small vehicle, otherwise indiscernible. There are two other men in the background, other mutable selves who could be standing in front of the trees along شارع الحبيب بورقيبة [Şarıo al-Hɑbib Burqibɑë, or Avenue Habib Bourguiba], the central avenue in downtown Tunis bearing the name of the Habib Bourguiba, the first President of the Republic of Tunisia and national hero of the movement for independence of the nation from French colonial rule. It could be tree-line Vali Asr Street in Tehran, the centerpoint of the June 2009 protests against the Iranian presidential election. It could be Zuccotti Park in lower Manhattan, before New York City Mayor Michael Bloomberg and NYPD Commissioner Ray Kelly ordered that Occupy Wall Street protestors be forcibly removed and the park surrounded by police barricades.

If the image were released more recently, the trees in the background could be those in Parque Central of San José, Costa Rica and the protestor in the foreground could be demonstrating at the March of the Invisible (Rincón Parra, 2012). The image could be a still from the video of the human rights demonstration produced by students at University of Costa Rica's Student TV Channel 15, or by those produced by citizen activist groups, Colectivo Alma Prima and Colectivo Creativo 98. While the June 16, 2012, march highlighted equal rights for same-sex couples, the legalization of In-Vitro Fertilization and the separation of State and Church, the demonstration is part of a larger *Movimiento Invisibles pour una Costa Rica en igualdad y libertad*. Equality and liberty metanarratives are consistent whether the activist engagement is situated in Tunis, Cairo, Toledo, Tehran, Manhattan, or San José.

"WE ARE ALL ..."

The story of Tunisia is not the only story from the Arab Spring to be so reconstructed within the metanarrative. Similar to the way that Mohammed Bouazizi and Sidi Bouzid became the several focal points for the Tunisian uprisings, Tahrir Square in Cairo, infused with its historical significance and centrality to the city and the nation, was a crucial space for the Egyptian uprisings, other individuals provided opportunities for identity construction of protesters in the region and beyond.

Such is the case of Khaled Said. The hero-construct in this case is again made clear. Identity construction aids the development of collective citizen-lead action as it promotes a heroic persona to which local and global audiences can relate. Yang (2000) argues the transformation of individual identities is "created by the experience of movement participation" (p. 593) (see also Calhoun, 1994). The "We are All Khaled Said" effort is an illustration of the transformation of the activity self, and functions to illustrate how a mutable self, created in a hero image, can become part of the iconography of the also-heroic new media. Khaled Said, a 28-year-old small business professional from Alexandria, Egypt, was beaten to death by police in June of 2010. After learning the story, MENA Google executive Wael Ghonim created a Facebook page as a tribute to Said which became focal point for Egyptian protesters (Alqudsi-ghabra, 2012; Baker, 2011; Khamis & Vaughn, 2011) and opened a global online dialog about Egyptian democracy. This story, allowing audience members to relate to the heroic figure of Said and Said's narrative, reflects the same metanarrative told about Mohamed Bouazizi and Rodney King.

Social media fora like "We Are all Khaled Said" provide opportunity for the construction of group activist identity through the heroic metanarrative of "Facebook changing the world." Valenzuela et al. (2012) argue, "by allowing multiple channels for interpersonal feedback, peer acceptance, and reinforcement of group norms, these sites also promote the construction of personal and group identities that are key antecedents of protest behaviour" (p. 302) (see also Dalton, Van Sickle, & Weldon, 2010). Activists and interested parties from all over the world can relate to Said's story through this site, and the interactivity of the site reinforces that ideal that all of the voices shared there have a consolidating effect. This heroic, relatable identity construction is also enhanced by the similar lived experience articulated on social media spaces like "We Are all Khaled Said": "Social network sites therefore emerge as resources that may create the kinds of collective experiences that are necessary conditions for successful protest movements" (Valenzuela et al., 2012, p. 303).

"We are all Khaled Said" also provided during the uprisings and, thereafter, has continued to allow for a wide-based inclusive community structure for citizens in and outside the MENA to engage in collectivist action and identity building. Social media spaces such as "We are all Khaled Said" have been created for other types of collectivist action and community building so that individuals could participate "without worrying about having to consent to a politically organized group, ideology, or internal hierarchy and to disconnect smoothly if the movement swayed from its fundamental openness and core issues" (Maireder & Schwarzenegger, 2012, p. 190).

The collective "We are all ..." rhetoric of such social media spaces allows for the mutable identity inscriptions of Khaled Said, Mohamed Bouazizi, Lasheen Naji, and others. The mutable cyberself can reflect multiple aspects of identity and embody the lived experience of multiple activist selves. The characterizations of Said, Bouazizi, and Naji, as the heroic figures in metanarrative can garner support from a wider community of activists and aligned supporters.

The role of social media in the Arab Spring merits continued investigation because social media provide opportunities to examine the constantly shifting identities, interactions, and actions of citizen activists in the MENA. More symbolic interactionist scholarship is needed on MENA identities and social movements, and on crowd interaction and activism outside the West. The nuanced nature of MENA political activism and complex processes of the development of activists' mutable selves, fluid and resistant to symbolically defined social roles, interactionist scripts and reflexivity, and public communication practices will illuminate the understanding of the vast political and social transitions occurring in the MENA.

NOTES

1. See, for instance, Andoni, 2010; Beaumont, 2011; Borger, 2010; Carr, 2011; Chick, 2011; Cornwell, 2011; De Soto, 2011; Fallows, 2011; Ikhide, 2011; Knickmeyer, 2011; Luca, 2011; Ryan, 2011a; Sadiki, 2011; Spencer, 2011; Thorne, 2011; Villa-Vicencio, 2012; Whitaker, 2010; Worth, 2011.

2. Please see Stonebanks (2008), Yanay (1996), and Yomtoob (2008).

3. By contrast to the efforts to transcend geophysical boundaries of emotionally charged spaces, other mediated discourses return to such spaces. One example is the August 10, 2012, Agenda France Presse article, "Tunisia revolution birthplace rises again" published as well by *The Jordan Times* at http://jordantimes.com/tunisia-revolution-birthplace-rises-again.

4. Facebook's shift to "Timeline" illustrates how an overall narrative voice and structure are significant to audience understanding.

5. A series of protests in 2013 and 2014, fueled by the assassinations of Democratic Patriots' Movement leader Chokri Belaid on February 6, 2013 and People's Movement leader and member of parliament Mohamed Brahmi on July 25, 2013, were widely reported in regional and international media (see, for instance, Amara, 2013, July 28; Berman, 2014, January 7; Beissinger, Jamal, & Mazur, 2013, April 15; Thorne, 2013, July 26).

REFERENCES

Aaron, N. (2009). The so-called mission school. In A. Jacoby (Ed.), *Street art San Francisco: Mission Muralismo* (section "Heart", pp. 44–87). New York, NY: Abrams.

Adbusters Media Foundation. (n.d.). *Activist tools: Corporate America flag*. Retrieved from http://www.adbusters.org/cultureshop/corporateflag

Agence France Presse. (2012, August 10). *Tunisia revolution birthplace rises again*. Republished on *The Jordan Times*. Retrieved from http://jordantimes.com/tunisia-revolution-birthplace-rises-again

Alqudsi-ghabra, T. (2012). Creative use of social media in the revolutions of Tunisia, Egypt & Libya. *International Journal of Interdisciplinary Social Sciences*, *6*(6), 147–158.

Amara, T. (2013, July 28). *Police clash with protesters in Tunisia's Sidi Bouzid*. Retrieved from http://www.reuters.com/article/2013/07/28/us-tunisiadeath-idUSBRE96Q01Z20130728

Andoni, L. (2010, December 31). The rebirth of Arab activism. *Al Jazeera (Opinion.)*. Retrieved from http://www.aljazeera.com/indepth/opinion/2010/12/20101231161958792947.html

Apps, P. (2011, *October* 11). *Wall Street action part of global "Arab Spring"?* Reuters. Retrieved from http://www.reuters.com/article/2011/10/11/uk-global-politics-protest-idUSLNE79A03Z20111011

Baker, A. (2011). How Egypt's opposition got a more youthful mojo. *Time*, World. Retrieved from http://www.time.com/time/world/article/0,8599,2045446,00.html

Balles, P. (2012, February 18). "The Butterfly Effect" and "Bouazizi was followed by self immolation of Mohsen Bouterfif in Algeria, Yacoub Ould Dahoud in Mautritania" (tag line from Manama, Bahrain). *Salem-News*. Retrieved from http://www.salem-news.com/articles/february182012/butterfly-effect-pb.php. Also published on *Studies and research on middle East and Africa*. Retrieved from http://blog.studi-me-africa.org/2012/02/butterfly-effect.html

Barrows-Freedman, N. (2012, January 17). Video of MLK Day protest outside Combined Systems, Inc., in Pennsylvania. *Electronic Intifada*. Retrieved from http://electronicintifada.net/blogs/nora/video-mlk-day-protest-outside-combined-systems-inc-pennsylvania

Beaumont, P. (2011, January 20). Mohammed Bouazizi: The dutiful son whose death changed Tunisia's fate. *The Guardian* (UK). Retrieved from http://www.guardian.co.uk/world/2011/jan/20/tunisian-fruit-seller-mohammed-bouazizi

Beinin, J., & Vairel, F. (2011). *Social movements, mobilization, and contestation in the Middle East and North Africa*. Stanford, CA: Stanford University Press.

Bennett, W., & Segerberg, A. (2011). Digital media and the personalization of collective action. *Information, Communication & Society, 14*(6), 770–799.

Benslimane, M., & Badaoui, S. (2011, January 24). Le maire à Mohcin Bouterfif: «Si tu as du courage, fais comme Bouazizi, immole-toi par le feu ». *Dernières nouvelles d'Algérie*. Retrieved from http://www.dna-algerie.com/interieure/le-maire-a-mohcin-bouterfif-si-tu-as-du-courage-fais-comme-bouazizi-immole-toi-par-le-feu

Berman, C. (2014, January 7). *Inside Tunisia's postrevolutionary protests*. Retrieved from http://mideastafrica.foreignpolicy.com/posts/2014/01/07/inside_tunisias_post_revolutionary_protests

Bessiner, M., Jamal, A., & Mazur, J. (2013, April 15). *The anatomy of protest in Egypt and Tunisia*. Retrieved from http://mideastafrica.foreignpolicy.com/posts/2013/04/15/the_anatomy_of_protest_in_egypt_and_tunisia

Bhatnagar, B. (2010, December 28). Tunisia jobless protests rage. *Al Jazeera*. Retrieved from http://www.aljazeera.com/video/africa/2010/12/20101228182021539319.html

Blood, J. (2011, June 28). CIA/"Wikileaks" spread fake rumor about Hugo Chavez death in Cuba. Retrieved from http://deadlinelive.info/2011/06/28/cia-wikileaks-spread-fake-rumor-about-hugo-chavez-death-in-cuba/

Borger, J. (2010, December 29). Tunisian president vows to punish rioters after worst unrest in a decade. Retrieved from http://www.guardian.co.uk/world/2010/dec/29/tunisian-president-vows-punish-rioters

Bormann, E. G. (1972). Fantasy and rhetorical vision: The rhetorical criticism of social reality. *Quarterly Journal of Speech, 58*(4), 396–407.

Bulawayo24News. (2011, January 16). *Algeria, man set himself on fire, yelling Tunisia!* Bulawayo, Zimbabwe. Retrieved from http://bulawayo24.com/index-id-news-sc-africa-byo-697-article-algeria,+man+set+himself+ on+fire, +yelling+tunisia!.html

Calhoun, C. (1994). Social theory and the politics of identity. In C. Calhoun (Ed.). *Social theory and the politics of identity* (pp. 9–36). Oxford, England: Blackwell.

Carpenter, J. S., & Schenker, D. (2011). Will Egypt's "Day of Rage" become a revolution? *Middle East Transparent*. Retrieved from http://www.metransparent.com/spip.php?page=article&id_article=12661&lang=ar

Carr, J. (2011, January 15). In Tunisia, cyberwar precedes revolution. *Frontlines of Revolutionary Struggle*. Retrieved from http://revolutionaryfrontlines.wordpress.com/2011/01/15/in-tunisia-cyberwar-precedes-revolution/

Cassara, C., & Lengel, L. (2013). Breaking the fear barrier: Cell phones, facebook and the Tunisian revolution. In R. Berenger (ed.), *Social media go to war: Rage, rebellion and revolution in the age of Twitter* (pp. 353–366). Spokane, WA: Marquette.

Chick, K. (2011, January 11). In town at center of Tunisia uprising, 23 years of repressed emotions burst forth. *Christian Science Monitor*. Retrieved from http://www.csmonitor.com/World/Middle-East/2011/0119/In-town-at-center-of-Tunisia-uprising-23-years-of-repressed-emotions-burst-forth

Cohn, A. M. (2012). Members of Congress excited to meet Ben Affleck. *The Hill*. Retrieved from http://thehill.com/blogs/twitter-room

Cornwell, R. (2011, December 3). Ten people who changed the world: Mohammed Bouazizi, an ordinary man who became the Arab Spring's figurehead. *The Independent* (UK).

Retrieved from http://www.independent.co.uk/news/world/politics/ten-people-who-changed-the-world-mohammed-bouazizi-an-ordinary-man-who-became-the-arab-springs-figurehead-6282311.html

Dahlgren, P. (2009). *Media and political engagement: Citizens, communication and democracy*. Cambridge, England: Cambridge University Press.

Dalton, R., Van Sickle, A., & Weldon, S. (2010). The Individual-institutional nexus of protest behaviour. *British Journal of Political Science*, *40*(1), 51–73.

De Soto, H. (2011, December 11). The real Mohamed Bouazizi. Retrieved from http://www.foreignpolicy.com/articles/2011/12/16/the_real_mohamed_bouazizi

Denzin, N. K. (1980). A phenomenology of emotion and deviance. *Zeitschrift Für Soziologie*, *9*, 251–161.

Denzin, N. K. (1983a). Interpretive interactionism. In G. Morgan (Ed.). *Beyond method* (pp. 129–146). Beverly Hills, CA: Sage.

Denzin, N. K. (1983b). A note on emotionality, self and interaction. *American Journal of Sociology*, *8*(9), 402–409.

Denzin, N. K. (1984). *On understanding emotion*. San Francisco, CA: Jossey-Bass.

Denzin, N. K. (1985). Emotion as lived experience. *Symbolic Interaction*, *8*(2), 223–240.

Elshahed, M. (2011, February 27). Tahrir Square: Social media, public space. *Design Observer*. Retrieved from http://places.designobserver.com/feature/tahrir-square-social-media-public-space/25108/

Eltantawy, N., & Wies, J. B. (2011). Social media in the Egyptian revolution: Reconsidering resource mobilization theory. *International Journal of Communication*, *5*, 1207–1224.

Estes, A. C. (2011, December 16). How Occupy Influenced Egypt's Arab Spring (and vice versa). *The Atlantic Wire*. Retrieved from http://www.theatlanticwire.com/global/2011/12/how-occupy-influenced-egypts-arab-sprong-vice-versa/46334/#

Fallows, J. (2011, September). Arab spring, Chinese winter. *Atlantic Magazine*. Retrieved from http://www.theatlantic.com/magazine/archive/2011/09/arab-spring-chinese-winter/308601/1/

Faris, D. (2008a). Revolutions without revolutionaries? Network theory, Facebook, and the Egyptian blogosphere. *Arab Media & Society*, *6*, 1–11.

Faris, D. (2008b). The web, the cell phone, and the Mubarak death crisis of 2007. *Politics and Technology Review*, *1*, 51–57.

Feldman, A. (1991). *Formations of violence: The narrative of the body and political terror in Northern Ireland*. Chicago, IL: University of Chicago Press.

Fernandez, L. A. (2008). *Policing dissent: Social control and the anti-globalization movement*. New Brunswick, NJ: Rutgers University Press.

Foucault, M. (1979). *Discipline and punish: The birth of the prison*. New York, NY: Vintage.

Garfinkle, H. (1967). *Studies in ethnomethodology*. Englewood Cliffs, NJ: Prentice-Hall.

Gaworecki, M. (2011). Organizing tool and a "space of liberty" in post-revolution Egypt? *Social Policy*, *41*(4), 66–69.

Gladwell, M., & Shirky, C. (2011, March/April). *From innovation to revolution: Do social media make protests possible?* Retrieved from http://www.foreignaffairs.com/articles/67325/malcolm-gladwell-and-clay-shirky/from-innovation-to-revolution

Goffman, E. (1959). *The presentation of self in everyday life*. New York, NY: Doubleday.

Goffman, E. (1974). *Frame analysis: An essay on the organization of experience*. London, England: Harper & Row.

Hermida, A., Lewis, S. C., & Zamith, R. (2014). Sourcing the Arab spring: A case study of Andy Carvin's sources on Twitter during the Tunisian and Egyptian revolutions. *Journal of Computer-Mediated Communication*, *19*(3), 479–499.

Huffington Post. (2012, March 4). George Takei vows gay marriage talk with Donald Trump. Retrieved from http://www.huffingtonpost.com/2012/03/04/george-takei-gay-marriage-donald-trump-_n_1319560.html

Ikhide, E. (2011, December 9). A day for human rights. *Focus Nigeria*. Retrieved from http://www.focusnigeria.com/human-rights.htm

Islam, H. (2011, October 27). The significance of Occupy Wall Street and the Arab Spring. *The Express Tribune* (Pakistan) Blogs [Web log post]. Retrieved from http://blogs.tribune.com.pk/story/8569/the-significance-of-occupy-wall-street-and-the-arab-spring/

Jade. (2012, March 22). Chinese government bans the word Ferrari. *Global Lingo* [Web log post]. Retrieved from http://www.global-lingo.com/chinese-government-bans-the-word-ferrari

Janmohamed, S. (2011, March). One ordinary individual can be the catalyst for change [Web log comment]. Retrieved from http://www.emel.com/article?id=83&a_id=2296

Jansen, F. (2010). Digital activism in the Middle East: Mapping issue networks in Egypt, Iran, Syria and Tunisia. *Knowledge Management for Development Journal*, *6*(1), 37–52.

Jasper, J. M. (1998). The emotions of protest: Reactive and affective emotions in and around social movements. *Sociological Forum*, *13*(3), 397–424.

Jasper, J. M. (2011). Emotions and social movements: Twenty years of theory and research. *Annual Review of Sociology*, *37*(1), 285–303.

Jenkins, H. (2004). Game design as narrative architecture. In N. Wardrip-Fruin & P. Harrigan (Eds.), *First person: New media as story, performance, game*. Cambridge, MA: MIT Press. Retrieved from http://web.mit.edu/cms/People/henry3/games&narrative.html

Jenkins, H. (2006). *Convergence culture: Where old and new media collide*. New York, NY: New York University Press.

Juris, J. S. (2004). Networked social movements: Global movements for global justice. In M. Castells (Ed.), *The network society: A cross-cultural perspective* (pp. 341–362). Cheltenham, England: Edward Elgar.

Juris, J. S. (2012). Reflections on #occupy everywhere: Social media, public space, and emerging logics of aggregation. *American Ethnologist*, *39*(2), 259–279.

Khamis, S., & Vaughn, K. (2011, Summer). Cyberactivism in the Egyptian revolution: How civic engagement & citizen journalism tilted the balance. *Arab Media and Society*, *14*. Retrieved from http://www.arabmediasociety.com/?article=769

Knickmeyer, E. (2011, February 9). Tunisia's hope deficit. *Vanity Fair*. Retrieved from http://www.vanityfair.com/politics/features/2011/02/tunisia-201102

Lalate. (2012, April 23). Hugo Chavez not dead: President battles false death reports. Retrieved from http://news.lalate.com/2012/04/23/hugo-chavez-not-dead-president-battles-false-death-reports/

Langlois, G., Elmer, G., McKelvey, F., & Devereaux, Z. (2009). Networked publics: The double articulation of code and politics on Facebook. *Canadian Journal of Communication*, *34*(3), 415–434.

Lekas Miller, A. (2012, January 13). *Street art: Mohamed Bouazizi*. Retrieved from http://www.annalekasmiller.com/2012/01/03/street-art-mohamed-bouazizi/

Lewis, B. (2011, December 11). Chinese law firms get social on weibo, "China's Twitter". *Asian Lawyer*. Retrieved from http://www.law.com/jsp/law/international/LawArticleIntl.jsp?id=1202535442885&slreturn=1

Lister, T. (2011, November, 21). *Many similarities in Arab Spring, European chaos*. Retrieved from http://edition.cnn.com/2011/11/21/world/europe/arab-spring-europe/index.html

Loader, B. D., & Mercea, D. (2011). Networking democracy? *Information, Communication & Society*, *14*(6), 757–769.

Lotan, G., Graeff, E., Ananny, M., Gaffney, D., Pearce, I., & Boyd, D. (2011). The revolutions were tweeted: Information flows during the 2011 Tunisian & Egyptian revolutions. *International Journal of Communication, 5*, 1375–1405.

Luca, J. (2011, January 23). Tunisia, Martin Luther King, and main street: What do we do with pain? *The Santa Barbara Independent.* Retrieved from http://www.independent.com/news/2011/jan/23/tunisia-martin-luther-king-and-main-street/

Maireder, A., & Schwarzenegger, C. (2012). A movement of connected individuals. *Information, Communication & Society, 15*(2), 171–195.

Mak, T. (2011, October 14). Occupy Wall Street uses Arab Spring model. *Politico.* Retrieved from http://www.politico.com/news/stories/1011/64993.html

Mattley, C. (2002). The temporality of emotion: Constructing past emotions. *Symbolic Interaction, 25*(3), 363–378.

McLuhan, M. (1964). *Understanding media: The extensions of man.* New York, NY: McGraw-Hill.

Miller, H. (1995, June). *Goffman on the internet: The presentation of self in electronic life.* Paper presented at the Embodied Knowledge and Virtual Space Conference, Goldsmiths' College, University of London. Retrieved from http://www.dourish.com/classes/ics234cw04/miller2.pdf

Newsom, V. A., Lengel, L., & Cassara, C. (2011). Local knowledge and the revolutions: A framework for social media information flow. *International Journal of Communication, 5*, 1303–1312.

Octavio, M. (2011, December 8). How an email saying Hugo Chavez was dead grew Venezuelan bond prices. Retrieved from http://www.csmonitor.com/World/Americas/Latin-America-Monitor/2011/1208/How-an-email-saying-Hugo-Chavez-was-dead-grew-Venezuelan-bond-prices

Parker, L. (2011, January 16). Death hoaxes: RIP Justin Bieber and Nelson Mandela topped Twitter trends. *All Voices.* Retrieved from http://www.allvoices.com/contributed-news/7907116-death-hoaxes-rip-justin-bieber-and-nelson-mandela-topped-twitter-trends

Pearce, K. E., & Kendzior, S. (2012). Networked authoritarianism and social media in Azerbaijan. *Journal of Communication, 62*(2), 283–298.

Pollack, R. (Producer), & Husain, M. (Presenter). (2011). *How Facebook changed the world: The Arab spring [Documentary motion picture].* London, England: BBC.

Randeree, B. (2010a, December 26). Protests continue in Tunisia: Clashes erupt between security forces and residents in Sidi Bouzid. *Al Jazeera.* Retrieved from http://www.aljazeera.com/news/africa/2010/12/2010122682433751904.html

Randeree, B. (2010b, December 28). Tensions flare across Tunisia. *Al Jazeera.* Retrieved from http://www.aljazeera.com/news/africa/2010/12/20101228197243635553.html

Rincón Parra, J. (2012, June 21). Costa Rica: Thousands march in capital for human rights. *Global Voices.* Retrieved from http://globalvoicesonline.org/2012/06/21/costa-rica-in-the-capital-city-thousands-marched-for-human-rights/

Robinson, L. (2007). The cyberself: The self-ing project goes online, symbolic interaction in the digital age. *New Media & Society, 9*(1), 93–110. doi:10.1177/1461444807072216

Routledge, P. (1994). Backstreets, barricades, and blackouts: Urban terrains of resistance in Nepal. *Environment and Planning D, 12*(5), 559–578.

Ryan, Y. (2011a, January 20). The tragic life of a street vendor. *Al Jazeera.* Retrieved from http://www.aljazeera.com/indepth/features/2011/01/201111684242518839.html

Ryan, Y. (2011b, January 6). Tunisia's bitter cyberwar. *Al Jazeera.* Retrieved from http://www.aljazeera.com/indepth/features/2011/01/20111614145839362.html

Sadiki, L. (2011, December 29). The Bouazizi "big bang". *Al Jazeera Opinion*. Retrieved from http://www.aljazeera.com/indepth/opinion/2011/12/20111217132155670692.html

Schradie, J. (2011, November 24). *Why tents (still) matter for the Occupy movement*. Retrieved from https://www.commondreams.org/view/2011/11/24-1

Sewell, W. (1996). Historical events as transformations of structures: Inventing revolution at the Bastille. *Theory and Society*, *25*(6), 841–881.

Sewell, W. (2001). Space in contentious politics. In R. R. Aminzade, J. A. Goldstone, D. McAdam, E. J. Perry, W. H. Sewell Jr., S. Tarrow, & C. Tilly (Eds.), *Silence and voice in the study of contentious politics* (pp. 51–88). Cambridge, England: Cambridge University Press.

Shott, S. (1979). Emotion and social life: A symbolic interactionist analysis. *American Journal of Sociology*, *84*(6), 1317–1334.

Siddiqi, K. (2011, January 16). Unemployed Algerian sets himself ablaze. *All Voices*. Retrieved from http://www.allvoices.com/contributed-news/7904595-unemployed-algerian-sets-himself-ablaze

Sinclair, J. (2011, September 13). Is Nelson Mandela dead? *Long Island Press.com*. Retrieved from http://www.longislandpress.com/2011/09/13/is-nelson-mandela-dead/

Slaughter, A.-M. (2011, October 11). Occupy Wall Street and the Arab Spring. *The Atlantic*. Retrieved from http://www.theatlantic.com/international/archive/2011/10/occupy-wall-street-and-the-arab-spring/246364/

Solidarité Maroc. (2011, January 16). "Si tu as le courage de Bouazizi, vas-y": Vague d'auto-immolations par le feu en Algérie. Solidarité Maroc [Web log post]. Retrieved from http://solidmar.blogspot.com/2011/01/si-tu-as-le-courage-de-bouazizi-vas-y.html

Solnit, R. (2011, October 18). How the Arab Spring and Occupy Wall Street started with one Tunisian man. *Mother Jones*. Retrieved from http://www.motherjones.com/politics/2011/10/arab-spring-occupy-wall-street-protests

Spencer, R. (2011, January 14). Tunisia riots: President Ben Ali flees as chaos hits country. *The Telegraph (UK)*. Retrieved from http://www.telegraph.co.uk/news/worldnews/africaandindianocean/tunisia/8260989/Tunisia-riots-President-Ben-Ali-flees-as-chaos-hits-country.html

Sterling, J. (2011). A Year Later Bouazizi's Legacy Still Burns. *Inside the Middle East*. CNN. Retrieved from http://www.cnn.com/2011/12/17/world/meast/arab-spring-one-year-later/index.html

Stonebanks, C. D. (2008). Spartan superhunks and Persian monsters: Responding to truth and identity as determined by Hollywood. In Norman K. Denzin, J. Salvo, & M. Washington (Eds.), *Studies in symbolic interaction* (Vol. 31, pp. 207–221). Bingley, UK: Emerald Group Publishing Limited.

Strømsnæs, P. (2011, March 24). *What Anonymous could do to promote human rights* [Web log post]. Retrieved from http://blog.pascual-stromsnes.com/2011/03/24/what-anonymous-could-do-to-promote-human-rights/

Suárez, S. L. (2011). Social media and regime change in Egypt. *Campaigns & Elections (2010)*, *32*(300), 30–31.

Swami, P. (2012, March 15). Some lessons in Barbarism. *The Hindu*. Retrieved from http://www.thehindu.com/opinion/lead/article2995534.ece?homepage=true

The Telegraph. (UK). (2011). Arab Spring: Timeline of the African and Middle East rebellions. *The Telegraph* (UK). Retrieved from http://www.telegraph.co.uk/news/worldnews/africaandindianocean/libya/8839143/Arab-Spring-timeline-of-the-African-and-Middle-East-rebellions.html. Accessed on October 21, 2011.

The Telegraph. (UK). (n.d.). Image of the self-immolation of Mohamed Bouazizi. *The Telegraph* (UK) multimedia archives. Retrieved from http://i.telegraph.co.uk/multimedia/archive/02033/fire_2033047c.jpg

Thorne, J. (2011). Bouazizi has become a Tunisian protest "symbol". *The National (Australia)*. Retrieved from http://www.thenational.ae/news/world/bouazizi-has-become-a-tunisian-protest-symbol

Tilly, C. (2000). Spaces of contention. *Mobilization*, *5*(2), 135–159.

Thorne, J. (2013, July 26). *Political assassination unsettles fragile Tunisian democracy*. Retrieved from http://www.csmonitor.com/World/Middle-East/2013/0726/Political-assassination-unsettlesfragile-Tunisian-democracy

Valenzuela, S., Arriagada, A., & Scherman, A. (2012). The social media basis of youth protest behavior: The case of Chile. *Journal of Communication*, *62*(2), 299–314.

Vico, G. (1968). Principi di Scienza nuava d'intorno alla communi natura delle nazioni. (T. Bergin & M. Fisch, Trans.). *The new science of Giambattista Vico*. Ithaca, NY: Cornell University Press. (Original work published 1744.).

Villa-Vicencio, C. (2012, January 18). Foreign policy: Making up is hard to do [Web log post]. Retrieved from http://reconciliationbarometer.org/2012/01/making-up-is-hard-to-do/

Wheeler, D. (2009). Working around the state: Internet use and political identity in the Arab world. In A. Chadwick & P. Howard (Eds.), *Handbook of internet politics* (pp. 305–320). Abington, England: Routledge.

Whitaker, B. (2010, December 28). How a man setting fire to himself sparked an uprising in Tunisia. *The Guardian (UK)* [Web comment]. Retrieved from http://www.guardian.co.uk/commentisfree/2010/dec/28/tunisia-ben-ali

Williams, C. (2012, February 17). Syrian situation is complex and unpredictable. Opinion. *The Sydney Morning Herald*. Retrieved from http://www.smh.com.au/opinion/politics/syrian-situation-is-complex-and-unpredictable-20120216-1tbs2.html?skin=text-only

Wilson, C., & Dunn, A. (2011). Digital media in the Egyptian revolution: Descriptive analyses from the Tahrir data sets. *International Journal of Communication*, *5*, 1248–1272.

Worth, R. F. (2011, January 21). How a single match can ignite a revolution. *New York Times*. Retrieved from http://www.nytimes.com/2011/01/23/weekinreview/23worth.html

Yanay, N. (1996). National hatred, female subjectivity, and the boundaries of cultural discourse. *Symbolic Interaction*, *19*(1), 21–36.

Yang, G. (2000). Achieving emotions in collective action: Emotional processes and movement mobilization in the 1989 Chinese student movement. *The Sociological Quarterly*, *41*(4), 593–614.

Yang, G. (2005). Emotional events and the transformation of collective action: The Chinese student movement. In H. Flam & D. King (Eds.), *Emotions and social movements* (pp. 79–98). London, England: Routledge.

Yomtoob, D. (2008). The vultures which attended my birth. *Studies in Symbolic Interaction*, *32*, 179–181. doi:10.1016/S0163-2396(08)32013-4

Zajko, M., & Béland, D. (2008). Space and protest policing at international summits. *Environment and Planning D: Society and Space*, *26*(4), 719–735.

Zurcher, L. A. (1977). *The mutable self: A self-concept for social change*. Oxford, England: Sage.

Zurcher, L. A. (1982). The staging of emotion: A dramaturgical analysis. *Symbolic Interaction*, *5*(1), 1–22.

STRUCTURAL ROLES IN MASSIVELY MULTIPLAYER ONLINE GAMES: A CASE STUDY OF GUILD AND RAID LEADERS IN WORLD OF WARCRAFT

J. Patrick Williams, David Kirschner and Zahirah Suhaimi-Broder

ABSTRACT

Role is an under-studied topic in research on virtual game worlds, despite its centrality in the ubiquitous term "massively multiplayer online role-*playing game (MMORPG)." In this article, we report on a study of the role concept and its relevance to virtual worlds, with emphasis on the MMORPG World of Warcraft (WoW). In particular, we focus on the concept of structural role, a term introduced to delineate a certain kind of social actor that carries greater-than-average responsibility for facilitating the diffusion of culture across interlocking groups. Beginning with a brief discussion of structural roles, this paper draws on ethnographic research in a raiding guild and interviews with hardcore WoW players to investigate the roles of guild and raid leaders in building and*

Symbolic Interaction and New Social Media
Studies in Symbolic Interaction, Volume 43, 121–142

ISSN: 0163-2396/doi:10.1108/S0163-239620140000043016

maintaining collaborative group play. Our study explores not only the expectations and obligations for players in key structural positions, but also specific processes through which they are embodied in everyday life online. Data show that an interest or willingness to learn the intricacies of gameplay, to take responsibility for players' emotional well-being, and to manage a shared definition of the situation are all basic components of the guild and raid leaders' roles, and guild or raid success is often reducible to the extent to which leaders master these components.

Keywords: Guild; massively multiplayer online game; MMORPG; role; virtual world; World of Warcraft

ROLES AND THE WORLD OF WARCRAFT

Traditional sociological definitions characterize roles in terms of their functional attributes. Individuals inhabit status positions (e.g., guild leader, girlfriend, healer) that exist within a social system and which have expectations and obligations attached to them (Parsons, 1952). A role in this sense has to do with stereotypical representations of what an individual in a certain status position does. An interactionist conception of role recognizes that these expectations and obligations are not static external structures that impinge upon an individual inhabiting the role (Dolch, 2003). Rather, individuals purposefully act in ways that project to others a desired impression. Individuals understand the expectations for their behavior in a particular situation based on the status identity they are performing, but beyond those expectations there is a potential for performing the role in creative, idiosyncratic ways.

Role is an under-studied topic in research on virtual game worlds, despite its centrality in the ubiquitous term "massively multiplayer online *role*-playing game (MMORPG)." In this article, we report on a study of the role concept with the specific intent of exploring its relevance to virtual worlds and especially the MMORPG World of Warcraft (WoW). In particular, we focus on the concept of structural role, a term introduced to delineate a certain kind of social actor that carries greater-than-average responsibility for facilitating the diffusion of culture across interlocking groups (Fine & Kleinman, 1979). MMORPGs are based on specific kinds of role performances. This is not always clear to new players, some of whom understand only that they play a character who must "kill" virtual creatures in order to progress through the game world. Yet with progression comes increased pressure from the game's design to band together with others, at least temporarily, to accomplish increasingly difficult tasks. During this process, players come to recognize different character roles such as "healer" (tasked with keeping other players alive) or "DPS" (the acronym of "damage per second;" primarily responsible for eliminating enemies). As the likelihood for engaging in collaborative play increases, so does the likelihood that players will band together in organized groups.

In WoW, two forms of organization are most common. The first is transient in nature and consists of players who band together for short periods of time (from a few seconds to a few hours) to accomplish some goal that is of mutual benefit. As characters progress through the game world, they encounter, with increasing frequency, circumstances that require them to work together with others. For example, a player may be offered a very powerful weapon as a reward for destroying some local evil power, but the player will find the enemy too strong to defeat alone. Players may invite others to join forces, thereby sharing the workload and benefitting from the increased strength of the group. Such groups are called "parties" and are limited to five players. Once characters reach level 60 (out of a current maximum of 90), they may join larger (up to 40 players) groups called "raids" to enter extremely challenging areas of the game world, with tougher resident evils and even more powerful rewards.

The second form of organization is more durable in nature and consists of players who band together to pool and share resources. The groups are called "guilds," which any player can join and leave at any time.

> You may discover that a guild greatly enhances your gameplay experience. You can meet friends, share adventures, and find people to protect you if you fight in faction versus faction combat. Typically, players in good guilds can go places and do things that players in poor guilds or no guild can't. This is especially the case at character levels 60–[max level], where the dungeons become very challenging. (WowWiki, 2007, "Background," para. 1)

Guilds are not only about helping players succeed at difficult challenges. Other advantages include developing networks of friends to socialize with, even when playing the game alone, and having a pool of fellow "guild members who are often a more reliable and more kind [*sic*] source of information than general chat" (WowWiki, 2007, "Advantages of a guild," para. 4). With these new organizations come new opportunities for leadership.

Anyone who can afford a "guild charter" from the vendor and then obtain signatures from nine other players can create a guild and be Guild

Master. Leaders often start guilds because of their interest in working with and/or managing others, building relationships, and organizing friends. The guild leader is primarily responsible for organizing collective action within the game, from recruiting players, to arranging group activities, to handling disputes and disruptions. Guilds may have up to 999 members, though most are much smaller. As they increase in size, it is likely that the Guild Master will identify responsible players and appoint them as guild officers. Regarding group activities, many guilds engage in "raiding," where groups of 10, 25, or 40 players will work together to overcome powerful enemies (see Williams & Kirschner, 2012).

Raid and guild leader roles are not mutually exclusive and often overlap. As we will show, leaders share many attributes and work to meet similar sets of obligations, yet we witnessed many unique forms of leadership during our data collection as well. Some guild and raid leaders were online "all the time" and were available to discuss strategy, technique, and other game-related issues. Some leaders were just as ready to talk about their offline lives as in-game play and thus fostered more intimate bonds among players. Others showed little tolerance for poor player performance and were relatively authoritarian in how they managed cooperative play. Yet despite these differences, leaders' roles were bounded by technical and social rules that govern gameplay. To the extent that leaders' role performances aligned with the expectations of other players, they became well-known and trusted individuals. When their role performances were poorly handled (or poorly received by others), individuals found their guilds or groups abandoned in favor of others managed by players who were better able or willing to organize cooperative activities.

In MMORPGs like WoW, leaders of guilds and raids are expected to be knowledgeable about the game and to be able to coordinate groups of players in various activities. Some studies have taken the roles of guild and raid leaders into account, but overlook the multiple frames and detailed interactional processes that make roles robust (e.g., Ducheneaut, Yee, Nickell, & Moore, 2007). Instead, studies have typically emphasized role performance in terms of stereotypical extremes, what one of Yee's (2006) respondents termed "Den Mothers" and "Bitch Goddesses."[1] These terms refer to ideal typifications of MMORPG leadership styles that are affected by structural and situational factors. Structurally, things like size matter, with smaller guilds often being more focused on social bonding and larger guilds being more focused on hierarchies that facilitate the achievement of in-game goals (Williams et al., 2006). Situationally, players' intentions, emotions, and interactions affect how leaders act as they manage groups of players (Chen, 2009; Prax, 2010). Such studies focus primarily on classifying and categorizing guilds and players based on a perceived dichotomy between raiding on the one hand, and everything else on the other. While the dichotomy takes into account situational demands placed upon leaders, it is focused on leadership style without sufficiently considering the analytic depth that the role concept contains.

In theorizing the unique status of guild and raid leaders, we draw upon the concept of structural role. In its subcultural formulation, structural role referred to individuals whose actions diffuse cultural information across groups of people that otherwise might not have direct ties. Our study found that guild and raid leaders were regularly responsible for the dissemination of information that bore on players' experiences with and within the virtual world of Azeroth. For newer players, guild leaders were especially useful in helping them solve a variety of problems, from finding quick routes to level their character(s) to developing efficient play styles for a particular character class. For more advanced players, guild and raid leaders were often helpful in advising how to set up keyboard shortcuts or use macros[2] to maximize character performance. We identified other sets of expectations and obligations as well, and in what follows we focus on three aspects of structural roles for players in these positions. First, leaders dedicated extensive amounts of time to mastering their knowledge of the game, its characters, and its players. Second, they engaged in policy-making decisions that affected dozens or even hundreds of players and worked within and among player groups as a type of public relations officer. Such work required leaders to deal with both their own and other players' emotions. Third, guild and raid leaders were instrumental in maintaining a collective definition of the situation that was necessary for success in advanced forms of collaborative play. An interest or willingness to learn the intricacies of gameplay, to take responsibility for players' emotional well-being, and to manage a shared definition of the situation were all basic components of the guild and raid leaders' roles, and guild or raid success was often reducible to the extent to which leaders mastered these components.

METHODS

This report on the structural roles of guild and raid leaders is part of a larger multi-year study of WoW, a Tolkienesque, fantasy-based virtual game world that has boasted more than 12 million concurrent subscribers worldwide (Blizzard Entertainment, 2004, 2010). Using ethnographic methods including participant observation, in-depth interviewing, and writing personal diaries and field notes, we participated in the social world of guilds and raiding. Patrick and David had been playing WoW recreationally since 2005 and were familiar with many aspects of the game world, each having created multiple characters and played them to the maximum available level. However, we had no more than fleeting experiences raiding. Therefore, in 2009 Patrick and David joined a respected raiding guild to begin studying experiences and interactional processes among cooperative teams of players. Zahirah joined the research team in 2010 and began playing WoW on a different server in order to collect data outside the primary raiding guild.

During 2010, Patrick and David participated regularly in scheduled weekly raids as well as other events both in and out of the guild. In 2011, they conducted a series of informal discussions with guild members about collaborative action, and all three authors completed semi-structured interviews with four individuals who held objectively defined leadership positions within the guild (i.e., Guild Master and Guild Officers). In discussions and interviews we sought an understanding of the responsibilities and strategies they took on as leaders in the guild and of weekly raids. In all cases, interviewees had played WoW for a minimum of five years. Additionally, each had served as Officer or Guild Master of at least one guild prior to joining The Cleaning Crew[3] and thus had largely internalized the roles of guild and raid leadership. Patrick was promoted to Guild Officer in late 2010. In this role, he experienced leadership firsthand and was privy to discussions and debates among a small group of core guild leaders that most guild members were unaware of. These discussions were also treated as data that provided additional insight into the everyday constitution of guild and raid leader roles.

We conducted interviews through Ventrilo, an online voice communication platform, as it was the preferred method of communication among players, partly because of the sense of familiarity and comfort it affords to people who play together in computer-mediated contexts (Chen, 2009). We subsequently transcribed these interviews for analysis. On average, Patrick and David spent 10–15 hours per week during much of 2010 and half of 2011 raiding and otherwise playing with fellow guild members, establishing a large degree of rapport with interviewees in advance. Despite this amount of time, we never asked for, nor did other guild members typically disclose their "real-life" identities. We did, however, offer information about ourselves and our research project to members of the guild by providing links to Patrick's university website as well as both of our email addresses should players want to contact us privately.

We collected additional data through two methods. First, we used software to automatically record all text chat that occurred while our characters were logged in. Chat logs provided us the opportunity to look for patterns of interaction among guild and raid members which we could compare with players' reports from interviews. Second, we tapped into WoW development blogs and internet forums that related to guild and raid leadership. For example, one developers' blog entry aimed at new players was called "New player tips: building foundations" and directed readers to a thread within the Raid and Guild Leadership community forum where players from around the world posted comments. Many posts were from experienced players who gave advice on how a guild should be managed and/or shared anecdotes from their own experiences. Another thread that we analyzed was created specifically to seek opinions on how to create a successful raiding group, and consisted of players who shared their opinions on populating a raid guild and about decision-making processes for leaders.

FINDINGS

Although we were interested in exploring the potential utility of the structural role concept, we treated it as a sensitizing concept that helped us begin the process of analysis without allowing it to impose itself on themes that emerged from the data. Our subsequent analysis was further driven by recognition that roles are embodied in at least three analytic forms: cognitive, emotional, and behavioral. In what follows, we divide our analysis according to these analytic forms as we consider how each form improves an understanding of the leadership roles within WoW.

Knowledge

We found guild and raid leaders to be among the most knowledgeable members of the gaming community. Leaders were expected to either know the answer to any question or to be able to point players to an answer. Leaders were therefore obligated to maintain their knowledge of a game world that was constantly expanding through developers' and players' actions. Three facets of knowledge are relevant to our discussion: knowledge of the game environment, knowledge of characters that act within that environment, and (especially for guilds that raided together weekly), knowledge of the players that controlled those characters.

Azeroth is a vast virtual landscape that has expanded regularly since WoW's launch in 2004. Originally comprised of two continents, the Eastern Kingdoms and Kalimdor, Azeroth subsequently grew to include two newer continents (Northrend and Pandaria) and part of a separate, sundered planet called Outland. In 2010, Azeroth was redesigned so that many old areas of the game world were replaced with new content. The world was divided into interconnected zones where players of different experience levels could find challenging content. All players progressed through some of these zones, but guild leaders typically maintained knowledge about all of them. In addition to single-player content, some of these zones contained instances where groups of players, from as few as five (called "dungeons") up to groups of 10, 25, or 40 (called "raids"), quested together. These areas contained much more difficult content that required that players learn to act cooperatively (Williams & Kirschner, 2012).

Guild and raid leaders generally took it upon themselves to master the intricacies of group encounters with bosses in order to lead effectively. The amount of knowledge they dealt with was in no way trivial and was crucial to the development of a "theory of task" (Bastien & Hostager, 1992) that guided role performance via a common set of behavioral conventions. First, there was a basic set of group play-related tactics that covered all role types that leaders were expected to understand and sometimes had to teach to newer players (see Fig. 1). Leaders also had to maintain knowledge of all current top-level bosses, including their abilities and behaviors. In only the *Cataclysm* expansion of WoW, which serviced level 80–85 characters, there were approximately 100 unique bosses to be encountered, each with a host of abilities to be understood.

A single example should suffice in suggesting the amount of knowledge to deal with. In the Bastion of Twilight raid, the second boss encounter involved a pair of dragons, named Valiona and Theralion. Together, the pair had eight unique abilities through which they attacked players. One was called "Blackout," a magical attack that could seriously injure or kill all players within eight yards of the spot where Valiona cast it. Worth noting is that the damage was split evenly among affected players. Raid leaders had to know exactly when Blackout was coming and ensure that other members of the group knew what to do. To handle this particular ability, raid leaders would mark a location on the floor and instruct players when

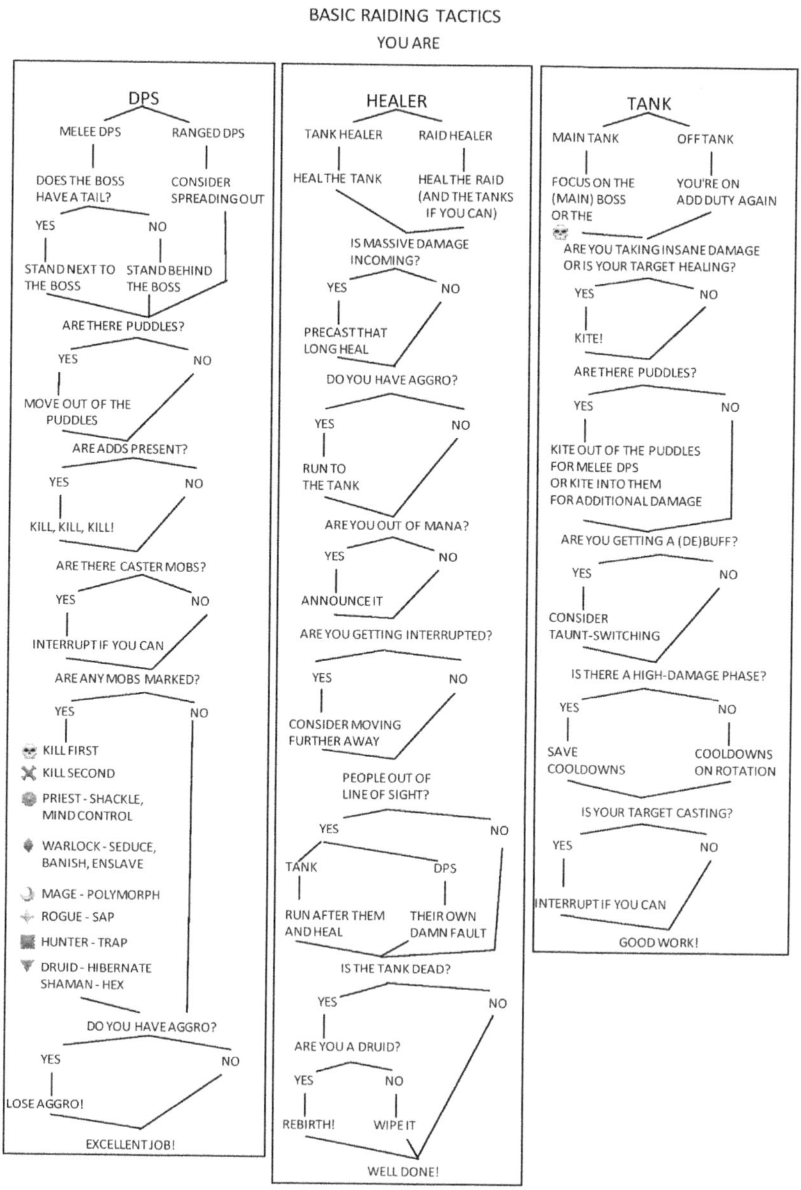

Fig. 1. Raiding Role Obligations in WoW. *Note:* This is based on the illustration by a player named "Aear" and published on many WoW raiding websites.

to collapse onto that spot so that the damage was split among as many players as possible, thus minimizing damage to any single character.[4] Raid leaders were responsible for knowing how each of Valiona's and Theralion's seven other abilities also worked, when and in what order they would come, and then instructing raid members as necessary. Although ideally players would come into a raid with at least some of this knowledge already mastered, it was not uncommon to witness leaders coaching individual players on specific aspects of boss encounters.

In order to coach players and otherwise manage a group, leaders had to keep up with the abilities and skills of each character class. There are 11 character classes in WoW – death knight, druid, hunter, mage, monk, paladin, priest, rogue, shaman, warlock, and warrior – and each has three distinct sets of talents. A player could master a set of talents that provided certain potential advantages or disadvantages when playing in a group. Certain situations might call for healers who had the ability to provide moderate healing to many players simultaneously, while other situations might call for healers who could restore large amounts of health to single targets instantly, or a group might need one or more of each type. Guild and raid leaders therefore needed to understand not only which classes were capable of healing, but how each class did so. In addition, guild and raid leaders had to know about the accoutrements of play, including weapons, armor, foods, potions, and other magical items that affected individual performance. There was thus a *burden of knowledge* unique to the structural role of guild and raid leader, as one interviewee described:

> Gotta be gemmed. Gotta make sure you've got the right item level, the right gear. You've gotta make sure that you have things reforged, now, to what your class requires and your [talents]. When you're a raid leader, it's that times 10 or 25 because not only do you have to know what you have to do, but now you have to know what everybody else has to do … to be a raid leader you really have to know everybody else's class too. You've gotta know what their cooldowns are, you have to know what kind of trinkets they currently have. You have to know when to [use] certain spells from a certain … class. You have to know when to call things out …. [Interview]

Such knowledge comes from a variety of media and may be passed on through the guild or raid leader to group members via an equally diverse set of media, including text chat within the game world, VoIP software, internet forums, and YouTube videos, to name a few. For this knowledge to impact the lives of players, it must be known, usable, and functional for guild and raid leaders (see Fine, 1979). To the extent that any particular bit of knowledge was triggered as situationally appropriate, leaders used it to improve the collaborative experience of online play.

Guild and raid leaders also regularly sought knowledge about the players behind the characters. Getting to know other players served several leadership-related functions. For example, knowing something about the players behind the characters on screen might assist a raid leader in building the best team possible. "If I'm like inviting, say for Icecrown, and I know there's a lot of mobility fights, I have four or five people that I consider friends that I wouldn't invite just because I know they can't move" [Interview]. Sometimes leaders had to split up these friends in order to achieve group goals, for example, if two players were redundant for a team or if one was not well suited for a particular raid. Leaders explained that knowing which players were more or less capable could make all the difference in keeping the larger group happy. This was true for the long-term stability of the guild as well as for the short-term stability of the raid. Having players online who were both able and willing to help other players or to craft armor, weapons, enchantments, or consumables was important for a guild's sustainability.

Getting to know the player behind the character helped guild leaders make informed decisions about the guild's current situation and its future direction. Officers talked regularly about well-known characters who could possibly be recruited, as well as about the "personalities" of players and how well or poorly they fitted with the guild's collective identity. This information was gleaned through months of participating in the everyday life of Azeroth, typically by interacting with other players in both private (e.g., "guild") and public (e.g., "general" and "trade") chat channels. When The Cleaning Crew experienced a void in upper management, the Guild Master turned to Patrick because she had learned through many months of almost-daily interaction that he was a university professor, he logged in regularly, and he offered advice or feedback when asked. Thus, she decided he would be relatively dependable in a leadership position. As an officer in the guild, Patrick became a regular participant in discussions about guild membership issues and was even sent as an envoy to another guild's raid when a possible guild merger was being considered. On that occasion, he reported that the other guild seemed to be made up of relatively immature players who seemed as much interested in one-upping each other and telling vulgar jokes as actually playing the game. Given this feedback, the guild leadership began questioning the consequences of such a merger.

Hanging out with other players in voice and text chat channels was equal part getting to know them in terms of their personal lives and getting to know what type of players they were online. Unstable family or work environments, for example, often affected players' online participation.

Some leaders avoided players whose outside lives would disrupt guild or raid progression, while others wanted their guilds and raids to be a home-away-from-home, that is, something players could look forward to. In sum, understanding the role of guild or raid leader was partially encapsulated in the knowledge they developed about the game world and its denizens. To look more deeply at the relations among leaders and other players, we need to consider emotions, which are important in interpersonal relations. Switching our discussion thusly is also important because emotions are a key component in an interactionist conception of roles.

Emotions

Unlike traditional single-player video games, where a player's success is predicated on her ability to anticipate what the program will do next, MMORPGs are distinctly social worlds within which individuals are connected to one another. The connections are not only among players but also among roles. When playing games face-to-face with friends, there may be, on the one hand, a desire to *win* while, on the other hand, there is a need to maintain (the appearance of) in-group solidarity (see Williams, 2006). The desire to win, and the emotional experiences that surround it, are determined not so much by the person, but by the rules of the game and the roles that players perform within the context of the game. We therefore need to distinguish between two frames that shape individuals' orientations toward gameplay: the play frame and the game frame (see Table 1). The play frame refers to the orientations *players* exhibited toward

Table 1. Orientation Frames.

Play frame	Achievement-oriented: the player seeks to progress; to accumulate resources and status
– orientation of the *player* toward the game world	Relation-oriented: the player enjoys establishing relations with other players; likes to help or offer advice
Game frame	Competition-oriented: the character seeks status; to be recognized for goals achieved; to be better than other characters
– orientation of the player's *character* toward the game world	Collaboration-oriented: the character enjoys working with a group; puts the team before herself; wants to be recognized in terms of group achievements

the game world, while the game frame refers to the orientation of players' *characters* toward the game world. Rather than being mutually exclusive, individuals orient as both players and characters and their orientations are shaped by a negotiated definition of the situation. This is a feature of all role-playing games and highlights the significance of in-game role identities and performances on interpersonal relationships (see also Weninger, 2006).

Players regularly demonstrated their orientation to these frames through talk and other actions. Sometimes members of guilds or raids had divergent frames, which resulted in moments of "drama." Managing drama was almost always the leader's responsibility, as leaders typically agreed that "having one person the entire guild knows as the final authority can be a huge benefit" [Forum post]. A leadership role involved responsibility toward and responsiveness to players' emotions. It required the cognitive tools to sense members' expectations and then manage the emotions arising out of conflicts in a way that maintained, or repaired disruptions to, players' frames. Such definitions were not always democratically derived, as leaders regularly staved off bases for conflict in advance by setting rules regarding players' etiquette, by defining the situational limits of characters' roles, and by stating consequences for deviation. When drama arose, guild leaders had to decide how to handle the situation, whether by relying strictly on pre-existing rules or mitigating negative emotions on the fly. Either way, there was demand for emotional responsiveness on the part of the leaders that required them to engage in emotion work – "the process of evoking, suppressing, or otherwise managing [players'] feelings" (Hochschild, 1979, p. 561) – to align their behavior with the feeling rules that characterized the situation at hand. The emotional dimension of guild and raid leader roles was most salient during raiding.

Raids, being purposefully designed to require coordinated action, demanded a high level of skill and knowledge and all players therefore expected each other to know how to perform class roles. Failure to perform, however, elicited varying responses. Data demonstrated an overarching assumption that members of "elite" raiding guilds were achievement (play frame) and collaboration (game frame) oriented. One guild leader called these the "hardcore" players who "put together a team that is actually consistent" and whose members were "always prepared. People who are … pretty anal about getting stuff done and about progression" [Interview]. Drama emerged when one or more members of such groups failed to perform. How leaders managed such drama "depends on the raid I'm in. A lot of times in high-end raid guilds they'll demean people on the spot for any problem they have. If you failed on one little portion of a fight, they'll just rip you in half and replace you with somebody from a waitlist … I guess if that's what you come in with the expectation of, it's fine" [Interview]. This might suggest that leaders gave little consideration to players' feelings, yet other interviewees discussed the emotional labor that occurred as leaders prepared for group play:

> I … start figuring out who's going to come … who we're going to have to sit, whose feelings we're going to have to hurt … which is … it's hard sometimes because I don't …. I want everybody to be able to come, but usually I have to log in a little bit early so I can explain to some people why they have to sit … and you know, explain to people sometimes …. [Interview]

Some leaders' role performances shifted across situations as they moved between the "den mother" role before and after raids to the "bitch goddess" extreme during raids (Yee, 2006). For other leaders, in so-called "social guilds" especially, the roles were more consistent and leaders had to work less to maintain collaborative and relation-oriented frames where players felt relatively little stress.

Our experience was with a guild that was transitioning from one of the top raiding guilds on the server to a more social guild. It was populated by a mixture of players and as the Guild Master told us, "if you are only here for gear and progression, you're probably in the wrong guild, because yes, we have a lot of skilled players, but we're also a lot of skilled players who have a lot of real life stuff going on. That's why it's a casual raiding guild" [Interview]. Players who didn't appreciate the increasingly relaxed nature of guild life vis-à-vis raiding would leave the guild, only to be replaced by others seeking a similar approach to gaming. Despite the more relaxed atmosphere in late versus early 2010, we continued to observe moments where discontinuities between play and game frames negatively impacted group play. During raids, failures in character role performance were most common, for example, when a mage did not dispel an enemy attack or when a tank did not taunt at the right moment. Out-of-game issues also affected the play frame – work stress, bad mood, and "wife aggro" were often cited as reasons behind emotional outbursts. Leaders had to consider such contingencies as well as the identities of players when mediating problematic behaviors. "There's a huge diversity in WoW, and you never know who you're playing with. And your best healer could be a grandmother, might be a mother of three children. You know, you can't just … expect everybody to get along" [Interview].

Leaders had to take the players behind the screen into consideration and anticipate the diversity of play and game frames as they dealt with management issues. The previous quote exemplifies both leaders' awareness of feeling rules and their engagement in "emotional role-taking," the imaginative experience or anticipation of moments of guilt, empathy, or shame for others (Shott, 1979). Upon reflection of our own opinions about who were "good leaders," we found they were individuals who made efforts (or undertook emotional labor) to avoid or mitigate the negative effects of such emotions. They were players who typically acted only after considering the many others involved. Emotional role-taking, and emotion work more generally, is significant in social life as it promotes self-control, creates trust, and consequently, maintains social organization (Cahill, 1995). Interpersonal conflicts often led to disrupted play and game frames, which could make raiding and guild life unpleasant:

> Sometimes you have to be the mediator. You have fights between ... members. Happens quite a bit, people whispering you, telling you "wow this guy sucks" and then the other person saying "hey, this guy's bothering me." So you end up playing mediator. Sometimes it feels like you're playing the nanny. As a leader, you're cleaning up everybody else's messes, so to speak. [Interview]

Leaders had a responsibility to act in conflict situations in order to protect others from drama and maintain the sanctity of the definition of the situation. In doing so, "good" leaders appeared neutral or objective when possible, ousted troublemakers when necessary, and projected confidence and poise during moments of intense emotional fervor. "There's nothing I respect more than a guild leader that knows when a player is souring his/her guild, and knows the best way to handle it" [Forum post]. Leaders' actions earned them the respect of many guild and raid members, a point that was repeatedly found to be important for a guild's long-term success in field notes, interviews, and forum data.

Action

Leaders who effectively manage their and others' emotions are able to solidify legitimacy in the eyes of their followers. Role legitimacy increases leaders' likelihood to be able to project or reinforce a definition of the situation, which is a crucial feature of managing social action. In the course of managing guilds, running raids, and frequenting forums, leaders learned to leverage their knowledge, feelings and authority to overcome numerous threats to the interaction order. The visible behaviors leaders engaged in to maintain a collective definition of the situation comprised the embodied leadership strategies that were diffused as cultural knowledge. As leaders strived to maintain a collective definition of the situation, they constantly negotiated interactions through both the play and game frames. We previously looked at how an emotionally informed definition of the situation is dialectically related to each of these two frames. A collective definition of the situation achieved frame alignment in *guilds*, resulting in a relatively drama-free social environment for like-minded players (Williams et al., 2006) as well as frame alignment in *raids*, facilitating the coordinated action necessary for advanced group play (Williams & Kirschner, 2012).

Guild or raid leaders needed to act responsibly, maintaining a vested interest in members' emotions and in the validity of their own positions in order to maintain a collective definition of gameplay. The significance of a shared orientation toward gameplay cannot be overstressed, especially when it comes to advanced forms of collaborative play. After all, collaborative play is the primary reason guilds exist, as they provide an organizational structure that facilitates the development and maintenance of a shared definition of the situation. Sometimes, however, leaders acted in ways that were best for them rather than in ways that were best for the groups they managed. The following two vignettes exemplify individuals acting in ways counter to collective expectations for guild and raid leader roles.

The first example comes from our first weeks of fieldwork and highlights the performative nature of roles by focusing on how a guild and raid leader made expert use of his knowledge and of feeling rules to mask his play and game frame so as to con other players. Not recognizing the significance of the event at the time, we later combined anecdotal recollections with recorded chat logs to reconstruct our initiation into the social world of expert raiding guilds. Patrick had obtained invitations for himself and David to join a new guild that was expressly organized for raiding. The Guild Master, Lolether,[3] had recently created the guild and attracted a number of well-geared and knowledgeable players to begin raiding. A group of 25 players immediately started raiding the Crusader's Coliseum, at that time the most advanced raid instance in WoW. During our third week of raiding, an extremely rare and prized item was found. Many raids operate under the rule that any character who (a) is eligible for an item and (b) needs it to upgrade her equipment has an equal chance of winning it through a random, computer-generated dice roll.[5] In this case Lolether, who was the raid leader as well as guild leader, was responsible for transferring the item to the winner. Yet after everyone had rolled, Lolether transferred the item to his own character, telling the raid that his internet connection was creating lag between his computer and the game server and he did not want to risk losing the item by disconnecting. When pressed by many raid members to pass the item to the winner, he was silent for a time, then typed "splled Pepsii onn kyboard," misspelling the words to support his performance as a player with a technical issue. As one player recollected, he then "went afk ['away from keyboard'] for 20 mins in hopes people would leave and he could take the gear" [Chat log]. Players did not leave, however, wanting to believe that he was attempting to resolve internet connectivity and keyboard issues and would return to transfer the item fairly. But his character eventually disappeared, and he was gone. Given his roles as raid and guild leader, Lolether wielded considerable power and control over the definition of the situation by retaining all managerial responsibilities, including those related to distributing items. He also engaged in careful emotion work, declining to respond to any questions or comments while he was idling and several times exhorting others not to complain or otherwise stir up "drama." His prior actions had reassured the group that everyone's play and game frames were compatible. We therefore shared a definition of the situation until he went idle after taking the item, introducing conflict into the situation, inducing strong negative emotions among the group, shattering the cohesive play and game frames, and reducing the shared definition of the situation to an angry and buzzing confusion. Not only did the raid group break up after he logged off, but the entire guild disbanded within 24 hours. We encountered him once more several days later in a public area of the game world where he was advertising a service. Another player responded: "Oh it's Lolether again the ninja who even steals stuff from his own guildies! he might just take ur stuff and log!" [Chat log]. His reputation and therefore his ability to lead a guild or raid ruined, Lolether transferred his character to another WoW server not long after, where players would be unlikely to know him.

Our second example came in 2011 after nearly a year and a half of active participation in The Cleaning Crew. One of the guild's officers and most trusted raid leaders, Xeky, left the guild after several weeks of poor raid participation and performance. He was well-liked and well-respected by many guild members and was responsible for teaching many, including us, how to become better raiders. Yet by his own admission, he was struggling to reconcile his own play frame between being achievement- and relation-oriented. "Sometimes I really like to be that progression guy that has the best gear, but most of the time now, I just like to be the guy that everybody wants to be around and still get things done you know?" [Interview]. He enjoyed time online with his guild friends but also felt that guild members were not doing all they could to be prepared to raid each week. Regular raid members would not show up sometimes; other times they would not know the details of boss fights and thus cause unnecessary setbacks for progression. In the end, the leader felt he needed to move to a guild that made faster progression. The emotional toll on the guild was evident in the reflective comments of another leader from the guild:

> [His leaving] makes me question what he was ever really here for and all the conversations we had and all the things that we play about and all the, you know, inside jokes that we had ... It's like, one of those things, where you start building a relationship with someone and then all of a sudden, they're gone and all you got was a small whisper, and it ... vaguely ... vaguely describes why they're leaving and there's no ... you know, sympathy or remorse involved in it. You start to really question, you know, the people around you. [Interview]

These vignettes bring the raid and guild leader roles down to earth. First, they illuminate the significance of emotions and behaviors in shaping the cultural definition of these roles. Second, they show that leaders are simultaneously similar to and distinct from other group members. Leaders are players like everyone else, and like everyone else they play games with their own goals in mind; goals which may or may not align with those of others.

The disruptions emphasized in these vignettes are partly attributable to the leader being distinct from other players. Players place their trust in leaders more than in other "random" players. They trust, for example, that the leader will facilitate a collective definition of the situation, or that the leader will be there every week to take charge and literally *lead* the group to success. Part of the role responsibility of the leader is the obligation to followers. When Lolether acted in ways that disrupted his role obligations, play was interrupted and people quit having fun. When Xeky left for a more achievement-oriented guild, those that had put faith in his orientation toward relationships felt cheated. In both cases, we must recognize "the precarious position in which these performers place themselves" (Goffman, 1959, p. 59). Whereas some leaders enjoy managing player groups, seeing it as an end in itself rather than as a means to an end, others lead because of a variety of benefits the role performance may provide. Generally, leaders enjoyed achieving high social status and with it the ability to wield power over collective definitions of situations, as we have highlighted above. In addition, they seemed to enjoy personal in-game rewards that they and their fellows received in part due to their effective leadership skills. Lolether's case involved each of the aforementioned benefits, which together facilitated his "misrepresentation," wherein he used his role capacity to deceive others for personal gain. Such a *faux pas* represents "that moment in their performance when an event may occur to catch them out and badly contradict what they have openly avowed, bringing them immediate humiliation and sometimes permanent loss of reputation" (Goffman, 1959, p. 59). Similarly, the precariousness of Xeky's position was rooted in the conflict between play frames that pulled him back and forth between managing player groups as a means versus as an end, between wanting to achieve and wanting to be in a guild where "friends" came first. Because roles are reciprocal, Xeky expected that followers would do what was expected of them. But several weeks of poor raid performance betrayed the expectations Xeky had placed on guild members to do their part. Analyzing his leaving illuminates the dialectic nature of roles, though the responsibility to maintain a shared definition of the situation rests more on the leader's shoulders than any other player because the leader is in a more structurally significant position.

CONCLUSION

Individuals performing structural roles diffuse culture across groups of people who may not otherwise have direct ties. For Fine and Kleinman (1979), a person in a structural role traveled physically among groups spreading culture (their examples included drug dealers, rock musicians, and itinerant preachers). In WoW, raid and guild leaders occupy structural positions around which other players gravitate, coming and going and in doing so bringing and taking culture with them. Guild and raid leaders also "travel" across internet websites and forums as they collect information, discuss problems, and search for best practices. Over time, many move as guilds merge and split, and they move among groups as they invite random players into their raids. The subsequent interactions between leaders and the other players/groups create or modify knowledge that is taken onward to other groups and to other roles.

In closing, we need to assess the utility of the *structural role* concept for virtual worlds, and for MMORPGs such as WoW in particular. Since the early days of WoW in 2004, games and other digital technologies have changed significantly with the integration of mass and social media into many MMORPGs. Game-related information has never been more available. The number of voices in online forums has proliferated, and

WoW-related forums and websites are no exception. WoW players routinely tap into the collective intelligence of the community online and in doing so learn about how to think, feel and act as players. This has affected the structural nature of guild and raid leader roles, mainly by reducing the amount of knowledge that a leader must carry around in her head. As one leader described it, "I used to know everything about unusual or difficult quests, all the locations to buy or earn certain pieces of gear, gold prices, and other things that were later helped by informational websites and specific addons" [Interview]. But today, "none of us can know everything; each of us knows something; and we can put the pieces together if we pool our resources and combine our skills" (Jenkins, 2006, p. 4). In 2004, a would-be guild leader had fewer sources from which to learn the art of guild leadership. In 2014, that aspiring leader has access to ten years' worth of distributed digital knowledge via forum posts, fan websites, wikis, and the millions of players that have tread on Azeroth's virtual soil. Leaders are, to some extent, relieved of the burden of knowledge.

As such, the *structural* nature of guild and raid leader roles has become less significant. Yet in terms of emotion work and managing a collective definition of the situation, guild and raid leaders still inhabit an important position in virtual worlds. Guild and raid leaders have the daunting task of bringing together diverse sets of players' frames of action and managing their own and others' emotions in order to maintain a shared definition of the situation that facilitates successful social interaction. The collective intelligence of gaming cultures provides increasingly ubiquitous resources upon which guild and raid leaders may draw to perform their roles effectively. Yet such collective intelligence does not do the work of leading; individuals must still step up to the challenge of managing computer-mediated networks of players with diverse interests and goals.

NOTES

1. Not all guilds engage in raiding as a primary activity and not all raids are comprised of members of guilds. Most research on guilds and/or raids has proceeded under the assumption that the two fit together.
2. A computer science term that refers to abbreviated sets of instructions or commands that reduce the number of keystrokes/mouse clicks necessary to perform a function.
3. All guild and character names are pseudonyms.
4. To get a feel for how this is experienced by players, you may search YouTube for "Valiona and Theralion guide."

5. Each eligible player types "/roll" in a command line and the game generates a number between 1 and 100. The person with the highest value wins. The raid leader usually then inspects the winner's role and gear to ensure the new item would in fact be appropriate and an improvement for that character.

REFERENCES

Bastien, D. T., & Hostager, T. J. (1992). Cooperation as communicative accomplishment: A symbolic interaction analysis of an improvised jazz concert. *Communication Studies*, *43*, 92–104.

Blizzard Entertainment. (2004). World of Warcraft. Platform: PC. Blizzard Entertainment.

Blizzard Entertainment. (2010). World of Warcraft subscriber base reaches 12 million worldwide. Retrieved from http://us.blizzard.com/enus/company/press/pressreleases.html?101007

Cahill, S. E. (1995). Embarrassability and public civility: Another view of a much maligned emotion. In M. Flaherty & C. Ellis (Eds.), *Social perspectives on emotion* (pp. 253–271). Greenwich, CT: JAI Press.

Chen, M. G. (2009). Communication, coordination, and camaraderie in World of Warcraft. *Games and Culture*, *4*(1), 47–73.

Dolch, N. A. (2003). Role. In L. T. Reynolds & N. J. Herman-Kinney (Eds.), *Handbook of symbolic interactionism* (pp. 391–410). Lanham, MD: AltaMira Press.

Ducheneaut, N., Yee, N., Nickell, E., & Moore, R. J. (2007). The life and death of online gaming communities: A look at guilds in World of Warcraft. In *CHI '07 Proceedings of the SIGCHI conference on human factors in computing systems* (pp. 839–848). New York, NY: ACM.

Fine, G. A. (1979). Small groups and cultural creation: The idioculture of little league baseball teams. *American Sociological Review*, *44*, 733–745.

Fine, G. A., & Kleinman, S. (1979). Rethinking subculture: An interactionist analysis. *American Journal of Sociology*, *85*(1), 1–20.

Goffman, E. (1959). *The presentation of self in everyday life*. New York, NY: Anchor Books.

Hochschild, A. R. (1979). Emotion work, feeling rules and social structure. *American Journal of Sociology*, *85*, 551–575.

Jenkins, H. (2006). *Convergence culture*. New York, NY: NYU Press.

Parsons, T. (1952). *The social system*. New York, NY: Free Press.

Prax, P. (2010). Leadership style in World of Warcraft guilds. In *Proceedings from DiGRA Nordic: Experiencing games: Games, play, and players*. Stockholm: University of Stockholm.

Shott, S. (1979). Emotion in social life: A symbolic interactionist perspective. *American Journal of Sociology*, *84*, 1317–1334.

Weninger, C. (2006). Social events and roles in magic: A semiotic analysis. In J. P. Williams, S. Q. Hendricks, & W. K. Winkler (Eds.), *Gaming as culture: Essays in social reality, identity and experience in fantasy games* (pp. 57–76). Jefferson, NC: McFarland.

Williams, D., Ducheneaut, N., Xiong, L., Zhang, Y., Yee, N., & Nickell, E. (2006). From tree house to barracks: The social life of guilds in World of Warcraft. *Games and Culture*, *1*(4), 338–361.

Williams, J. P. (2006). Consumption and authenticity in collectible strategy games subculture. In J. P. Williams, S. Q. Hendricks, & W. K. Winkler (Eds.), *Gaming as culture: Essays in social reality, identity and experience in fantasy games* (pp. 77–99). Jefferson, NC: McFarland.

Williams, J. P., & Kirschner, D. (2012). Coordinated action in the massively multiplayer online game World of Warcraft. *Symbolic Interaction*, *35*(3), 340–367.

WowWiki. (2007). Guild. Retrieved from http://www.wowwiki.com/Guild

Yee, N. (2006). Life as a guild leader. *The Daedalus Project*. Retrieved from http://www.nickyee.com/daedalus/archives/001516.php

(RE)EMBODIMENT OF THE DIGITAL SELF AND FIRST LIFE BODY IN A NEW SOCIAL MEDIA ENVIRONMENT: PAID SEX WORK IN *SECOND LIFE*

Justin A. Martin

ABSTRACT

Using the perspectives of dramaturgy and symbolic interactionists like George Herbert Mead and Carl Couch this study focuses on paid sex work in the hypermodern, virtual world of Second Life. *Using seventeen semi-structured interviews and six months of ethnographic fieldwork, I find that the employment of sexual scripts, carrying off a successful erotic scene, and the creative use of communication and embodiment are highly valued in escorts' performance of* Second Life *sex work. Escorts craft an online persona that is a digital representation of the self, which is manifested in the embodiment of their digital body or avatar. In addition to digital representations of the physical self,* Second Life *allows for multiple methods of computer-mediated communication, and escorts are able to re-embody the first life body through the trading of first life*

Symbolic Interaction and New Social Media
Studies in Symbolic Interaction, Volume 43, 143–171

ISSN: 0163-2396/doi:10.1108/S0163-239620140000043017

pictures, voice cybersex, and web cam cybersex. The data allow the conclusion that most escorts are unwilling to re-embody the first life body for reasons of personal safety and the desire to restrict access to the first life self. I find, however, that there is a porous boundary between first life and Second Life *in which the first life self comes through in the* Second Life *persona. In the concluding remarks, I explore the implications this study has for the negotiation of privacy for new social media actors who are reluctant to fully disclose their lives yet perform a persistent, archived persona for friends and followers on the Internet. This study contributes to a small, but growing, body of literature on* Second Life *and expands the existing work on embodiment and privacy in the digital realm.*

Keywords: *Second Life*; embodiment; paid sex work

This afternoon between bouts of reading and writing, I find myself sitting on a teak Lutyens bench situated in a garden with lush green grass, a breeze rustling the azalea bushes in full pink bloom, and a marble fountain gurgling nearby. As I am enjoying the tranquility, a white-haired gentleman dressed in a simple black t-shirt and jeans approaches and asks if he can join me. We engage in idle chat, asking what each other does for a living. I explain that I am a student, and he tells me that he is an art teacher from Copenhagen. As Scandinavian modern furniture is a passion of mine, the conversation quickly turns to the influence of Mies van der Rohe on contemporary design. Bemoaning the bastardization of the Charles and Ray Eames and George Nelson in IKEA's offerings, Halvor tells me that it is late in his part of the world and we begin to wrap up our conversation. As Halvor stands up and gives me a wave, my cell phone starts to vibrate and make its raucous noise. The caller-ID tells me that my mother is calling for our weekly chat about how my stepfather's eyesight is doing and her tribulations in the classroom. It is not an altogether unpleasant experience to talk to my mother every Sunday, but I am annoyed at her call. It has broken the peaceful time I was spending in the garden and brings to the fore that I cannot smell the azaleas but rather the coffee slowly burning in the next room; I am not a muscular young man dressed in slacks and a nice shirt but a flabby guy in pajamas who has yet to have a shower; I am no longer surrounded by beauty but am now acutely aware of the little red and black bug crawling up the wall beside my desk. My mother's call brings me back to my immediate situation. While talking with Halvor, I was in another world. While talking with Halvor, I was in *Second Life*.

Second Life is a persistent, computer-mediated virtual world in which users are represented by avatars.[1] Through these avatars, residents[2] can interact with one another and their environment. The focus of this study is on paid sex work in *Second Life*. Both males and females engage in paid sex work; however, the industry appears to be dominated by females. There are multiple media through which paid sex work takes place, each with increasing degrees of first life[3] embodiment: in-world text cybersex, voice cybersex, and web cam cybersex. In *Second Life*, the self is embodied in a seemingly disembodied environment in such a way that the sex worker offers his or her self, virtual body, and potentially the re-embodied first life body for sale; the self and the body become commodities.

The *Second Life* economy is based on the Linden, a token which is used in-world and purchased with first life currency. With Lindens, residents can purchase items designed by other residents or from commercial outlets that construct items for use in-world. Such items include clothes, buildings, cars, and avatar shapes. In addition to buying virtually tangible items, residents can trade Lindens between themselves. This ability allows for payment for any kind of service, including sex.

This project uses the perspectives of symbolic interaction and dramaturgy to examine a hypermodern, consumer society to expand on the small, but growing, body of literature on "life" and sex in *Second Life*. An examination of paid sex work in *Second Life* matters because it provides insight into how people arrange their intimate relationships, both paid sexual encounters and increasingly in romantic couplings, into mutually constructed sensual play (Couch, 1989); and it matters because it allows us to understand how we increasingly introduce agency into the technology in our life (Vannini, 2009). It matters because it tells us about the porous nature of the online and offline self: the encounters that we co-author and our value of privacy. For some, *Second Life* is just a game, but as Brookey and Cannon write, "it is a game that matters" (2009, p. 160).

SCRIPTING COMPUTER-MEDIATED SEX IN A CONSUMER SOCIETY

To undertake this examination of the commodification of the self and the body, it is necessary to lay a theoretical and empirical understanding of computer-mediated communication and sex; dramaturgy and sexual scripting; and hypermodern consumer society. Computer-mediated communication, be it textual, aural, or visual is the means of performance of an erotic encounter between escorts and their clients. Dramaturgy and sexual scripting provides a lens through which to understand paid sex work in *Second Life*. Commodification of the self and the virtual body takes place in an increasingly consumer society.

The Internet is not a noun, it is a verb; it is a production, a doing, a being, an act of communication and collective activity. All content on the Internet was conceived of and posted by someone to be consumed by some other. The most static webpage is a symbolic form of interaction between users. The most transparent incarnation of the Internet as an act of communication is when it serves as a conduit for the exchange of information in the instantaneous, spontaneous, and co-constructed interaction of computer-mediated communication. In her study of computer-mediated communication, del-Teso-Craviotto finds that "people participate in chats and other recreational varieties of computer-mediated communication for several reasons, but in most cases, there is a high level of personal satisfaction derived from the social contact with other participants" (del-Teso-Craviotto, 2006, p. 465). This high level of personal satisfaction through social contact is a function of communicative acts, an exchange of symbols and language. del-Teso-Craviotto writes further that "online experiences are constituted in and through language and as the joint accomplishment of the participants in interactions" (2006, p. 462). In online communications, there is an increased degree of intimacy and self-disclosure between the participants as they continue to enjoy the personal satisfaction derived through personal contact. As in first life interactions, as the participants begin to "grow old together" (Schutz, 1967, p. 140) the barriers between first life and online interactions begins to break down, which allows for the sharing of intimacy between the participants. This intimacy and a concern for privacy creates a tension which must be negotiated through the continued interaction and collective definitions of the participants.

Often in discussions of a sexually charged nature in chat rooms and other venues for computer-mediated communication, the participants are more willing to be open, frank, and honest about their lives, desires, and interests, which is in part facilitated by the anonymity provided by the medium (Mileham, 2007, pp. 15–16). According to Giddens, the intimacy and disclosure of the like that can be found in computer-mediated communication results in mutual trust and more open sharing of information. "Intimacy means the disclosure of emotions and actions which the individual is unlikely to hold up to a wider public gaze. Indeed, the disclosure of what is kept from other people is one of the main psychological markers likely to call forth trust from the other and to be sought after in return" (1992, p. 138).

The intimacy and disclosure in computer-mediated communication makes it a prime market for the sharing of sexuality. As Ross writes, "Discussions of sexuality would by definition involve the disclosure of intimate details ... It is likely that the intimacy shared on the Internet occurs much more rapidly than in most cases of conventional socially-mediated interaction ... [and] may lead to greater and more rapid intimacy" (2005, p. 346). Computer-mediated communication, with its increased degree of intimacy, rapidity, and anonymity makes the Internet the perfect venue for sexual exploration and computer-mediated sex. According to Ross and Kauth, computer-mediated sex is "carrying on via computer proxy sexual activity through rich description with accompanying sexual activity, often to orgasm" (2002, p. 47). Rich description, communication, and co-authored interactions heighten sexual experience even though they take place in separate physical spaces. McRae writes that this intimacy can be just as fulfilling as first life encounters. "While some may find technologically facilitated eroticism to be a disembodied, alienating, and ultimately meaningless experience, others, however, have discovered that it can be as involving, intense, and transformative as the best kinds of embodied erotic encounters" (1997, p. 73). Paid sex workers in *Second Life*, many of whom are not new to computer-mediated communication, use the skills they have honed over their years of chat-based Internet sex-play to produce a more satisfying and enjoyable sexual encounter for their clients and are, therefore, able to present themselves as having the skills that justify their remuneration.

The fantasy of computer-mediated communication and computer-mediated sex is a reality created through interaction. The Thomas dictum tells us that "if men [sic] define situations as real, they are real in their consequences" (Thomas, 1929, pp. 571–572). As Waskul and Lust (2004) note, fiction cannot be made of fiction alone but must have some basis or foundation in "reality." Frank (1998) and Zheng (2008) write that the manifestation of desire in a gentlemen's club is based on a fantasy that is constructed in the negotiation of intimacy through interaction between sex workers and customers. This manifestation may be a fabrication, but the fabrication is realized through the interaction. This fantasy is the foundation for a meaningful and heightened sexual experience in computer-mediated sex. Mileham writes about chat-based sex, "One can project onto the screen one's wildest imaginings. The conversation is limited only by the very limits of one's imagination. The lack of identifying information, of visual input, of a real body next to one's own leads individuals to co-create an imaginative fantasy ambiance whose magnetism can be very strong" (2007, p. 17). Mileham points out that it is the sense of personal security, derived from a "lack of identifying ... visual input" that allows for the sharing of intimacy which leads to a successful sexual encounter. As I will show, some *Second Life* sex workers are willing to transgress that boundary to (re)embody the first life body, but only for recompense. Privacy, or rather a breach in the wall of anonymity, comes at a price. Fantasy and reality, real and simulation, become blurred in computer-mediated sex in such a way that the reality is subsumed by the fantasy in the creation of an atmosphere and experience that can surpass even the "real" sexual encounter.

METHODS

There is no shortage of places in *Second Life* that attract paid sex workers, and all of these are places in mature or adult areas. Several simulations in *Second Life* advertise sex workers in much the same way that areas in metropolitan cities are known to cater to paid sex workers. As many escorts wear a name tag that identifies them as paid sex workers or escorts, there is no difficulty in finding them in *Second Life*. Respondents were drawn from those areas that cater to people looking for sex and those advertising their services. Snowball sampling was utilized on the basis that many paid sex workers got their start or learned from others who engage in paid sex work. There exists a network of paid sex workers, and many sex workers are friends with others who engage in that work in *Second Life*.

Interviews were based on loosely formed, semi-structured questions. Semi-structured interviews are free flowing but rely on the use of an interview guide (Bernard, 1995). Interviews lasted from thirty minutes to over an hour. The interviews began from an interview guide; however, the interviews were allowed to flow wherever the interviewee took the conversation.

A total of 17 interviews were conducted between January 10, 2010, and March 19, 2010. Of these, fourteen respondents were female and three were male. Participants ranged in age from 19 to 41, with a mean age of 28. Six of the respondents were Europeans or Americans living in Europe; the balance lived in North America. All except one had Caucasian avatars. The escorts I interviewed had avatars which conformed to exaggerated standards of beauty with chiseled, youthful bodies, stylish hair, and faces that could belong to runway models.

Four of the seventeen respondents indicated that they currently are college students. Janet Bull (39, northeast U.S.) is a psychology major; Ellen Cyberscriber (23, Midwest U.S.) is a library science master's student; Katherine Bailey (22, Chicago) is an animal science major; and Pam Cunard (35, Holland) is undergoing employment retraining. The people who approached me about my research displayed a level of familiarity with doing scientific, if not social scientific, research. Porn Glace (28, Berkley, technical consultant) asked if I had trouble getting the topic approved by my Institutional Review Board. Alyssa May (41, New York) said that she's "been reading a lot about 'what is cheating in a virtual environment'" and asked about the purpose and methods of my study. Ellen Cyberscriber said "I don't want to be paid for this [...] this is a good survey, it is making me think about why I am doing this [escorting], haha, a little self-analysis :)."[4]

Participants reported a variety of occupations. Alyssa said that she is "something that's rather close to being a courtesan. I'm a corporate wife." She went on to indicate that she has experience in sex work in her first life: "well ... once upon a very long time ago, I worked briefly as a dancer in rl [real life] ... changed jobs ... went to college."[5] Two of the respondents are unemployed and not in school. Two respondents work in information technology; Pam referred to herself simply as a "scholar." Jennakatana Furrpaw (30, England) has "been poledancing for 10 [years] in rl [real life]." Jackie Colbert (22, New York) says that her occupation is an "escort in SL."

Residents I interviewed had been in *Second Life* for various amounts of time; however, the most common length of time in *Second Life* was two to three years. Jennakatana Furrpaw was only "a month old," but she and Brad Moore (21, Midwest U.S.), who has been online only a few days, were the exception. Interviewees reported that they started working as paid escorts relatively quickly after joining *Second Life*. The shortest amount of time was one week after joining. The norm was within two to three months.

Most of the residents I approached for interviews were at a large simulation called Escort Oasis. Escort Oasis advertises itself as "a different kind of place. It is a busy freelance club, lots of hot girls and guys. Dancers and escorts keep 100% of their tips. Free ad boards, 12 private free sex skyboxes, 20 dance poles, freebies, MALL & shops, Freelance escorts." The skyboxes provide sex beds and pose balls, and there are actually thirty, not twenty, dance poles. These are usually all occupied and surround a large dance area flanked with chairs. Although the description indicates that there are male escorts, this is rarely the case. Dancers at Escort Oasis offer escorting services in addition to accepting tips for their dancing, which they perform to attract clients. As indicated in the description, Escort Oasis is a freelance club meaning that the owners of the club do not take any portion of the tips earned by the dancer/escorts. Smaller clubs, those which do take a portion of the tips, have regular escorts who fill out an application, interview, and join the club. As Porn Glace told me, "If you join a club, the tips are better, a good club has good traffic. As a freelancer, I hang around places like this [Escort Oasis] where a lot of guys are not interested in paying. At a club, the patrons generally know that the girls are not free."

Because Escort Oasis is so large and there are so many avatars there, the simulation is characterized as "laggy." Lag refers to the length of time it takes for the simulation to load and the reduced responsiveness in manipulating the environment. Smaller clubs do not experience this lag, and the interaction with the environment is more fluid. The smaller clubs tend to attract a clientele that is willing to pay a little more for the experience.

Five of my interviews came from escorts working at these smaller clubs, which have a more regular employment. Patrick Ward (24, Holland), the owner of G Club, advised that he requires his escorts to work a minimum of five hours per week to hold their position at the club. In contrast to Escort Oasis, smaller clubs like G Club and Platinum Lotus have six to eight dance poles, usually with no more than three or four of them occupied at a given time. These more intimate settings allow escorts to focus on residents entering the club, strike up a conversation with them, and entice them with their avatar representations and interactional abilities in a way that is hampered by the scale and volume of residents at a simulation like Escort Oasis.

FINDINGS: DRAMATURGY, COMMODIFIED VIRTUAL BODIES, AND RE-EMBODIMENT

Paid sex work in *Second Life* is a complicated, mediated communication between escort and client. The virtual body and Meadian self of the escort are commodities offered to their clients. Escorts' avatars are embodied through the attachment of enhancements and the representation of the self through advertising, profile information, and pictures. There is a porous separation between first life and *Second Life*, and a progression of re-embodiment of the first life body through the addition of voice and web cam cybersex to the more common text form. The findings support theories that there is a working consensus (Goffman, 1959) in an erotic encounter. Mutuality and sensual play (Couch, 1989) are important components of the sex work transaction. *Second Life* is a hypervirtual destination in which participants can engage in playful deviance (Redmon, 2003). Escorts engage in a third-person mode of communication that facilitates the scripting (Gagnon & Simon, 1973) of an erotic scene. The self and the virtual body are commodified, and the first life body is re-embodied through the use of voice chat and web cam cybersex (Waskul, 2002).

Defining the Situation

Burke (1969) lays out five elements of a dramaturgical performance in his famous pentad: act, scene, agent, agency, and purpose. The act is what happened. The scene is where the action took place. The agent is who is involved in the action. Agency is how the agents act. Finally, purpose is why the agents acted. In the development of an erotic encounter between an escort and a client, there emerges a working consensus of the situation (Goffman, 1959) in which the parties understand the roles they are to play to carry off a successful erotic encounter. This working consensus is central to Couch's (1989) understanding that the parties involved must relate to one another and hint at pleasure. Porn Glace told me what the escort must do to carry off a successful encounter:

> Focus on the other person and their *relationship* to you ... be empathetic. Try to *listen* to what is going on in their head without playing with their head. Get to a space where both parties are comfortable letting a little of their desires and fantasies out into the open. *Share*, even if that sharing is playing at being somewhat abusive. Make sure you are playing, and that the other person is at their *comfort* level. Be 100% totally into the person you're with at the time. Don't be afraid to enjoy the experience along with them. (emphasis added)

The emphasis that Porn places on the "relationship" and being at her clients' "comfort level" indicates that she is interested in giving her clients more than just a "quick fuck." The creation of a successful erotic scene is based on "mutuality." Couch writes:

> In mutual encounters both parties willfully relate to each other and offer or hint at pleasurable excitation. Mutuality is frequently sexual ... those who construct a mutual

> encounter at least hint that they are interested in becoming implicated with each other ... The involvement may be as minimal as two strangers winking at each other. (1989, p. 65)

Or, the involvement may a one-time erotic encounter or as protracted as a long-term relationship that an escort has with a client. Mutuality in *Second Life* does more than hint at "pleasurable excitation;" it is an expected outcome of an encounter between an escort and a client. Mutuality begins with the attention focused on the escort's alluring body, continues through the initial conversation, and culminates, often, in first life sexual satiation.

Couch (1989) also writes about the importance of sensual play. Developing this sense of play is nowhere more important than in the interaction between an escort and a client in *Second Life*. Darkflower Worth (32), Dee Allison (24, Canada), and Porn Glace offer advice to new escorts concerning the development of a regular clientele. They each told me that regulars are not so regular, that they come and go, and some are less desirable than others.

> Every so often I get it where I have a client many times in a week or two. Then I go through a dry spell like all the other girls here. Men come and go. Some stay with you, some don't. That's how it is in the business of an escort. (Darkflower Worth)

> Most men are 1 to 3 times, and then I guess they move on. I have one client that has been with me for almost exactly two years. All the other freebies are history, never see them again. For the most part, I wouldn't want to see them either. [They are] boring and you might not believe this but some men in SL [*Second Life*] are jerks. (Porn Glace)

> You find they [regulars] are often only regular for a while, then they either drift off to find something new, or in some cases leave sl [*Second Life*]. New = exciting, bb [baby]. There are only so many things you can do here, well in rl [real life] too, really. After a while it becomes the same things repeated. (Dee Allison)

Couch writes about the requirement for "something new" in first life relationships. "Romance is the source of variation, excitement, and adventure. On the other hand, relationships are constant. Constancy generates boredom. When all is certain, interest tends to fade" (1989, p. 177). Couch's observation applies to the data in that clients often seek out new and exciting erotic opportunities. Variety, whether in the choice of erotic partner or the scene played out, is the spice of first and *Second Life*. In constant relationships, such as being a long-time regular with an escort, sensual play (Couch, 1989) becomes less spontaneous and unexpected. Successful escorts can cater to the needs of their clients and keep the encounters fresh and stimulating. Learning how to portray the self as a skilled sex worker comes from other escorts, and learning how to advertise those skills is a part of commodification.

Dramaturgy and Sexual Scripting

The significance of using dramaturgy and sexual scripting is that these perspectives lend themselves to developing an understanding of the intimate interactions that are carried out in *Second Life* sex work. Sex work in *Second Life* is predicated on symbolic interaction: the exchange of ideas and emotions through symbols. Dramaturgy requires that we examine the position of actors in their environment, how they define their situation, and the actions that they undertake in that environment. Sexual scripting allows us to examine the interaction that paid sex workers have with their clients. As Gagnon and Simon write:

> Without the proper elements of a script that defines the situation, names the actors, and plots the behavior, nothing sexual is likely to happen ... Elements of such scripting occur across many aspects of the sexual situation. Scripts are involved in learning the meaning of internal states, organizing the sequences of specifically sexual acts, decoding novel situations, setting the limits on sexual responses, and linking meanings from non-sexual aspects of life to specifically sexual experience. (1973, p. 13)

The interactionist perspective tells us that the human being is a social person; sex work in *Second Life* cannot be carried out in a vacuum by one person alone. We also know that humans must be understood as thinking beings. Dramaturgist Charles Edgley (personal communication) furthers this by saying that "man is by nature an active creature."

By studying paid sex workers in *Second Life* with these understandings, we can see that they move beyond the sometimes static-appearing representation on the screen. The interaction between sex workers and their clients are more than the words that they type and the animations that appear in the environment: there is an active negotiation, an active co-authoring process that is occurring in order to carry out the scene. Both parties creatively co-author the interaction to bring off the sexual encounter. Other interactionist elements mirror dramaturgical aspects of symbolic interaction: humans make a definition of their situation, their action is predicated by what is going on in their environment, and again, they are active beings within their environment. Symbolic interaction, including dramaturgy and sexual scripting, is the most appropriate perspective to use in studying the communication that takes place between sex workers and their clients.

Sexual scripts vary in *Second Life*; however, there is some continuity. Escorts tend to utilize similar methods of gaining the attention and interest of potential clients: talking to them first and establishing a mutual connection or desire, being attentive to the needs of their client, getting into their head to make their fantasy come true. Alyssa May claims that she follows no script; however, she does provide some classifications of her clients: men who just want to "hit the sack," men who want to talk, and men who follow definite scripts in their sexual desires.

> Typical ... I'd have to say, not really ... I've had clients who simply want to get right into bed ... and others that mostly want to just chat. (The bulk of my clients are older, married men, btw [by the way]) many of which just want a woman that will pay attention to them. I've had a few ... odd ... ones and more than a few that are into BDSM,[6] since it's a service I offer, and enjoy personally. [Clients who just want to talk chat about] a wide variety of things ... sometimes they just want to vent ... wife doesn't listen ... isn't sexually interested ... things like that ... and in many instances, I'll give out advice ... (I'm not a mental health professional, but I do have a wealth of knowledge about sex, dating, relationships and the like ...) [On men who just want to hit the sack] I happily oblige ... :) Part of the appeal of what I do in here is that it's wonderfully erotic ... very often ... most times, in fact, I'll end up having an orgasm or two in RL [real life], while playing here. Just like in RL [real life], there's a good range of tastes, and techniques ... some men want to lay back and be served ... and others get enjoyment more out of satisfying their partner. Chuckles ... I do remember one client ... haven't seen in a while, who was interesting ... his fetish was to have me put on seamed nylons, a lacy bra and panties, and stilettos ... then just to walk around the couch he was on. We didn't talk, beyond the occasional "direction" ... "Stop please ... now turn ... good ... now continue ..." and we never once had sex ... but he paid me twice my usual fee to do that for him every few weeks. (Alyssa May)

Dee Allison says that luck plays a part in attracting a new client, but that her approach remains consistent. She also hints at the fact that you get what you pay for in that some escorts charge little for their services and the experience is worth exactly that. "My approach is to make them feel special, by giving them attention and chatting to them. Price of course plays a part. We all know there's nothing a guy can get from me or any other girl here they can't get 100 times over, in many cases it's just luck talking to the right guy at the right time." Ellen Cyberscriber says that she is normally the one in control of the sexual script, putting the needs of her clients first. "I am usually the one who takes the lead and does all the typing and focus on their pleasure. I think I definitely put the guy first, I am also pretty sweet and witty." Alyssa May knows when her client is about to achieve orgasm and changes the tone or flow of the conversation so that she is in greater control of the fantasy and is able to create a scene:

> It's a telling point that when my partner begins to falter ... to type less ... or less often ... at the "right" moments in play ... that he's masturbating in RL [real life] ... I'll usually pick up on that ... and give him a little extra attention at that time ... to let him come ... when my client starts to shorten up, I'll do more and more ... another thing I'll do, is to run two "conversations" at once ... the "scene" takes place in the main chat window ... and out-of-character chat, in the IM [instant message] window ... so we can use the IM to give each other hints ... "Oh yes Alyssa ... talk slutty, ... I love that ..." .... in here ... and I'll respond in the "scene" by doing so. (Alyssa May)

Although there is variation in the sexual scripts employed by paid sex workers in *Second Life*, the dramaturgical elements Gagnon and Simon (1973) outline are present. Escorts and their clients create a shared definition of the situation, the actors are named, and the behavior is plotted. Given the presence of these elements, "something sexual" can happen. As Alyssa May makes clear above, she responds to the "scene" by performing an act consistent with the desires of her client. She also manages the communication with her clients in such a way that allows the first life body to be manipulated to sexual satiation. This recognition of the porous relationship between the *Second Life* interaction and the pleasuring of the first life body creates a definition of the situation in which the participants model their interaction to meet the desired outcome of the erotic encounter.

Consumer Society

Computer-mediated sex has emerged in a hypermodern world and that world is a consumer one. In an era that has witnessed the replacement of production to one of complete consumption, even fashioning the self has become a consumerist task. Anthony Giddens writes, "To a greater or lesser degree, the project of the self becomes translated into one of the possession of desired goods and the pursuit of artificially framed styles of life ... The consumption of ever-novel goods becomes in some part a substitute for the genuine development of the self" (1991, p. 198). Zygmunt Bauman echoes this sentiment: "Individual needs of personal autonomy, self-definition, authentic life or personal perfection are all translated into the need to possess, and consume, market-offered goods" (1989, p. 189). Consumerism is imbued with sexuality; sex sells and the market sells sex. As Bourdieu (1984, p. 367) writes, the new bourgeoisie has a "morality of pleasure of duty" and a part of seeking out pleasure is found in seeking out sexuality. "Sexuality generates pleasure; and pleasure, or at least the promise of it, provides a leverage for marketing goods in a capitalistic society"

(Giddens, 1992, p. 176). Bauman writes that *homo sexualis* is now *homo consumens* leading people to "treat other humans as objects of consumption and to judge them after the pattern of consumer products by the volume of pleasure they are likely to offer" (2003, p. 66). Sex on the Internet is a commodity offered up for consumption to members of a consumer society. "Whatever the explanation, sex on the Internet has become a consumer phenomenon, providing a huge array of sexual possibilities for cybersex all over the world" (Ross, 2005, pp. 346–347).

Residents in *Second Life* act toward the sexuality of the avatar and judge the amount of pleasure it is likely to afford them based on the perception of the ability of the avatar to provide an intense and rich sexual experience. The assessment of a meaningful sexual interaction in *Second Life* is based on the ability of the avatar to carry on a performance that is likely to lead to orgasm. This perception of performance "consists on the assumption of responsibility for a display of communicative competence," the evaluation of which is based on the "relative skill and effectiveness of the performers' display of competence" (Bauman, Babcock, Gossen, & Abrahams, 1977, p. 11). In their discussion of Internet relay chat, Danet, Ruedenberg-Wright, and Rosenbaum-Tamari write that "players show keen interest in showing off, and express admiration for their own and each others' skills" (1997, Frame #5: PERFORMANCE, para. 1). The appreciation of their skills is shown to paid sex workers in *Second Life* through the transfer of money. Admiration for communicative skills and the ability to craft a sexual performance is shown through payment.

Escorts as Commodified Virtual Bodies and Selves

Bauman writes, "The most prominent feature of the society of consumers … is the transformation of consumers into commodities" (2007, p. 12). Escorts in *Second Life* use a variety of techniques to commodify their virtual bodies. As we will see, the importance of the looks of the avatar is apparent in how escorts reinvest most of the money earned into their avatar's clothes, appearance, and accessories. Their selves are commodified through the creative, thick description of the emote,[7] their notecards, picture books, and advertisements.

The more description, creative, thick accounts of what the avatar is doing beyond the animation helps in creating and carrying off a performance through the mental visualization of the action. "We are missing a few key things in here … scent … touch … hearing … so the more … the better … we can 'fill in' those missing things, the closer we can come to a 'real' encounter," said Alyssa May. The missing items limit the scene, forcing the residents to creatively co-author a setting in which to enact their performance. Even though *Second Life* provides a structure, the setting is made more manifest through the co-authored description of what is taking place. In much the same way that Alyssa indicates that the corporeal senses are limited by the medium of *Second Life*, so too are the social cues that indicate gender, age, and ethnicity.

The Avatar

The avatar's appearance and the profile are two ways to fill in the missing cues and commodify the person behind the avatar. Another way, one most important for an escort, is a notecard. I collected several notecards during data collection and there were some consistent themes. Most indicated the escort's avatar name, age, and location, and some indication of their first life physical attributes:

> Hello! I am an escort of 21 years old very hot, I live in Portugal, I do anything you may ask. I'll create a great and pleasant time for you to enjoy, a warm moment for us to be alone in intimacy, and in case you love to be with more than one people let me know, and we will make your dreams come true! (Andre Jones)

> Hey baby, thanks for requesting my notecard. I'm Dee Allison (you can call me Dee or Allison I don't mind), I'm a 24 year old English rose currently living in North America. If you want some idea what I look like RL [real life] please check out the 1st Life tab in my profile. Although I don't sell RL [real life] photos I do have a couple more I'm happy to give out on request with 30 min sessions or longer. For those of you who like to get Xcited![8] I'm fully Xcite! compatible, including clit & vagina, nipples, ass, lips and various accessories! (Dee Allison)

> Thanks for looking at my card. I am a 39 year old buxom Boston girl who is full of life, wit, intelligence and humor, not to mention an insatiable sexual appetite. Skilled in eroticism from many cultures throughout the world and history, you are guaranteed to have a fabulous sexual experience with me. I have no limits when it comes to pleasing you, except of course age play, scat and bestiality. (Janet Bull, 39, student, Northeast U.S.)

The Interaction

Communication is important for attracting new clients. Katherine Bailey says that she genuinely likes people, always chats with potential clients first, and never gets "right to business": "I don't treat everyone like just business. I meet them at clubs, I meet them while I'm shopping, I meet them where I dance. I go to freelance places and meet them there, and I never ever get right to business. I genuinely like people and if that's what they end up liking to do with me, I give them my card." Similarly, Porn Glace places importance on conversation and interaction with her potential clients as a precursor to a sexual encounter. She also distinguishes herself from her competition in her abilities to talk dirty and to improvise. "I chat them up. I'm real … I can talk about most any subject. Once I get them interested, I'm pretty good with the dirty talk. Most escorts seem pretty canned to me. I'm spontaneous." Darkflower Worth approaches new clients with a demure demeanor and gets them interested in her ability to talk to them. "It's not just the look. It's my demeanor, my attitude with men … How I talk to them and attract their attention that gets them interested. It's the same for most of the girls here. It's all in the way you attract a man in to get them as your client."

Ellen Cyberscriber, who claims to be a virgin in first life, shares her virginity with some of her clients to enhance their experience with her in a symbolic loss of her virginity. This is commodification of not only the virtual body but also the symbolism of her virginity. The performance of the loss of virginity is a dramaturgical act; however, it is reified in that act and because both she and her clients act toward that performance as real. "Nope, if anything it [her virginity] adds, but it is not something that I share too much or too often. I think on some level, guys want to be the first to 'plant their flag' so to speak. They love someone who will let them take charge and doesn't know the difference if they are bad or not." But, Ellen is not naïve about her abilities to create a scene. A creative writing major in first life, Ellen is articulate and knowledgeable about her clients' desires. Jennakatana Furrpaw, an erotic dancer in first life, draws on her experience as a paid sex worker to enhance her interactions in *Second Life* and to "work" men, to get in their heads. At first she gives them "an ego boast then compliment them on something." She says, "I found I do better than a lot of girls here. I know how to work the men, how to get in their heads, and make them think I love them which is mean I know and believe me it hurts sometimes [be]cause some I really do like."

Katherine Bailey makes the distinction when she says that she is visually alluring, but her real talent is her communication skills. "My avatar is stunning, my ability to text/cyber is fantastic, and my voice turns heads. Of course I will charge [for] what I do." Similarly, Brad Moore underscores the importance of the ability to roleplay in the creation of a scene and the enhancement of the fantasy when he is aware that his clients experience orgasm in first life:

> Don't get me wrong, the visual is a fun aspect of SL [*Second Life*] sex. But the real fun is actually creating what happens […] That's one thing I'm heavy into, I love making

> men orgasm in real life just by being a talented roleplayer [...] Sometimes your partner isn't very good at roleplaying, so you have to take the reins. Sometimes your partner won't shut the fuck up and over describes things. And sometimes you get guys that like watching the pose-ball animations while typing things like "Ohhh, fuck ya!" While others do the description route.

The "description route" is valued and esteemed in *Second Life* sexual encounters, and those who are talented with it use their abilities to make money.

Good Looking Avatars

The ability to creatively co-author an erotic encounter is reported to take precedence over the visual aspects of *Second Life* sex; however, the visual does play its part. "Good looking" avatars are highly esteemed. Club owner, Patrick Ward said that during his interviews with prospective escorts, he looks for "good looking avatars." He says, "This club has very high standards. Good looking avs [avatars] [...] maybe that's why this club is doing well ..." Darkflower Worth said that "when I made my final design of my avi [avatar] or even my first, I made her to be alluring, appealing, sensual, attractive. I am every man's desire." When seeking out a potential client, Katherine Bailey looks first for a "hot" avatar. I asked her what she considers "hot," pointing out that a resident could simply buy a new shape or skin to meet her desires. She said, "I would change your clothes and give you an AO [animation override]." She said that a "hot avi [avatar] is great shape/skin/ao and hair and clothes." Based on the shape and skin of the majority of the avatars seen in *Second Life* a "great shape/skin" would be one that conforms to Western ideals of beauty. Where everyone can be beautiful, everyone is. After buying my current shape, I was told countless times "you look good," "hey sexy," "you look so hot, you're turning me on." This commodification of the virtual body is an important part of crafting a highly desirable "peg" (Goffman, 1959) on which to hang the virtual self.

While the avatars in my study are exaggerations of the Western ideal of beauty, the relationship between the first life body and the *Second Life* avatar is one in which the fantasy is based on at least some adherence to reality. Although the avatars in *Second Life* represent idealized versions of the self, they are just that: representations. As Waskul and Martin (2010) found in our exploratory study of sex in *Second Life*, residents sometimes devote a great deal of energy and concern to constructing their avatars in as a re-embodiment of the self so that they can relate to that representation visually during virtual sexual encounters. For example, even though gender-bending does occur in *Second Life*, when the topic arose in this study, most respondents indicated that they prefer their avatar to have the same sex as their first life selves. The issue is one that relates to creatively constructing a sexual scene that is relatable to the first life user. If the scene breaks the boundary beyond which the first life user can no longer relate in any fashion to what is being creatively co-constructed, the fantasy is shattered and the encounter cannot be pulled off successfully. Although the bounds of what is possible in the construction of an avatar are seemingly limitless in *Second Life*, residents typically manufacture an avatar that is relatable to the first life body even if that resemblance would be only recognizable to the user herself.

One resident commented on how sexy my eyes are. My eyes are not sexy; I bought them. I also bought my good looking, sexy, and hot, skin. The focus on the shape, skin, eyes, and hair of the avatar is valued over the appearance of the person behind the keyboard; the persona is acted toward as an authentic, embodied extension of the person. In addition to skins, avatars attire themselves in the hottest, coolest fashions. Clothes, shoes, and hair styles all portray a sense of beauty the likes of which would be seen in an Abercrombie and Fitch catalog or from the pages of *Elle* or *GQ*. The sexy, hot, beautiful avatar is real; it is the focus of physical attention because it is acted toward as an embodied representation of the physical self. Waskul, Douglass, and Edgley examine the relationship of the "body-to-self-to-society" in their study of online chat participants. They write:

> Because on-line chat participants can present any body they choose, they will be more likely to do so in a manner supportive of the situational self they are currently enacting. These on-line self-enactments are dramaturgical performances that do not materialize out of thin air. Rather, they occur on a metaphorical stage that contains scripted socio-cultural performances to which participants tend to adhere. (2000, p. 389)

These scripted sociocultural performances are based on norms of beauty. In *Second Life*, the avatar is the "peg" on which not only the self, but also embellishments are hung. The docile body (Foucault, 1978) is commodified along exaggerated norms of the "beauty myth" (Wolf, 1990) in an environment where the myth can be achieved. The docile body of the *Second Life* avatar is one that is selected, purchased, and represented in such a way that others act toward it as if it were real.

As in first life, the *Second Life* body becomes a consumer of body enhancement products and a beautified commodity to be consumed by others. Millard writes that "to be part of the beauty elite requires a carefully managed set of semiotic resources, including long, shiny hair; clear, smooth skin; cosmetics; thin body; straight, white teeth; and trendy clothes" (2009, p. 150). All of these products of avatar enhancement are available in multiple forms from a wide array of providers. The commodities available to purchase to enhance the "peg" not only allow residents to perform a body that is exaggerated, but other residents act toward that body as an authentic representation of the self. Shilling notes that the transformation into a consumer culture has meant that beauty enhancements become a part of the negotiation of identity. "Analysts of consumer culture identified appearance, body shape and physical control as having become increasingly central to people's sense of self-identity" (2007, p. 7). By meeting the demands of the beauty myth, an avatar enables others to act toward it as an encapsulation, a digital re-presentation of the peg on which the self is hung. My eyes are beautiful because my avatar's eyes are beautiful. The working consensus (Goffman, 1959) among *Second Life* residents is that not only can an avatar achieve the beauty myth, but that they should and will be acted toward as though the person behind the persona meets the expectations of beauty. This "looking-glass body" (Waskul & Vannini, 2006, p. 5) encourages escorts to adorn and enhance their virtual bodies and enables the client to observe the virtual body of the escort as a beautiful, sexy, and alluring representation of the self. This reflexive embodiment (Crossley, 2006) – adornment and attention – adds to the working consensus of the erotic encounter. Escorts' virtual bodies and selves are commodified through avatar enhancements, notecards, advertisements, and profiles. The body-to-self-to-society concept allows us to see that the escort's virtual body is a peg on which to hang the self, and society, their clients, act toward that body and self as a commodified object.

From Text to Voice to Cam: Embodiment and the Porous Separation of First and Second Life

The increased re-embodiment is a part of commodification of the self, the virtual body, and in some cases the first life body. Pictures associated with escorts' notecards were in all but one case images of the resident's avatar and not of the person at the keyboard. Brittney Dunn (30, American in Europe) gives prospective clients a sophisticated picture book, which has shots of Brittney's avatar in seductive poses in various states of undress, nude, or wearing lingerie. Jackie Colbert (22, New York) and Jennakatana Furrpaw offer their potential clients professionally shot first life photographs without charge, and they use these photos as a way to attract clients. Mandy Ellison (19, unemployed, Ohio) sells pictures of her first life body. When I asked Mandy to describe the pictures she sells, she replied "hahaha, [they are] headshots, breast shots, vag[ina] shots." She explained that she charges different prices depending on what is depicted. She charges "200[$L] for face, 300[$L] for tits, 400[$L] for vag[ina]."

Mandy values her breasts and vagina, parts of the body that probably could not be used to identify her, more than she does her face, for which she charges the equivalent of approximately eight U.S. cents. The pictures of her body parts earn more money than pictures of her face, what Waskul (2002) found to be the most intimate part of the body in web cam cybersex. Waskul writes that "the body is protected by stringent rules and filled with profound meaning to the individual ... access to the sacred naked body of others means power and privilege ... A large part of the eroticism and feelings of liberation that come from televideo cybersex stem precisely from the cultural heresy of breaking these rules" (2002, p. 221). In contrast to Waskul's findings (2002), Mandy's devaluation of the "face" marks a divergence from the importance (and marketability) of what Davis (1983, p. 51) calls the body's "erotic generators" – the breasts, buttocks, thighs, and genitals. The value Mandy places on her erotic generators is increased because she works as an escort; the value she places on the face indicates that she does not believe it adds to the erotic encounter. Similarly, Jackie Colbert shows her face on web cam cybersex if her client requests it. She said that she does not charge extra for that. But Mandy and Jackie's devaluation of the face indicates that the erotic capacity of other parts of their bodies carry more value in *Second Life* sexual transactions than do parts of the body that are not typically highly eroticized.

Others indicated that with greater first life embodiment comes a higher price. Katherine Bailey sold topless photographs of her first life body, but did not show her face. Even still, it was a source of discomfort for her. "I've taken a couple of topless pics [pictures] for Lindens, but for a LOT ... I agonized over doing that, but I couldn't say no to 40,000 Lindens [~U.S.$160] for a picture." This begs the question: is the embodiment of the avatar not enough? The fantasy when coupled with first life photos, voice, and video is then carried over into the first life body, which is nothing more than a pornographic image could convey. However, *Second Life* is interactive porn (Reid, 1994), which weaves a new level into Vannini's (2004) Dante-inspired pornographic Hell. Images of the first life body may be mere titillation, but the real fantasy is created in interacting with the digital representation of that first life body. Katherine's client paid the equivalent of around U.S.$20 for a picture of an erotic generator, her breasts. Similar photographs are freely available at any of millions of Internet websites. But the point is that they were *her* breasts, someone with whom her client could interact and create an erotic encounter. What is puzzling is that Katherine's client had no way of knowing if the photograph he bought was an authentic representation of her breasts or one that she harvested from the Internet. The power of the self-induced illusion and willing suspension of disbelief on the part of her client is that he can act toward the picture of the breasts he purchased as though they were Katherine's breasts. He can act and interact with a representation of the body because he believes that the picture is actually Katherine; for him, it is. Given Katherine's reported agonizing over selling pictures of her first life body, it seems reasonable that she did, in fact, sell a photograph of her breasts. Because of Katherine's candor during our interview, I believe she would have told me if she duped her client. However, even if she had sold "fake" pictures of someone else's breasts, the fact remains that her client could act toward them as though they were Katherine's.

There is a progression of first life re-embodiment from text sex work to using voice and video. Of the seventeen escorts interviewed only one offers video. Most expressed concerns about videos or pictures being placed on the Internet, being recognized by others, concerns about their personal safety or the fact that embodying the *Second Life* sex experience is too close to cheating as reasons that they do not participate in video or share photos.

For Ellen Cyberscriber, there is a religious reason for not embodying her avatar with voice or video. Ellen is a devout Roman Catholic who makes a clear distinction between first life and *Second Life*. Early in her interview she said that she is a "Roman Catholic in RL [real life]." When I pointed out that she made the distinction that she is Roman Catholic in first life, she said the following:

> While I may not "sin" in RL [real life], I come to SL [*Second Life*] and I am much more free and I don't really feel like it is sinning. There is a divide [between *Second Life* and first life], because I feel like sl isn't really my body, it is just an avi [avatar] that looks like me, so it is more like looking at porn, and using my creative writing skills to have fun, so while it may be a "sin" to some people that I am looking at porn, thinking impure thoughts and masturbating, I don't. And I believe God is very forgiving, and would probably prefer me doing things in SL than in RL.

Ellen does not feel as though what she is doing is sinning. She uses *Second Life* to create a sense of moral distance (Chatterjee, 2003). By separating her first life self from her *Second Life* persona, she feels that God will forgive her for her transgressions and prefers her "sinning" in *Second Life*. However Ellen may feel that there is a separation, it should be clear from the preceding that there is only a porous separation between first life and *Second Life*. Her first life desires and ability to communicate them are made manifest in her *Second Life* interactions.

Anthropologist Marc Augé (2008) theorizes that certain places such as subway stops, airports, and vacation resorts to be non-places, that is, spaces in which we remove ourselves from the Schtuzian durée and cease to grow old with our fellows. However, Augé does not trouble his construction with the people who regularly inhabit these non-places: the stewards, cooks, and agents who creature these places on a daily and ongoing basis. By omitting the experience of those who perform a personal front in these places on a daily basis, Augé's analysis is incomplete. In the daily lives of residents of *Second Life* the online, the virtual world represents one such non-place that is inhabited on an ongoing basis by people who creatively co-construct virtual lives there. To the casual observer, *Second Life* is a game; however, it is also a place of performance. As dramaturgists have shown, what is backstage to some is front stage for others. As Turner and Edgley (1976) show in their analysis of the American funeral home, the front stage of the parlor is managed by the funeral director; however, the normally back stage place of the embalming room is a front stage for the people who occupy on a daily basis only that place in the production of the funeral. For the embalmers and other technicians, the morgue is their front stage. In this way, what is front stage for some is back stage for others. This complicates the model from Goffman (1959) but offers a more complete theory of the places we inhabit. The morgue in Turner and Edgley's analysis represents what I will call a performative backstage region: a region shrouded from daily experience of the masses, but a non-place region inhabited by the few for whom it is a place in which the personal front, at least for a time, matters.

Second Life is one such performative backstage region. As a performative backstage, *Second Life* represents a place in which residents can play with stigmatizing identities without the need to also create an account for their behavior (Scott & Lyman, 1968). As a performative backstage, *Second Life* is a kind of non-place in which we temporarily enter into engagement with our fellows and exit at will. It is a place in which we can perform or drop our personal fronts at will, and it is a place in which the potential for the adherence of the stigmatizing defect of character, as would normally be evidenced by our performance of sexual acts with strangers for money, gains little saliency. Stigmatizing performances which would normally earn one the label of slut or whore can be brushed aside because they are enacted in a performative backstage region. It is in this way that Ellen

Cyberscriber is, in fact, not really sinning because she is performing sinful acts in a performative backstage region in which the potentially stigmatizing identity has little opportunity to transcend the boundary between first life and *Second*. This is one example where the boundary between these two regions is firm: identity markers from *Second Life* have little chance of "infecting" the first life of residents. In this way, the barrier between first life and *Second Life* is permeable mostly in one direction: from first life to *Second*. However, with increasing degrees of embodiedness, as would be the case in the addition to the sexual script of voice chat and camera play, the barrier becomes more porous and the potential for stigma to flow from the online world into the first world. With increasing levels of displays of the first life personal front (thereby bringing the performative backstage into the front region of first life), the resident makes herself more vulnerable to having a stigmatized identity stick.

The boundary between the first life and performative backstage region of computer-mediated communication is a factor in the openness with which we interact with friends, colleagues, and others in some forms of new social media. Where social distance is great and the potential for the adherence of stigma is low, we are likely to be less guarded in our online communications through such tools as Twitter and Facebook. Viewed as performative backstages, we can enact a personal front in which we are free to open discourses otherwise unthinkable in a first life front stage; the barrier of the computer screen acts as a barrier to stigma. Updates and tweets may be forgotten; we do not suffer the consequences of a negative appraisal of our actions in real time; and we can explore the creation of an identity which may be unsavory to some but allow that identity to grow without having to immediately offer accounts of our behavior because we may be unaware of the immediate reactions of others.

DISCUSSION

The significant findings of this study can be summarized along the following lines which deal with how residents act toward others: the commodification of the self, the importance of scripts, and the escalating embodiment and decreasing levels of privacy of the various types of services offered. Residents act toward the avatar of the other as though it were an authentic representation of the self because the self emerges in the digital medium through communication. By selecting and attracting new clients with the approach that it is the interaction with others for the symbolic exchange of money, the self and the virtual body become a commodity because the client acts towards the escort's representation of the self as if it were real. Sexual scripts and the awareness of the escort that interaction skills are what are for sale is important to the successful creation of an erotic scene. There is a continuum from text sex work to voice and video that escorts recognize but do not engage in due to the increasing levels of embodiment for preservation of the separation of first life from *Second Life*.

The exchange of wealth for interaction and symbolic sex puts the self and the virtual or first life body on display for consumption by others. All wealth is symbolic – just as is the economy of *Second Life* – and the positive, reciprocal exchange of interaction is what makes good sex work valuable. The self becomes a symbolic commodity and the exchange in *Second Life* sex work is based on the co-authored presentation of the self, whether in the form of the embodied avatar or the re-embodied first life body. The exchange value of the self surpasses the tokens of symbolic money, calling forth a need to revisit an analysis of wealth in a tertiary, libidinal economy. Putting the self for sale is the ultimate wealth, the ultimate power – the power to give or exchange the self for sexual gratification in the symbolic barter of intimacy in return for a mutually authored and gratifying fantasy.

Playful Deviance in a Hypervirtual, Telecopresent Environment

To be copresent, Couch (1989) writes that it is merely necessary for two people to be aware that they are in the perceptual field of the other. He makes no distinction that two people must be physically proximal, but allows for the possibility that a digital representation of the selves will suffice. This computer-mediated place in which two people may be mutually aware of each others' position in the perceptual field is the mode through which escorts and clients interact in telecopresence. Shanyang Zhao (2003) writes that in a telecopresent environment, actors also construct a "sense of being with" one another. This sense of being together is created from the interaction the client and the escort share with one another. Zhao writes, "hypervirtual telecopresence is a form of human colocation in which individuals on both sides are virtually present at the site through digital representations that are located in each other's electronic proximity" (2003, p. 449, emphasis added).

David Redmon writes that "playful deviance occurs most often when small groups of tourists travel to symbolic spaces of leisure to participate in temporary forms of transgressions that they will not perform in places where they live" (2003, p. 27). There can be, perhaps, no more a symbolic space than the environment of *Second Life* to which a virtual sex tourist may travel to participate in temporary forms of transgressions privileged from access by others in places where they live in first life. These symbolic places in which users participate in transgressions allow what Redmon calls a "secret self" to emerge. Redmon reports that "none of [his] respondents were concerned with what strangers thought of their behavior" (p. 34). Because of the anonymity of the medium, clients and escorts alike in *Second Life* are free to explore and expose their secret selves. As Waskul and Martin (2010) found, this expression of sexual desire in *Second Life* often influences or takes the place of first life sexual desires and fantasies. Because *Second Life* is a hypervirtual, telecopresent environment, both clients and escorts are willing to explore and express sexualities and sexual behaviors they would be unlikely to enact in first life. Several of the escorts I interviewed told me that being paid for sex in *Second Life* adds to the thrill of the encounter. They also expressed, however, that they would never "whore themselves out" in first life. Similarly, it is doubtful that many of the clients would hire a prostitute in first life. Because of the telecopresence of the environment, *Second Life* acts as a virtual tourist destination in which escorts and clients can enact behaviors that allow the secret self to emerge.

For the most part, those escorts who were unwilling to re-embody the first life body were reluctant to do so because of the potential consequences to their first lives. The hypervirtual environment allows residents to temporarily transport themselves to a tourist destination where few, if anyone, would know their first life person. There they can engage in activities in which they control the re-embodiment of the first life body. The stigma of the "transgression" of working as or hiring a paid sex worker in a hypervirtual world is minimized. The secret self can flourish when re-embodiment of the first life body is controllable.

Couch writes of intimate relationships that they take different forms, but follow along similar lines of escalation. "Robust romantic relationships are (1) based on sensual play; (2) establish emotional and physical intimacy; (3) include repetitive lovemaking encounters; (4) produce sensual satiation; and (5) project intimacy indefinitely into the future" (1989, p. 178). Erotic encounters on *Second Life* do not meet all of Couch's categories. Rarely do escorts and clients establish robust emotional intimacy or project a sense of future intimacy. *Second Life* relationships are present-based; however, there is some level of repetitive "lovemaking." There is most definitely an occurrence of sensual play; in fact, that may be the seminal factor of *Second Life* erotic encounters between clients and escorts. "Sensual play occurs whenever two people are more attentive and responsive to each other than required by the situation and at least hint that they have a passing sensual interest in the other" (Couch, 1989, p. 179). Even when this sensual play is ephemeral and distanciated, which Couch points out may occur in first life (as in the case of erotic dancers and their audience), it is none the less sensual play. He writes further that "physical intimacy usually proceeds by individuals physically locating themselves next to each other, to incidental touching, to hand holding and kissing, to caressing" (1989, p. 182). In *Second Life* this physical proximity is not available; however, the intimate touching is accomplished via discourse in the form of text, voice, or video cybersex.

Escorts in *Second Life* are free to explore and enact a commodified virtual body and self. They engage in performances of scripted sexual encounters that blur the boundary between first life and *Second Life*. The embodiment of the avatar and the re-embodiment of the first life body and self allows residents, both escorts and clients, to act toward the digital representation of the body and self as though it is real; in fact, it is real. The power of the commodified embodiment is that residents can craft a persona that exudes sexuality and transforms of the cartoon-like avatar and environment into a scene that often leads to first life sexual satiation.

Privacy in New Social Media Environments

New social media environments, of which *Second Life* is an extreme example, allow for the display and consumption of selves and bodies on the Internet. While we may post multiple pictures of our lives on Facebook, MySpace, and myriad other sites, *Second Life*, with its especially sexual content, allows us to examine the tension between sharing and our valued concern about internet privacy. *Second Life* allows users to re-embody the first life body in connection with the development of intimate relationships, some of which are extremely sexual in nature. This marriage between the highly intimate, sexual self-presented online and the desire to remain anonymous and morally distant in our first life concept of the self is indicative of the types of fears that we have about giving employers, students, and close associates full access to our online selves as presented in Facebook posts or Twitter tweets. We want our friends to share in our lives, but only to a certain extent. We filter some content to alternate accounts, and censor our posts for fear that someday someone may judge us for our online presentation of self. The Internet is a vast archive of the presentation of self, and it is one that is accessible and amenable to breaches of privacy. The tension between full participation in the presentation of an online self and the desire that we exclude some from access to that self is typified in the extreme case of *Second Life* sex work. As new social media environments progress toward more fully developed virtual presentations of self, the kind of tensions that are being negotiated now on *Second Life* will become commonplace it our online vernacular.

NOTES

1. The word avatar comes from Sanskrit, and in the Hindu religion is used to denote the manifestation of a deity on the physical plane. In computing, avatar refers to a digital representation of a user, typically in a human or anthropomorphic form.
2. Users of *Second Life* are referred to as "residents."
3. First life will be used in this study to refer to the offline world. Residents typically refer to being offline as "real life." As Waskul and Martin (2010) note, however, interactions in *Second Life* are no less real than those in first life.
4. Ellipses will be included as they appear in the transcripts; bracketed ellipses indicate a break from the quote as in the case of probing or information that is not relevant to the quote.
5. As stated above, the distinction between the online realm and offline is referred to in this research as *Second Life* and first life; however, it is the convention to use the terms "rl" and "irl" [real life, in real life] by users in-world.
6. Bondage, domination, and sado-masochism.
7. A performance which the escort scripts in third-person, providing a rich description of their actions.
8. Xcite! is a purveyor of custom scripted avatar attachments such as genitalia.

REFERENCES

Augé, M. (2008). *Non-places*. London: Verso.

Bauman, R., Babcock, B. A., Gossen, G. H., & Abrahams, R. D. (1977). *Verbal art as performance* (p. 11). Prospect Heights, IL: Waveland Press.

Bauman, Z. (1989). *Legislators and interpreters*. Cambridge, MA: Polity.

Bauman, Z. (2003). *Liquid love*. Cambridge, MA: Polity.

Bauman, Z. (2007). *Consuming life*. Cambridge, MA: Polity.

Bernard, H. R. (1995). *Research methods in anthropology: Qualitative and quantitative approaches*. Walnut Creek, CA: Alta Mira Press.

Bourdieu, P. (1984). *Distinction: A social critique of the judgment of taste*. Cambridge, MA: Harvard University Press.

Brookey, R. A., & Cannon, K. L. (2009). Sex lives in *Second Life*. *Critical Studies in Media Communication*, *26*(2), 145–164.

Burke, K. (1969). *A rhetoric of motives*. Berkeley, CA: University of California Press.

Chatterjee, D. K. (2003). Moral distance: Introduction. *Monist*, *86*(3), 327–333.

Couch, C. J. (1989). *Social processes and relationships: A formal approach*. New York, NY: General Hall.

Crossley, N. (2006). The networked body and the question of reflexivity. In D. D. Waskul & P. Vannini (Eds.), *Body/embodiment: Symbolic interaction and the sociology of the body* (pp. 21–34). Aldershot, England: Ashgate Publishing.

Danet, B., Ruedenberg-Wright, L., & Rosenbaum-Tamari, Y. (1997). Hmmm. Where's that smoke coming from? Writing, play and performance on internet relay chat. *Journal of Computer-Mediated Communication*, *2*(4). Retrieved from http://jcmc.indiana.edu/vol2/issue4/danet.html

Davis, M. (1983). *Smut: Erotic reality/obscene ideology*. Chicago, IL: University of Chicago Press.

del-Teso-Craviotto, M. (2006). Language and sexuality in Spanish and English dating chats. *Journal of Sociolinguistics*, *10*(4), 460–480.

Foucault, M. (1978). *The history of sexuality: An introduction*. New York, NY: Vintage Books.

Frank, K. (1998). The production of identity and the negotiation of intimacy in a gentlemen's club. *Sexualities*, *1*(2), 175–201.

Gagnon, J., & Simon, W. (1973). *Sexual conduct: The social sources of human sexuality*. Chicago, IL: Aldine.

Giddens, A. (1991). *Modernity and self-identity*. Stanford, CA: Stanford University Press.

Giddens, A. (1992). *The transformation of intimacy*. Stanford, CA: Stanford University Press.

Goffman, E. (1959). *The presentation of self in everyday life*. New York, NY: Doubleday.

McRae, S. (1997). Flesh made word: Sex, text, and the virtual body. In D. Porter (Ed.), *Internet culture* (pp. 73–86). London: Routledge.

Mileham, B. L. A. (2007). Online infidelity in internet chat rooms: An ethnographic exploration. *Computers in Human Behavior*, *23*(1), 11–31.

Millard, J. (2009). Performing beauty: Dove's *real beauty* campaign. *Symbolic Interaction*, *32*(2), 146–168.

Redmon, D. (2003). Playful deviance as an urban leisure activity: Secret selves, self-validation, and entertaining performances. *Deviant Behavior*, *24*(1), 27–51.

Reid, E. (1994). *Cultural formations in text-based virtual realities*. M.A. thesis, University of Melbourne. Retrieved from http://www.aluluei.com/cult-form.htm

Ross, M. W. (2005). Typing, doing, and being: Sexuality and the internet. *The Journal of Sex Research*, *42*(4), 342–352.

Ross, M. W., & Kauth, M. R. (2002). Men who have sex with men and the internet: Emerging clinical issues and their management. In A. Cooper (Ed.), *Sex and the internet: A guidebook for clinicians* (pp. 47–69). New York, NY: Brunner-Routledge.

Schutz, A. (1967). *Phenomenology of the social world*. Evanston, IL: Northwestern University Press.

Scott, M. B., & Lyman, S. M. (1968). Accounts. *American Sociological Review*, *33*(1), 46–62.

Shilling, C. (2007). *Embodying sociology: Retrospect, progress, and prospects*. Malden, MA: Blackwell Publishing.

Thomas, W. I. (1929). *The child in America*. New York, NY: Alfred A. Knopf.

Turner, R. E., & Edgley, C. (1976). Death as theater: A dramaturgical analysis of the American funeral. *Sociology and Social Research, 60*(4), 377–392.

Vannini, P. (2004). Così Fan Tutti: Foucault, Goffman, and the pornographic synopticon. In D. Waskul (Ed.), *Net.seXXX: Readings on sex, pornography, and the internet*. New York, NY: Peter Lang.

Vannini, P. (2009). *Material culture and technology in everyday life: Ethnographic approaches*. New York, NY: Peter Lang.

Waskul, D. D. (2002). The naked self: Being a body in web cam cybersex. *Symbolic Interaction, 25*(2), 199–227.

Waskul, D. D., Douglass, M., & Edgley, C. (2000). Cybersex: Outercourse and the enselfment of the body. *Symbolic Interaction, 23*(4), 375–397.

Waskul, D. D., & Lust, M. (2004). Role playing and playing roles: The person, player and persona in fantasy role-playing games. *Symbolic Interaction, 27*(3), 333–356.

Waskul, D. D., & Martin, J. A. (2010). Now the orgy is over. *Symbolic Interaction, 33*(2), 297–318.

Waskul, D. D. & Vannini, P. (Eds.). (2006). *Body/embodiment: Symbolic interaction and the sociology of the body*. Aldershot, England: Ashgate Publishing.

Wolf, N. (1990). *The beauty myth: How images of beauty are used against women*. New York, NY: William Morrow.

Zhao, S. (2003). Toward a taxonomy of copresence. *Presence, 12*(5), 445–455.

Zheng, T. (2008). Commodifying romance and searching for love: Rural migrant bar hostesses' moral vision in Post-Mao Dalian. *Modern China, 34*(4), 442–476. doi:10.1177/0097700408319493.

SURFING TO AN ALTERNATIVE SELF: INTERNET TECHNOLOGY AND SEXUALITY AMONG "MARRIED STRAIGHT HOMOSEXUAL MEN"

Avi Shoshana

ABSTRACT

This article presents a theoretical and empirical discussion of the way in which computer technologies (the internet) influence the production of sexuality, sexual fantasies, and specific sexual behaviors. This discussion is based on the case study of an Israeli website for sexual encounters, which its users say has brought out (or enabled) a specific sexuality that would not have emerged were it not for the new technology. This article focuses on a particular population from among the sites users: married men who surf the site to find men with whom to have one-off sexual encounters, and who report a positive experience of "life in the closet." A total of 34 men were interviewed, 6 face-to-face and 28 in online interviews. The findings include three main accounts: (1) most of the interviewees said that the new technology (the website) enabled them to invent a

Symbolic Interaction and New Social Media
Studies in Symbolic Interaction, Volume 43, 173–200

ISSN: 0163-2396/doi:10.1108/S0163-239620140000043018

new existential category, that of "married straight men who sometimes have sexual encounters with other men." This category is seen as enabling a new sexuality, or a sexuality that would not have been enacted were it not for the internet; (2) the interviewees spoke of how "life in the closet," and in particular entering and exiting it (which was called a "zigzag sexuality" or the "revolving doors of the closet"), creates an experience of a vital sexuality that fits in with their marriage to a woman and their life as a "straight" man; (3) many interviewees explained how the technology enabled them to keep their sexuality secret, where the secrecy itself was said to create a unique sexual desire. The discussion section shows how the new technology enables individuals to invent a new sexuality, to enact unique sexual fantasies, and to maintain an alternative self, or alternative components of their concept of self.

Keywords: Self; virtuality; sexuality; internet; alternative self

SURFING TO AN ALTERNATIVE SELF

The relationship between technology, the body and (a new or improved) subjectivity has been discussed in various contexts (fertility technologies; surrogacy; anti-aging; cosmetic surgery; psychiatric medications; treatments to improve sexual function; and so on). An issue that has received less attention is the way in which computer technologies (the internet) influence the production of an alternative sexuality, sexual fantasies, and specific sexual behaviors (Waskul, 2003). This article describes how an Israeli website that offers sexual encounters (in contrast to websites aimed at helping people find romantic love) is portrayed by its users as bringing out (or enabling) a specific sexuality that would not have emerged (or been enabled) without it. This article looks at a very specific population among the users of the website, namely married men who surf the site looking for other men with whom to have one-off sexual encounters. The article also discusses the accounts of sexuality and the concept of self among married men who talk positively of their "life in the closet." It is assumed that these men experience sexuality differently from married men who view the closet as a suffocating space of denial (Seidman, Meeks, & Traschen, 1999).

The findings of the study point to three issues that link new technologies, sexuality, and the experience of an alternative self: (1) technology and the invention of new social categories. Most of the interviewees spoke of how the new technology (the website) enabled them to create a new existential category: "married straight men who sometimes have sexual encounters with other men." This category is said to enable a new sexuality, or a sexuality that would not have come about were it not for the internet; (2) an alternative experience of the closet. The interviewees described how their "life in the closet" – and mostly how they enter and leave it (described as a "zigzag sexuality," or "the revolving doors of the closet") – constructs an experience of a vital sexuality, and, moreover, a sexuality that they can integrate with their marriage to women and their lives as straight men. The interviewees say that this different experience of living in the closet is enabled by the internet; (3) technology, secrets and sexual desire. Many interviewees talked of how technology enables them to keep a secret (Simmel, 1950), which in turn is said to offer a unique type of sexual desire.

What these main findings have in common is the phenomenological association between technology and the construction of a unique self. Technological innovation is seen as bringing with it creative escape lines, or escape attempts (Cohen & Taylor, 1992), that help to construct new existential experiences. Given this, the article's discussion section proposes a synthesis of technology, new social categories and sexuality, one that shows how new technology enables individuals to invent a new sexuality, to act out sexual fantasies, and to strengthen an alternative self, or alternative aspects of their concept of self.

This article thus has two main objectives, one theoretical, and the other empirical. The theoretical objective is to widen the debate about new technologies, concepts of self, and alternatives. The empirical objective is to depict the understandings of self and the accounts of members of a unique group (married men having sexual encounters with other men) who make use of the internet to produce and maintain an alternative sexuality.

The paper is comprised of four sections. The first includes a review of the literature about the relationship between technology, subjectivity, and existential alternatives. The second section describes how the research on which this paper is based was designed. The third section presents the findings in terms of four central themes: a new existential category; a phenomenological negotiation with discursive orders; the sexuality of married men who have sexual encounters with other men; and technology, secrets and sexual desire. The final section offers a discussion that brings together technology, virtuality, and alternative sexualities.

TECHNOLOGY, SUBJECTIVITY, AND EXISTENTIAL ALTERNATIVES

New technologies are closely related to the processes of the social construction of reality, both in the ways in which they perceive the world, and in the ways that we become subjects (Foucault, 1983). Not only do new technologies challenge our "paramount reality" and the phenomenological taken-for-granted, but they also bring with them existential alternatives and new cultural scripts concerning the way in which individuals understand themselves and reinforce their concept of self (Shoshana, 2012).

The study of new medical technologies and subjectivity has shown how technological innovations entail changes in the ways that individuals experience their culture, their self, their body, the accounts they give, and the potential for a "different" or "new" life. In this regard one could mention a number of fascinating explications of how technologies relating to fertility (Ivry, 2010), surrogacy (Teman, 2010), plastic surgery (Atkinson, 2006), and skin lightening (Glenn, 2008) construct a new phenomenology for people in their everyday lives.

Atkinson (2006), for instance, shows how the consumption of technologies related to plastic surgery among men helps to fix a "damaged" self and to reinforce a story of self in the genre of "before and after." Teman (2010) argues that the medical technologies of surrogacy create a new type of talk about new life alternatives and special linkages between nature and culture (and technology), and thus new perceptions of the body and private concepts of self. Similarly, Ivry (2010) discusses how the use of fertility technologies (which are seen as secular) among ultra-orthodox Jews gives rise to new constructions of reality that incorporate religion and science, and ultimately produce a new subjectivity and novel life experiences. For Nikolas Rose (2003), the products of new medical technologies, such as psychiatric medications or anti-aging pills, construct neurochemical selves. These new technologies encourage a naturalistic (and essentialist) view of the self that reinforces the strict distinction between body and soul (and that actually negates the soul). Moreover, unlike the psychological discourse, for instance, these technologies operate on the movement from the outside (in the form of swallowing pills) to the inside, and not from the inside to the outside (in the form of confessions, for example). They also advance self-understandings that are entirely different from those posited by post-structural (Callero, 2003) or hermeneutic discourses (such as symbolic interactionism) (Blumer, 1969; Mead, 1934).

The technologies of the internet – which promote a technologically mediated subject (Yaszek, 2002), a cyberself (Waskul & Douglass, 1997), or a digital self (Zhao, 2005) – are seen as dramatically impacting on human experience, the way in which people grasp reality, and self-social world relationships. Garza (2002), for instance, describes how the internet has changed the human experience along the dimensions of temporality, embodiment, spatiality and sociality. Early writings about the internet underlined the uniqueness of life on the screen (Turkle, 1995) and argued that specific aspects of it (anonymity, fluidity and transgression) encourage a subversiveness that had not previously been possible. In particular, the internet has been said to "empower queer identities to negotiate with hegemonic sexuality" (O'Riordan & Phillips, 2007). It is suggested that "cyberspace creates new possibilities for exploring one's sexuality" (Wang, 2011). It has been argued that pornography sites for women for instance, are a case in point (Schauer, 2005). More contemporary writing about the connection between the internet and subjectivity questions its subversive potential, however, primarily because the hegemonic cultural orders (regarding sexuality, for example) are reproduced in virtual spaces.

The connection between the internet, subjectivity and alternatives has received special attention in three main contexts: the study of virtual communities, research into online dating sites, and sexuality. Research into virtual communities has detailed the growth of virtual or online support groups. Of particular interest in this regard is the emergence of alternative communities, such as pro-ana sites (Gailey, 2009), or sites for couples who have chosen not to have children (Donath, 2010). These communities are interesting because they show how the internet is tightly related to the expansion of the prevalent "typical biographies" (Schutz & Luckmann, 1974) in a given culture, to finding existential escape routes, and to challenging taken-for-granted cultural hierarchies.

Research into online dating sites has illustrated how, alongside stable gender hierarchies, counter-sites (or what Foucault would call heterotopias) are also available (Wang, 2011), sites that are able to construct new cultural repertoires about gender and sexuality. The literature also reports that the experience of surfing online dating sites is related to specific self-understandings and discursive orders. Illouz (2007), for instance, argues that the internet is clearly represented as a technology that detaches us from the body, making the internet self more authentic and real. At the same time, Illouz describes how online dating sites that require users to create a "profile" of the self enhance reflexivity and examination of one's self as a commodity. The self is defined by being broken down into categories of tastes, attitudes, characteristics, physical attributes, and its ranking on a scale. Given this, Illouz argues:

> Whereas the postmodern self implies there is no core self, only a multiplicity of roles to be played, the self that is posited by the conjunction of psychology and the Internet technology is "ontic" in the sense that it assumes there is a core self which is permanent and which can be captured through a multiplicity of representations (questionnaire, photo, emailing) and so on. The Internet revives with a vengeance the old Cartesian dualism between mind and body with the only real locus for thought and identity being in the mind. To have an Internet self is to have a Cartesian cogito, and to be involved in the world by looking at it from within the walls of one's consciousness. (2007, pp. 80–81)

The literature about the internet and sexuality largely deals with three issues: pornography (Seidman, Fischer, & Meeks, 2006; Waskul, 2003), cybersex (Waskul, 2003), and queer sexuality (O'Riordan & Phillips, 2007). A subject that has received insufficient attention in the research literature is the association between the internet and sexualities that are experienced as alternative to everyday, or offline, sexuality. We do not know enough about whether and how individuals use the internet to construct a sexuality that is perceived as an alternative to everyday sexuality. Moreover, we do not know how people maintain an alternative sexuality (an alternative self or alternative components of the concept of self) and incorporate it within their "regular" everyday life and alongside their "regular" sexuality. This article demonstrates, for instance, that there is population of married men who identify as "straight" in their everyday lives, and who even see themselves as straight, that uses the internet to express a sexuality, defined as "alternative," that exists alongside their "straight" and "regular" sexuality. Furthermore, the article shows how married men who have encounters with other men do so by managing a very particular structure: keeping these encounters a "secret." This structure can be seen to be vital, positive (and not pathological), sexually arousing, supportive of an alternative sexuality, and as producing existential innovations that would not have been possible without the internet. Before delving into the ways in which the interviewees for this research understand their self and their sexuality, I shall first present the study's methodology.

RESEARCH DESIGN AND METHODS

This article is part of a larger research project about technology, sexuality, alternative reality, and virtuality. The wider study looks at the sexuality and sexual fantasies of members of different groups on websites that offer sexual encounters. This article discusses a specific group: married men who have sexual encounters with other men. All of the people in this group use an Israeli website for sexual encounters.[1] Members of this specific group talk of two main experiences: a negative experience of "life in the closet," and a positive one.

Members of the first group report life experiences that are similar to those depicted in the research literature: repression, denial, suffocation, fear, and heteronormative pressures (Floyd & Stein, 2002). Members of the second group, however, offer quite a unique portrayal of life in the closet and of their sexuality. The current article is based on the phenomenological accounts of these people. It is important to emphasize that the members of this group see their unique sexuality as enabled by the technological innovations of the internet. A total of 34 men were interviewed: 6 face-to-face, and 28 in online conversations.[2] Between 2007 and 2012, I approached 412 men whose profile said that they were married to a woman and looking for discreet sexual encounters with men. One hundred and sixty-three responses were received. Eighty men agreed to be interviewed in an online chat on the site. Forty-six men spoke negatively of their life in the closet, and so the interviews with them are not included in this article. Thirty-four men, however, talked of a positive experience of living in the closet. Their ages range from 30 to 58. Eighty percent of the interviewees have a university degree and work in the professions (lawyers, doctors, bankers, advertising account managers, and so on). All of the interviewees live in the urban center of Israel.

Because discreteness is so crucial to the informants' life experience, very few of them agreed to meet with me face-to-face. The six that did meet with me only agreed to do so after months of correspondence through the site or by email. All six of these interviews were conducted at my home, and lasted between two to four hours.[3] Over the years I had many conversations with all of the informants about their sexuality. However, for the sake of uniformity one conversation was conducted based on a pre-prepared questionnaire which was presented to each informant. These conversations lasted between one and a half to three hours.

The interviews were comprised of five main sections: life story; description of the routine of their marriage and their relations with their (female) partner; sexuality (definitions of sexuality, sexual attraction and sexual fantasies); their experience on the website; and their sexual encounters with men. The interviews were analyzed in accordance with the stages of grounded theory (Strauss & Corbin, 1998). After identifying a number of dominant themes, five readings were carried out based on those themes: sexual self-definition; sexual practices and fantasies; the relationship between the internet and personal sexuality; understanding of the category "men in straight marriages who sometimes have sexual encounters with other men"; and identity position vis-à-vis the metaphor of the closet.

FINDINGS: A NEW CATEGORY, NEGOTIATIONS, AN ALTERNATIVE CLOSET AND SECRETS

A New Existential Category: "Men in Straight Marriages Who Sometimes have Sexual Encounters with Other Men"

Classifications, categories, and distinctions play a central role in making us into subjects (Bourdieu, 1984; Foucault, 1983; Schwartz, 1981). As Ian Hacking put it, "People are affected by what we call them and, more importantly, by the available classifications within which they can describe their own actions and make their own constrained choices. People act and decide under descriptions, and as new possibilities for description emerge, so do new kinds of action" (1991, pp. 244–245).

Hacking's main argument (and that of many others; see Shoshana, 2012 in this regard) is that new descriptions do not necessarily point to a social behavior that did not exist previously, but rather that the new classification offers new ways for people to be persons, or new conditions of personhood.[4] Given this, it is interesting to note the grievance expressed by *all* of the interviewees regarding existing social definitions of homosexual sexuality and the lack of a social category that accorded with their sexuality and the self that they manage.

Guy, a 43-year-old coffee shop owner, put it as follows:

> I don't know exactly how to define myself, not because I don't really know, but because no exact definition exists, there is no such thing. I am not a gay, I am not bi, I am a straight married man or a married man that sometimes also likes to spend time with men. There isn't, you see there just is no definition that describes my situation exactly. Something needs to be invented.

Guy's sense of unease concerning the category "bisexual" was expressed by all of the interviewees. Analysis of their accounts of this sheds light on two main reasons for it: resistance to the assumptions of "half and half" that accompany the prevalent definition of bisexuality, and resistance to the "hybridity" ("both this and that") that is seen as simplifying the interviewees' sexuality.

Alon, a 38-year-old accountant, described the first of these two resistances:

> I don't connect with the definition of bisexual, because it assumes that there's something mathematical, half and half, that you're 50% attracted to women, and 50% to men. That's ridiculous. It doesn't fit who I am. I'm a married man who is mostly happy with women, and sometimes I like to fuck with other men. It's totally different. It happened because of the internet. Before the internet, I couldn't have acted out this sexuality, and the fact is I did nothing about it. The frequency of sex that I need with men is different, the encounter is different, and I just don't feel that you can capture what happens through the simple definition of bisexuality.

Omer, a 33-year-old project manager at a high-tech firm, also conveys his discomfort with the category of bisexuality, mainly because of the hybridity it entails:

> It's an easy solution, to think I'm this and that, bisexual, attracted to men and attracted to women. But I've got news for you, I'm a more complex person than that, I'm not this and that. Today there's a whole thing about being this and that, masculine and feminine, feminist and chauvinist, women with two family names and stuff like that. Choosing the middle, the middle path – that lacks character, to me. My sexuality is different. *I'm a married man who sometimes needs sexual relations*[5] *with a man*. That's what I am. Complicated? Excellent, welcome to my life.

It is also interesting to note that not one of the interviewees felt comfortable with the category of "homosexuality," which they see as failing to express their different sexuality. Moreover, as emphasized by Ran, a 41-year-old analyst for an airline, it is a category that entails a "life scenario" that does not correspond with the sexuality of "men in straight marriages who sometimes have sexual relations with other men":

> The term homosexual doesn't reflect me. My sexual identity is really different from what that concept implies. I am not a man who likes men. I don't like men at all. *I'm a married man who sometimes likes to have sex with other men*. I like women, and so I'm married. Most of the time, I'm sexually attracted to women. And emotionally, I'm only attracted to women. You've got to understand that that term [homosexuality] paints a life scenario that is totally different from my life. With me there are no struggles over my sexual attraction, or about coming out of the closet or not coming out of the closet. I know what I find attractive. Without that site I don't think I would ever have fucked men. Before the site I didn't do anything. If you want to understand my sexuality you need a new definition.

Note also that Ran, as with the other men quoted above, stresses the need to come up with a new category in order to understand his sexuality.

The new category would not only point to the different types of sexual attraction between men, but would also include a different kind of sexuality. The quite conscious use by Assaf, a 48-year-old computer programmer, of the verb "to fuck," and not "to sleep with" or "make love" with men sheds light on this sexuality:

> I fuck men. I don't make love with men or sleep with them. That's why you need to understand that this is a different concept. *Married men who every now and then like to fuck other men*. Fucking them, not making love with them. It's a sexuality that's rooted in an urge for quick sex, not for ongoing love or a fixed lifestyle. You meet, you have sex, it's over. That's it. C'est tout. The urge is satisfied, and now there'll be quiet for a few months. So that's why you need a new definition for our situation.

The need to invent a new linguistic category is thus seen as related to a *different* sexuality that is made possible by the website, a sexuality that would have been controlled (or overcome) were it not for the site. Indeed, all of the men said that before "the age of the internet" they did not realize this sexuality of theirs. It is depicted as based on desire and urges, and not on love and the need for romantic relations; on short-term sexual satisfaction and not on lengthy relationships; and on a relatively infrequent need to put this sexuality into practice. On the other hand, their routine relationships with women are portrayed as meeting the need for love, ongoing intimacy and stable desire. The interviewees' concern with their different sexuality is also presented in terms of their phenomenological negotiations, or internal conversations (Archer, 2003; Mead, 1934), with people described as "professional homosexuals," as I shall now explain.

Phenomenological Negotiations and Internal Conversations with "Professional Homosexuals"

Foucault argues that the production of social discourses, and the emergence of some of them as dominant, plays a crucial role in the social construction of reality and the concept of self. What particularly interests Foucault is the way in which discourse is regulated. In his book, *The Order of Discourse*, Foucault (1972) discusses the processes that limit discourse and lead to its production, and points to three exclusions that participate in the production of discourse: the taboo ("what is prohibited"), the distinction between reason and folly, and the distinction between truth and falsehood. Inter alia, the division into true and false refers to the special status of "experts," who are seen as being able to speak the truth. People excluded from positions of power are seen as unable to speak the truth. Foucault (1972, p. 16) stresses that only those statements that are *dans le vrai* (or "within the true") will be disseminated. One of the results of this is "the rarefaction of speaking subjects," where "rarefaction" refers to the constant restrictions on the authority to speak. References to these dynamics of truth and falsehood, the rarefaction of speaking subjects, and primarily the disregard for variation within homosexual sexuality came up over and again in the interviews. The brunt of their criticism was directed at people they termed "professional homosexuals," or "[gay] community leaders," referring to familiar characters from the Israeli media, such as journalist Gal Uchovsky.

Their main points highlighted how "professional homosexuals" speak in the name of "the truth," the assumption of a single homosexual identity (and one that is out of the closet), and the way in which the script of sexuality (Simon & Gagnon, 1986) that they offer plays a central cognitive role in constructing the interviewees' selves. Nimrod, a 52-year-old doctor, explicitly discussed the two former issues:

> Gal Uchovsky and his husband, Eytan Fox [a film director] do us an injustice. They out whoever they want. Apart from being violent, it also works against them ... because I'm the proof that there are men who are attracted to other men and want to stay in the closet, or who don't fit the picture they're painting. It's like asking all women to be feminine and temptresses ... They are professional homosexuals who are speaking in the name of the truth, as if they're the experts in homosexuality, as if there's only one truth.

Omri, a 36-year-old public relations manager, also criticized people who speak in the name of the truth and who insist on the idea that men who are attracted to men can all be characterized in terms of a single sexuality. At the same time, though, Omri also talks of how the sexuality of professional homosexuals has helped him understand his own sexuality:

> Not only do they assume that all gay men must come out of the closet and look like them ... whenever I hear them talking I realize that I'm different, that the world is complicated, that there are men who are attracted to other men without wanting to make that a way of life, it's something else entirely. Only by comparing myself to them do I understand that. I explain to myself who I am. Kind of like talking with myself. When I see them I understand that I'm different, and so the site saves me, because it lets me meet men with a similar sexuality to mine. Without the website I'd have to come out, or only be married to a woman and never meet with men.

We should note that Omri, like most of the interviewees, points to two important themes: "talking with myself," and the association between his selfhood and the website. Paying cognitive attention to the "professional homosexuals" (or the "experts") and their discourse heightens the interviewees' reflexivity, which is played out in their "internal conversations" (Archer, 2003) and efforts to understand their own personal sexuality. In other words, many interviewees talked of how they carry out phenomenological negotiations with the "experts'" discourse, which in turn help them understand their own selves. The second issue brought up by Omri has to do with the linkage between the experience of a different sexuality and the website. The phenomenological negotiations or internal conversations that the interviewees conduct with the "professional homosexuals" conclude with an important insight into the way that the internet enables them to express (or bring out) a unique sexuality that is far from prevalent in the public discourse about homosexuality. Surfing the website and being exposed to other married men who are attracted to men (or the exposure to a similar sexuality to theirs) entails a life script that would not have been attained without the internet and could not have been derived from the experts' discourse. As mentioned, the experts' discourse is seen as demanding an out sexuality, and is not supportive of the category of "married men who sometimes have sexual encounters with other men." Tomer, a 46-year-old lawyer, points to these connections quite clearly:

> It's plain and simple. What I understand from all those spoilt professional homosexuals in Tel Aviv [familiar characters from the Israeli media] is that they wouldn't accept my story ... A married straight man who every now and then likes fucking with another man, and wants to stay in the closet. They'd want me to come out and confess to everyone that I'm gay. I'm not gay. I have a different sexuality. It was only after joining the site that I really understood that there is such a sexuality, and wonder of wonders, there are other men like me. I'm quite simply very happy that the site brought out my true sexuality, which never really existed in my life beforehand.

Zigzag Sexuality: "Oops, Now I'm Inside; Oops, Now I'm Outside"

The metaphor of the "closet" plays a central role in descriptions of homosexual identities. The closet operates as a "key symbol" (Ortner, 1973) that is "good to think with." It offers what Ortner (1973, p. 1341) calls a key scenario for managing the self.[6] The metaphor of the closet outlines a living space with two locations and a passage between them. The sociological and psychological literature discusses the emotions that accompany these spaces and locations and often "recommends" a preferred location. The closet itself is seen as an existential space of concealment, denial, suffocation, and secrecy. It is conceived of as a temporary position between two identities, one of which is "false" and the other of which is "true" (Turner, 1976); one is imprisoned while the other is liberated; one is full of life while the other is tinged with "death" (in this regard see the distinction between the life-self and the death-self in Shoshana & Teman, 2006). Moreover, the closet is often depicted as an oppressive space that requires exhausting and practically impossible maintenance, constant attentiveness and chronic tactical impression management (Bacon, 1998; Floyd & Stein, 2002; Roof, 1996; Rust, 1993; Seidman et al., 1999; Troiden, 1989).

The self in the closet is thus seen as a pathological self (Seidman et al., 1999). The research literature contains no alternative portrayals of a closeted self that is hedonistic, liberated and full of vitality. The closet is mostly represented as a liminal space that has no autonomous existence, but rather incorporates a self that is waiting to be discovered or revealed (Chambers, 2003). There is hardly any theoretical or empirical writing that sees living in the life space of the closet as a rational or strategic decision that an individual might make.

The interviewees for this study, however, did talk about an alternative experience of the closet. They described how "life in the closet" – and mainly leaving and entering it, or what was termed as a "zigzag sexuality," or "the closet's revolving doors" – constructs an experience of a vital and productive sexuality, and importantly one that can be integrated with married life and with being "a straight married man who is sometimes also attracted to men."

Tamir, a 39-year-old pharmacist, expressed himself as follows:

> This is exactly what I need. I don't need to live with a man or to have sex with only men. I really don't need that. It suits me to have sex with a man let's say once a month, or whenever I need to. There are months that I don't go into the website at all – it's this thing like "oops now I'm inside, oops now I'm outside" ... I am a straight married man who is sometimes also attracted to men .... The thing is that it is exactly the amount that suits me. I go shopping sometimes [laughs]. Most of the time I don't need to go shopping. Most of the time it suits me to be as if I'm straight, with my wife and the children.

Tamir goes on to emphasize his strategic choice of living "in the closet":

> I'm not sure if what they call The Closet aptly describes my situation. I don't know. But if it does, then I've chosen to be there. It's a strategic decision I've made. No one is forcing me. I'm sure there are people who find the closet suffocating, or feel that they have been forced into it by other people. No one put me in the closet. I chose it. More than that, I find it sexy. My life is more vivacious [laughs].

Shai, a 48-year-old lawyer, also used the word "vivacious" when he linked "vivaciousness and a sexuality that's full of vitality":

> I've felt really lucky ever since the website was set up. It has spiced up my life. It's given me vivaciousness and a sexuality that's full of vitality. I feel more colorful, more alive, vital. I don't want to be gay. I don't feel gay. I'm a married straight man who every now and then wants a man. The website lets me go in and out of the closet [laughs]. It reminds me a bit of that film, *Sliding Doors*,[7] with Gwyneth Paltrow, but with me it's not so glum, it revitalizes me, it gives me something that I wouldn't have were it not for that site.

When I asked Shai to explain his use of the term "revolving doors," he referred to the movement into and out of the closet ("zigzag"), or into and out of his unique self:

> The zigzag turns me on, it revives me, yes, when I think about it now I've got a zigzag sexuality, and I guess I like it that way. Because it's not only about sex. It's the whole excitement before and then getting back into my regular life for a few weeks or months. I find the zigzag sexy. I feel sexier [laughs].

I found this "zigzag" movement particularly interesting, especially when Nimrod, the 52-year-old doctor, used the same term as well:

> It's not only the sex. I swear on my life. It's the zigzag. It's the stimulating shift between my regular life and an intense encounter with a man. And it's always a one-off encounter. That's understood by both sides. There's no falling in love. There's something powerfully sexual. But again, not only because of the sex. Because of the secrecy. The transition and the zigzag. I feel like my life is in motion, that something inside me is alive.

Wishing to gain a more nuanced understanding of this movement and its association with vitality, I asked Ran to explain the significance of this movement to me:

> It makes me feel like I've got an alternative. There's something very sexual about that. Very alive. Sheer pleasure. It brings out an alternative in me that wouldn't be in me without the website. It also gives me a sense that I don't have to be stuck with a single identity, there's an alternative. I feel like I'm reinventing myself every time I have one of these encounters. The secret gives me life. So I'm not at all interested in exposing myself. I wouldn't find it sexy. The secret is my sexuality. I find the discreteness wildly sexy.

The prevalent depictions thus uncover an alternative experience of the closet that includes a conscious choice, vital sexuality, desire, and pleasure. All interviewees consciously rejected the popular conceptions of the closet and the sexuality it entails. They talk of their sexuality as a new and alternative "invention" that has emerged following a new technology (the internet). One of the main features that is said to offer "sexiness," "vivaciousness" or a "vital sexuality" is the *movement* in and out of the closet, or, more precisely, entering and leaving different types of sexuality that are attributed to the regular ("straight") self and the less regular self (one-off and relatively infrequent encounters with other men). As mentioned, this was described as a "zigzag sexuality." A further characteristic that is closely related to this vital sexuality is the "secret," the secret of being "a married man who sometimes have sexual encounters with other men."

Technology, Secrets, and Sexual Desire

> If human sociation is *conditioned* by the capacity to speak, it is *shaped* by the capacity to be silent .... (Simmel, 1950, p. 349)

When I asked Gabi, a 51-year-old architect, what is "different" about his sexuality, something he frequently emphasized, he responded:

> The secret. The secret is the essence of my sexuality. And I feel no need to expose it. More than that, the moment I let the secret out it's obvious that it will become something else, it won't turn me on so much. It adds intensity to my life. It broadens me, it makes my world bigger and opens me up to other places. Secrets are sexual. It makes who I am bigger. It's a different world, all mine, all privacy and discretion. It's mine. It's a whole extra world in addition to my regular life.

Liran, a 35-year-old lawyer, also stressed the "expansion" of his self, focusing especially on the sense of uniqueness and individuality that his "secret sexuality" gives him:

> My secret sexuality is mine and mine alone. It gives me an amazing feeling of being unique. It's a part of me that I keep to myself. I feel no need to reveal it or share it with my wife. Quite the opposite, the secret makes me feel like we're not a single body. Married life makes you operate like a single unit, and you can get lost. My relationships with men attract me because it's a secret, and the secret gives me a feeling of uniqueness.

These associations between secrecy and a broadening of the self and a sense of uniqueness resonate with Simmel:[8]

> The secret in this sense, the hiding of realities by negative or positive means, is one of man's greatest achievements. In comparison with the childish stage in which every conception is expressed at once, and every undertaking is accessible to the eyes of all, the secret produces an immense enlargement of life: numerous contents of life cannot even emerge in the presence of fully publicity. The secret offers so to speak, the possibility of

> a second world alongside the manifest world; and the latter is decisively influenced by the former. (1950, p. 330)

Simmel goes on to stress the connection between the secret and personal uniqueness:

> All these elements which determine the sociological role of the secret are of an individual nature ... The decisive point in this respect is that the secret is a first-rate element of individualization. It is this in a typical dual role: social conditions of strong personal differentiation permit and require secrecy in a high degree; and conversely, the secret embodies and intensifies such differentiation. (1950, pp. 334–335)

The connection made by *all* of the interviewees between secrets and sexuality helps us identify four main components: the sexuality of the secret; the frequency of performing the secret (and the sexuality); the secret and adventure; and the secret and an alternative self.

It is important to note that the interviewees' accounts suggest that their sexuality is not only related to their having sexual encounters with men, but also to the erotic experience of the secret. Conducting encounters secretly, preparing for the encounter, the excitement of anonymous meetings, guessing what the partner will be like and look like – all these are said to offer a broad erotic experience. As Tamir put it, "The secret is erotic. All the discretion turns me on no less than the sex itself."

Idan, a 41-year-old engineer, links the secret and its eroticism to the low frequency with which he meets up with men, similarly to many of the interviewees. The interviewees' subjective reports refer to infrequent sexual encounters with men (once a month, on average), which is said to enable the structure of the secret to be preserved:

> It isn't possible to describe the incredible feeling it gives, this whole business – whether he knows me or doesn't know me, how I will maintain discreetness, where we will meet, the names I make up for myself, professions. Wow, it is really heaven, virtual heaven [laughs]. It's what makes it special, even no less than the sex itself. And do you know what; it is also the reason not to meet with the man every day. If it was everyday then it would no longer be a secret, right?

The third way in which the interviewees link secrets and sexuality concerns what they define as "adventure" and as "escaping" from everyday life. Most of the interviewees described their relatively infrequent sexual encounters with men as having the structure of an adventure: it is a one-off, relatively short encounter, where both sides are clear about its objective (a short and non-committal sexual encounter), and that is a "non-regular" or "non-routine" experience. In other words, an adventure is an event that enables one to escape one's "normative" everyday routine or married life. This also appears in Simmel, "An adventure is certainly a part of our existence, directly contiguous with other parts which precede and follow it; at the same time, however, in its deeper meaning, it occurs outside the usual continuity of this life" (1971, p. 181).

Gad, a 43-year-old financial executive, spoke of this escape from one's permanent reality:

> The secret, which let me remind you again, is about an encounter of no longer than an hour, you come, present a fake identity, you do what you do, and you go, it's incredible, I love it, it lets me escape from my permanent reality. And it gives you a strong libido. I go back to my routine full of energy. It's a whole alternative world, which is only mine, and which is a secret.

This representation enables us to observe the interviewees' sexual encounters as "escape attempts," defined as "the search for some site outside everyday life which we might regard as 'alternative reality' or 'Other'" (Cohen & Taylor, 1992, p. 6). Of particular note here is the emphasis on *alternativeness*, which is closely related to the sexuality of the secret. The interviewees talk of the website as bringing out an entirely alternative self (and sexuality), or alternative components of their concept of self, that had existed but had not been enacted until their exposure to the site. Sixty percent of the interviewees said that the site (and in particular its category of "married men looking for men") brought an alternative sexuality out of them that they had not previously been aware of. Most of the interviewees said that they had had sexual thoughts about men, but that discovering the site (and the sexual categories therein) gave them the understanding that they are "married straight men who are attracted to other men." Raz, a 41-year-old industrial designer, put it as follows:

> Before the site, I didn't know that there was such a thing as married straight men who are attracted to other men, preferably other married men [laughs]. What I used to think was that you were gay or straight, and I wasn't one or the other, so I didn't have sex with men before the website. The site helped me to understand that I'm a strange bird, an alternative animal. I'm a straight man who likes sex with other men, preferably married men [laughs].

Doron, a 31-year-old fundraiser for an NPO, put it very concisely: "It wouldn't have happened before. The moment I saw the caption, 'straight married man looking for another married man for discrete relationship', my heart skipped a beat, and I realized that's what I am, that's what I'm really attracted to."

Ohad, a 51-year-old doctor, also talked about alternativeness:

> Until the site came along I didn't know you could be a 'gay straight married man' [laughs]. It's an amusing oxymoron that I was exposed to by the website ... I enjoy being alternative, on the condition that it's kept secret, of course. There's something naughty about it, and since then that's how I define myself. To myself, inwardly, of course, otherwise it wouldn't be a secret. And now only you and me know about it.

Other interviewees did not see the website as having brought out an alternative self, though they did see it has enabling alternative aspects of the selfhood to be realized. As Tal, a 36-year-old engineer put it:

> I won't lie to you, I had sex with men before the site, but really infrequently. It was impossible to be discrete. And I didn't really like it, because I wasn't looking for a relationship with a man. I was looking for non-committal sex. I wanted to keep my family life, my family is the holy of holies. I wanted someone who would understand me or who was in my situation. And then the site came along and you could search according to all sorts of criteria and find a man who was married, discrete, who understood that it's just about the sex, without falling in love unnecessarily, and most of all someone who can enjoy the secret without too many pangs of conscience.[9]

Like all of the quotations presented above, these comments challenge psychological conceptions of secrets. The dominant psychological discourse sees secrets in romantic relationships (and especially marriages) as pathological, or as a clinical oxymoron. The literature thus discusses the adversity of secret relationships and the way in which secrets are a burden and decrease relationship quality (Foster & Campbell, 2005).

Members of the specific group under study here, though, spoke of secrecy as structuring desire, eroticism, and vitality in a way that broadened the self and created an alternative. It was certainly not experienced as pathological. The various comments about secrecy suggest that it was made possible by new technologies. This connection between technology, sexuality and the invention of existential alternatives forms the basis of the following discussion section.

DISCUSSION: TECHNOLOGY, VIRTUALITY, EXISTENTIAL INVENTIONS, AND ALTERNATIVE SELVES

This article shows how a new technology is closely associated with discoveries about the self, new sexual definitions, and the reinforcement of an alternative self within a unique life structure. Furthermore, the article demonstrates how a new website, which includes newly invented sexual categories, encourages the subject to enter into creative phenomenological negotiations and internal conversations with existing discursive orders, taken-for-granted social categories, and thoughts about (cognitive and behavioral) escape routes from the cultural repertoires regarding sex and sexuality.

The research population of this study is comprised of married men who secretly have sexual encounters with other men. Prevalent discursive orders define this population in specific terms that call for the management of the self and personal sexuality in terms of "struggle," "falsehood," "pathology," and mainly of a self that needs therapy in order to be cured. The psychological discourse would see this population as managing a self that is not "real," that is suffering from emotional problems (repression, pressure) and a relatively low quality of life. Popular public discourse, in which the metaphor of the closet is central, might describe the life experience of the men in this study as one of suffering that could be alleviated by taking the dramatic step of coming out. The discourse among the leaders of the gay community in Israel, as elsewhere (Seidman, 2002), offers two main scripts regarding (gay and straight) sexuality. The experience of married men having sexual encounters with other men is seen as impossible, or as involving repression and denial. It is a discourse that explicitly encourages coming out of the closet, and is blind to alternative experiences of the closet and to the variety of sexualities that are entailed by sexual attraction between men.

In light of these discourses, the accounts given by the men who participated in this study are surprising. The dominant discursive orders make it hard for them to construct an alternative sexuality and maintain a hedonistic self that gains pleasure from its sexuality. The accounts given by "married straight men who sometimes have sexual encounters with other men" are surprising not only because they convey a positive experience of the closet, and not only because they see the closet (and their sexuality) as a sphere of life that gives them vitality, vivaciousness and a particular sexual desire, and not only because some of them do not formulate their (secret) sexuality in terms of the metaphor of the closet.[10] Rather, the interviewees' self-understandings and accounts are surprising because most of them do not experience themselves as "homosexuals" (or bisexuals). This finding is unexpected given that the sexual scripts about homosexuality do not encourage men having sexual encounters with other men (even if they are married) to produce (or invent) a definition of "married straight men having sexual encounters with men."

This definition is attributed to a technology, or more specifically, to a website. The internet is said to encourage and enable linguistic innovations, oxymorons, and new social categories. Not only does the new category not include the use of existing categories (gay or bisexual), but it also rejects the internal logic of the fixed categories of the dominant cultural repertoires. The prevalent discourses about homosexuality make assumptions about *being* gay, and not *becoming* gay.

Being assumes specific locations of identification (sexuality, ethnicity, gender, and others), of separation between locations, but mostly awareness of what is "real" and "false," or "original" and "imitation." This helps us understand why the metaphor of the closet, which assumes two existential positions (in the closet or out of it), plays a central role in the processes of being. Becoming, on the other hand, as underscored by Deleuze (1990, p. 39), does not tolerate this separation or distinction between before and after, or past and future. Deleuze and Guattari talk about becoming as follows:

> Becoming is a rhizome, not a classificatory or genealogical tree. Becoming is certainly not imitating, or identifying with something; neither is it regressing-progressing; neither is it corresponding, establishing corresponding relations; neither is it producing, producing a filiation or producing thorough filiation. Becoming is a verb with a consistency all its own; it does not reduce to or lead back to, "appearing," "being," "equaling," pr "producing." (1987, p. 239)

Becoming assumes multiplicity, abundance, movement, innovativeness, and finding escape routes from fixed cultural categories, none of which appear in being (gay, a woman, a man, a member of a minority, and so on).

The men in this study thus reject the fixed definitions of homosexuality and challenge the widespread scripts of sexuality, both in popular (and "normative") discourse, and in the gay community. In fact, according to my interpretation, they talk of becoming gay (or becoming a new identity, what they call "married straight men who have sexual relations with other men"). The movement entailed by becoming (zigzag sexuality) is also said to be one of the sources of the sexual desire and vitality of the category of "married straight men who have sexual encounters with other men."

By returning to a number of the findings from this study, I shall attempt to shed more light on the existential inventions referred to by the subjects. Sixty percent of the married men in this study had never had sexual encounters with men before being exposed to the internet site. All of the men in this group say they are sure that they wouldn't have had such encounters were it not for the site, and they would have continued to live their "straight" lives with their wives. All of the men in this group also said that their attraction to men is not so dramatic, and that their family life is the "holy of holies."[11] They report that their exposure to the site and the new category of "married straight men who have sexual encounters with other men" brought this new and more "exact" sexuality out of them. In other words, these men are saying that the prevalent cultural scripts of sexuality did not encourage them to have sex with men because they did not accord with their sexuality or sexual desires. Not one of the men in this study experiences himself as "homosexual" or "bisexual." Moreover, the dominant scripts of sexuality are seen as resting on a social structure (the "secret") that they do not find sexually stimulating. Their sexuality, therefore, is not only comprised of sexual attraction to men, but also of the adventure and movement entailed by their "secret."

Entering and leaving the site, the relative infrequency of encounters with other men, meetings with men who are not interested in a long-term intimate relationship, the discrete preparations before the encounter (making up a name, a profession, and so on), returning to one's "normative" ("straight") self (and sexuality) after the encounter – all these play a central role in sexuality of the men in this study and their ability to become "gay" (albeit for a short period of time) and realize a sexuality that had previously been "virtual." In other words, the new technology is responsible for the actualization of the virtual (Deleuze, 1994). Actualizing the virtual refers to new existential inventions, and is not an act of representation of something that had already existed.

In order to understand Deleuze's use of the concept of the virtual we need first to graph the notions of the real, the possible, and the actual. The real is that which exists here and now, while the possible is that which could exist. The possible, says Deleuze, is related to that which already exists. The possibilities of the future are related to the achievements of the present. Against the background of this (causal) relationship between the real and the possible, which in turn limits the potential for the invention of alternative life worlds, Deleuze uses the concepts of the actual and the virtual. The virtual need not be related to the actual or the possible. The distinction between the virtual and the actual is not the same as the distinction between the possible and the real. There are two main differences. First, "the possible does not exist, while the virtual does. It is real … the possible is what might become or might have become real, but as yet has not. The virtual is already real. It does not need to have anything added to it in order to become real." (May, 2005, p. 48). The second difference is that: "the possible is a mirror of the real, while the virtual does not mirror the actual … the possible is an image of the real, constructed just like it minus the real's character of factual existence" (May, 2005, p. 48). The virtual is not like an image. In this sense Deleuze distances himself from Platonic ways of thinking. Plato emphasizes the distinction between Model and Copy. The copy (the inferior idea) takes its content by resemblance to the model (the superior idea). For Deleuze "It is not the distinction between the Model and the copy, but rather between copies and simulacra" (1994, p. 39).

Something additional that should be recalled with regard to Deleuze's "virtual" concept is that it should be separated from the "popular" usage, especially with regard to the Internet (mainly "virtual reality"). Most dictionaries "conflate the virtual with the possible and define it as almost existing or almost real. But the possible is opposite to the real – it is an alternative form of present reality that has not yet been 'realized'" (Linstead & Thanem, 2007, p. 1492). Moreover the popular use relates to "virtual" or "virtual reality" that is connected to the Internet as not real or less real than (real everyday) reality. The popular virtual concept emphasizes the lack of reality (or realness) of virtuality because of the lack of face-to-face interaction. For Deleuze the virtual is not connected to relations with the real. For Deleuze the virtual concept is in terms of an *event* (and especially becoming). In other words, the process related to the virtual does not deal with realization, but rather with the actualization or becoming of other events that may, in turn, open up the future and change the "natural" constructions of reality (Deleuze, 1994). An event is "neither something that simply happens, such as … concert, nor something that reveals the essential truth about a general development. Rather, an event is inessential, unexpected, anomalous, seemingly impossible from the current state of affairs, and therefore capable of opening up the future, making a difference, and changing the world" (Linstead & Thanem, 2007, p. 1493).

The virtual event, according to Deleuze (1994), therefore enables us not to cling to regular events or common orders of discourse, and to invent new stories and in turn new life experiences (like new sexuality or new categories). I believe that an additional concept that Deleuze uses can assist us in comprehending the importance that he places on "virtual" for finding lines of escape from the hegemonic order or major truth. This concept, which Deleuze took from Bergson (1960 as cited in Deleuze, 1994) is "fabulation." Fabulation "challenges the received truths of the dominant social order, and in this regard it 'falsifies', but also produces its own truths through its inventions, and in this sense it manifests the creative 'power of the false'" (Bogue, 2006, p. 213). Accordingly, fabulation encourages thinking – in a structural existential way – about repetition (in the form of stereotypes, cultural hierarchies and fixed discourses about sexuality), the "real" (the here and now), and the "virtual" (relating to ideas of becoming different from something else) (Deleuze, 1968/1994).

In order to understand invention (or fabulation), the multiplicity and the openness (and not the closeness) involved in the virtual, Deleuze (1969/1990) uses the story of *Alice in Wonderland.* This description by Deleuze can assist us in understanding the decisions faced by my interviewees in this study when they surf a website and the invention of new sexuality involved in their decisions. Alice stands before the road sign that points in two possible directions for her situation: "Which way, which way" asks Alice, "sensing that it is always in both directions at the same time" (Deleuze, 1969/1990, p. 3). The potential of her situation stems not only from her ability to choose one direction and not another (i.e., "freedom" of choice), but also from the event itself, meaning two paths existing simultaneously, and not one of them existing until it happens. Deleuze emphasizes that there is no "good sense" in the right direction (among all the many possibilities) and no "commonsense as assignation of fixed identities" (Deleuze, 1969/1990, p. 3). The actualization of the virtual is not an action of representing something that already exists (in terms of this article the sexuality put forward by the dominant orders of discourse). The path receives actualization only via that which it executes. From the point of view of Deleuze we cannot think that there is a correct "direction" that exists upfront which the subject must go to. This choice of direction means responding to the major truths, which do not necessarily suit "other" subjects whose identity (or sexuality, in terms of this article) is experienced as "irregular" or "different." The actualization of the virtuality (inventing new sexuality in terms of the article) means choosing existential lines of escape, and moving from the mundane and regular, and especially *discontinuity* in history and opening the future.

When the individuals in this study surf the website, in addition to their "real" (homosexual *or* heterosexual) sexuality, they are exposed to a virtual sexuality. This virtual sexuality (in Deleuze's sense of the term) is not unreal. Rather, it is a proposal to follow paths (or to "fabulate") that had not existed in their world before. These are multiple paths that are not entirely clear (rhizomes, as Deleuze and Guattari, 1980/1987 put it) and that do not insist on the right direction or on "good sense" (Deleuze, 1969/1990). They chose not to follow the path of "real" (homosexual or heterosexual) or "possible" sexuality (men who define themselves as bisexual). Instead, their sexuality is virtual, in that it is becoming different from something else (Deleuze, 1968/1994). Thus, they produce a different sexuality from that put forward by the prevalent discursive orders (the psychological discourse and the popular discourse regarding homosexuals). This sexuality is actualized, or becomes a life script, through the new technology and the internet site. In fact, it is the website that encourages an alternative or virtual self (in the Deleuzian sense).

In order to fully comprehend the complexity of the current case study and the association between the internet and sexuality, two further issues need mentioning. First and foremost, there is need for a more nuanced discussion of the connection between morals and secrets. The interviewees for this study chose not to deal with the moral aspects of disclosure and concealment. They tended to say that the infrequency of their sexual encounters with men and their lack of desire for a long-term intimate relationship made their decision not to deal with the connection between morality and secrets an easier one to make. Closely and directly examining that connection may reveal more complex dynamics. Moreover, it could also help us understand the dark side of secrets and the paradoxes of secrecy (Bellman, 1981). The second issue that deserves more in-depth discussion involves the way that the many of the interviewees portrayed the internet as reinforcing their alternative self, or alternative components of their concept of self. Examining the everyday dialectic between alternatives and "normativity" (or being "straight"), the transitions between them (in other words, the movement), the reflexivity required to manage an alternative self, and especially the way the internet was used to maintain this alternativeness, could contribute to a more nuanced understanding of the relations between technology and the creative production of new life scripts.

I shall leave the final words of this article to one of the interviewees, Omer, a 41-year-old advertising agency executive:

> What's amazing about the invention of the internet is not that it turns the world into a global village or makes everything accessible, as researchers tend to say, but rather that culture has overcome nature. Things that weren't natural before the internet have become natural, at least as far as my sexuality is concerned. Thanks to the internet I can have an oxymoronic sexuality and say quite explicitly, though only to myself, and without wanting to reveal it to anyone: *I am a married, straight, homosexual man.* That's how I like to live, with culture winning out over nature [laughs], with technology helping us to sin a little and spice up our lives. It gives you hope and opens up the future, or as Oscar Wilde said, "The difference between the saint and the sinner is that every saint has a past, but every sinner has a future."

NOTES

1. The website was founded in 2002. As of April 2012 it had 278,941 members, most of whom live in the center of the country. Compared to other dating sites, this site is considered to be relatively permissive and aimed primarily at sexual encounters.

2. For a discussion of the dilemmas thrown up by the online interview method, see Orgad (2009).

3. The interviews took place at my home because the interviewees insisted on being discrete and refused to meet with me anywhere else (at a coffee shop, for instance).

4. These arguments resonate with labeling theory, "which asserts that social reality is conditioned, stabilized, or even created by the labels we apply to people, actions, and communities" (Hacking, 1986, p. 226).

5. The expression "sexual relations" is a literal translation for the word intercourse. In Hebrew the expression "sexual relations" can characterize long-term relations or one point in time acts. This expression may slightly confuse the reader who does not speak Hebrew. A number of interviewees sometimes used the word "encounter," which is more fitting to their interaction with the men that they met. All of the interviewees emphasized that they are not looking for long-term relationships. Moreover their preference is to meet a new man each time and avoid meeting the same man more than once (in order to avoid "relations") or to meet with the same man but very infrequently.

6. Ortner emphasizes that these metaphors are key symbols that act to sort out an experience and assist us in thinking (Ortner, 1973, p. 1341).

7. In Israel, the name of the film was translated as Revolving Doors.

8. A definition of the secret is offered by Frijn (2005, p. 15) "Secrecy is a social phenomenon, happening between or among people. It is also a conscious phenomenon that involves purpose and intent. Finally, it is an effortful phenomenon that requires active engagement in secret-keeping behaviors."

9. Most of the interviewees did not deal at all with the moral questions raised by the secrecy and concealment of information from their partner. Towards the end of the interviews I asked a direct question about the connection between secrets and morality. The vast majority of the interviewees refused to discuss it. The main reasons given were that their attraction to men was only sexual, their encounters were one-off, they had no desire for long-term intimate relationships with men, and that their attraction to women was more significant for them.

10. Forty percent of the interviewees said that the "closet" does not in any way characterize their life experience.

11. The sentence, "my family is the holy of holies" came up in 80% of the interviews.

REFERENCES

Archer, M. (2003). *Structure, agency, and the internal conversation*. Cambridge: Cambridge University Press.

Atkinson, M. (2006). Masks of masculinity: (Sur)passing narratives and cosmetic surgery. In D. D. Waskul & P. Vannini (Eds.), *Body/embodiment: Symbolic interaction and the sociology of the body* (pp. 247–261). Burlington, VT: Ashgate.

Bacon, J. (1998). Getting the story straight: Coming out narratives and the possibility of a cultural rhetoric. *World Englishes, 17*(2), 249–258. Retrieved from http://dx.doi.org/10.1111/1467-971X.00098

Bellman, B. L. (1981). The paradox of secrecy. *Human Studies, 4*(1), 1–24. Retrieved from http://www.jstor.org/stable/20008785

Blumer, H. (1969). *Symbolic interaction: Perspective and method.* Englewood Cliffs, NJ: Prentice-Hall.

Bogue, R. (2006). Fabulation, narration and the people to come. In C. Boundas (Ed.), *Deleuze and philosophy* (pp. 202–223). Edinburg: Edinburg University Press. doi:10.3366/edinburgh/9780748624799.003.0013

Bourdieu, P. (1984). *Distinction.* Cambridge, MA: Harvard University Press.

Callero, P. (2003). The sociology of the self. *Annual Review of Sociology, 29*, 115–133. Retrieved from http://www.jstor.org/stable/30036963

Chambers, S. A. (2003). Telepistemology of the closet; or, the queer politics of "six feet under". *The Journal of American Culture, 26*(1), 24–40. doi:10.1111/1542-734X.00071

Cohen, S., & Taylor, L. (1992). *Escape Attempts.* New York, NY: Routledge.

Deleuze, G. (1990). In M. Lester & C. Stivale (Trans.), *The logic of sense.* New York, NY: Columbia University Press. (Original work published 1969).

Deleuze, G. (1994). In P. R. Paton (Trans.), *Difference and repetition.* London: Athlone. (Original work published 1968).

Deleuze, G., & Guattari, F. (1987). In B. Massumi (Trans.), *A thousand plateaus: Capitalism and schizophrenia.* Minneapolis, MN: University of Minnesota Press. (Original work published 1980).

Donath, O. (2010). Pro-natalism and its "cracks": Narratives of reproduction and childfree lifestyles in Israel. *Israeli Sociology, 11*(2), 417–439. (in Hebrew).

Floyd, R., & Stein, T. (2002). Sexual orientation identity formation among gay, lesbian, and bisexual youths: Multiple patterns of milestone experiences. *Journal of Research on Adolescence, 12*(2), 167–191.

Foster, C. A., & Campbell, W. K. (2005). The adversity of secret relationships. *Personal Relationship, 12*(1), 125–143. doi:10.1111/j.1350-4126.2005.00105

Foucault, M. (1972). In A. M. Sheridan Smith (Trans.), *The archeology of knowledge.* London: Tavistock. (Original work published 1969).

Foucault, M. (1983). The subject and power. In H. Dreyfus & P. Rabinow (Eds.), *Michel foucault: Beyond structuralism and hermeneutic* (2nd ed., pp. 208–226). Chicago, IL: The University of Chicago Press.

Frijns, T. (2005). *Keeping secrets: Quantity, quality and consequences.* Utrecht: Free University of Amsterdam. Retrieved from http://hdl.handle.net/1871/9001

Gailey, J. A. (2009). "Starving is the most fun a girl can have": The Pro-Ana subculture as edgework. *Critical Criminology, 17*(2), 93–108. doi:10.1007/s10612-009-9074-z

Garza, G. (2002). The internet, narrative, and subjectivity. *Journal of Constructivist Psychology, 15*(1), 185–203.

Glenn, E. (2008). Yearning for lightness: Transnational circuits in the marketing and consumption of skin lighteners. *Gender & Society, 22*(3), 281–301. doi:10.1177/0891243208316089

Hacking, I. (1986). Making up people. In T. C. Heller, M. Sonsa, & D. E. Wellbery (Eds.), *Reconstructing individualism: Autonomy, individuality, and the self in Western thought* (pp. 222–236). Stanford, CA: Stanford University Press.

Hacking, I. (1991). The making and modeling of child abuse. *Critical Inquiry*, *17*(2). 253–288.

Illouz, E. (2007). *Cold intimacies: The making of emotional capitalism*. Cambridge: Polity Press.

Ivry, T. (2010). Kosher medicine and medicalized halacha: An exploration of triadic relations among Israeli rabbis, doctors, and infertility patients. *American Ethnologist*, *37*(4), 662–680. doi:10.1111/j.1548-1425.2010.01277.x

Linstead, S., & Thanem, T. (2007). Multiplicity, virtuality and organization: The contribution of Gilles Deleuze. *Organization Studies*, *28*(10), 1483–1501. doi:10.1177/0170840607075675

May, T. (2005). *Gilles Deleuze: An introduction*. Cambridge, UK: Cambridge University Press.

Mead, G. H. (1934). *Mind, self and society*. Chicago, IL: University of Chicago Press.

Orgad, S. (2009). How can researchers make sense of the issues involved in collecting and interpreting online and offline data? In A. Markham & N. Baym (Eds.), *Internet inquiry: Conversations about method* (pp. 33–53). Thousand Oaks, CA: Sage. Retrieved from http://eprints.lse.ac.uk/23979/

O'Riordan, K., & Phillips, D. J. (Eds.). (2007). *Queer online: Media technology & sexuality*. New York, NY: Peter Lang Publishing.

Ortner, S. (1973). On key symbols. *American Anthropologist*, *75*(5), 1338–1346. doi:10.1525/aa.1973.75.5.02a00100

Roof, J. (1996). *Come as you are: Sexuality & narrative*. New York, NY: Columbia University Press.

Rose, N. (2003). Neurochemical selves. *Society*, *41*(1), 46–59.

Rust, P. C. (1993). "Coming out" in the age of social constructionism: Sexual identity formation among lesbian and bisexual women. *Gender & Society*, *7*(1), 50–77. doi:10.1177/089124393007001004

Schauer, T. (2005). Women's porno: The heterosexual female gaze in porn sites "for Women". *Sexuality & Culture*, *9*(2), 42–64. doi:10.1007/s12119-005-1007-8

Schutz, A., & Luckmann, T. (1974). In R. M. Zaner & H. T. Engelhardt Jr. (Trans.), *The structure of the life-world*. London: Heinemann Educational Books.

Schwartz, B. (1981). *Vertical classification: A study of structuralism and the sociology of knowledge*. Chicago, IL: The University of Chicago Press.

Seidman, S. (2002). *Beyond the closet: The transformation of gay and lesbian life*. New York, NY: Routledge.

Seidman, S., Fischer, N., & Meeks, C. (Eds.). (2006). *Handbook of the new sexuality studies*. New York, NY: Routledge.

Seidman, S., Meeks, C., & Traschen, F. (1999). Beyond the closet? The changing social meaning of homosexuality in the United States. *Sexualities*, *2*(1), 9–34. doi:10.1177/136346099002001002

Shoshana, A. (2012). Classification, subjectivities, and personal visibility. *Sociological Forum*, *27*(1), 187–206. doi:10.1111/j.1573-7861.2011.01307.x

Shoshana, A., & Teman, E. (2006). Coming out of the coffin: Life-self and death-self in six feet under. *Symbolic Interaction*, *29*(4), 557–575. doi:10.1525/si.2006.29.4.557

Simmel, G. (1950). The secret and the secret society. In K. Wolff (Ed.), *The sociology of Georg Simmel* (pp. 304–355). New York, NY: The Free Press.

Simmel, G. (1971). The adventurer. In D. Levine (Ed.), *Georg Simmel on individuality and social forms* (pp. 187–199). Chicago, IL: University of Chicago Press. (Original work published 1911).

Simon, W., & Gagnon, J. (1986). Sexual scripts: Permanence and change. *Archives of Sexual Behavior, 15*(2), 97–120. doi:10.1007/BF01542219

Strauss, A., & Corbin, J. (1998). *Basics of qualitative research*. Thousand Oaks, CA: Sage Publication.

Teman, E. (2010). *Birthing a mother: The surrogate body and the pregnant self*. Berkeley, CA: University of California Press.

Troiden, R. R. (1989). The formation of homosexual identities. *Journal of Homosexuality, 17*(1–2), 43–74. doi:10.1300/J082v17n01_02

Turkle, S. (1995). *Life on the screen: Identity in the age of the internet*. New York, NY: Simon & Schuster.

Turner, R. H. (1976). The real self: From institution to impulse. *American Journal of Sociology, 81*(5), 989–1016.

Wang, Y. (2011). Internet dating as heterotopias of gender performance: A case study of Taiwanese heterosexual male dater. *International Journal of Cultural Studies, 15*(3), 1–16. doi:10.1177/1367877911422855

Waskul, D. (2003). *Self-games and body-play: Personhood in online chat and cybersex*. New York, NY: Peter Lang.

Waskul, D., & Douglas, M. (1997). Cyberself: The emergence of self in on-line chat. *The Information Society, 13*, 375–397.

Yaszek, L. (2002). *The self wired: Technology and subjectivity in contemporary narrative*. New York, NY: Routledge.

Zhao, S. (2005). The digital self: Through the looking glass of telecopresent other. *Symbolic Interaction, 28*(3), 387–405.

PART I
NEW EMPIRICAL STUDIES

"THE WALL IS THE CITY": A NARRATIVE ANALYSIS OF VANCOUVER'S POST-RIOT "APOLOGY WALL"

Jennifer A. A. Lavoie, Judy Eaton, Carrie B. Sanders and Matthew Smith

ABSTRACT

We conducted a narrative analysis of a collective narrative comprising inscriptions left on the locally famed "Apology Wall," written by thousands of community members in the immediate aftermath of the 2011 Vancouver Stanley Cup Riot. In considering the Apology Wall as an "evocative object," this study emphasized the significance of material objects as meaning-making devices. Interpretation of themes was conducted through a constructivist lens, specifically guided by literature concerning meaning-making following negative life events. Results bolstered the significance of the Wall as a sense-making device that provided a forum for the community to collectively share positive emotional expression, construct solidarity and collective identity, and express desires for restoration. By studying this collective narrative, the study not only illuminated how those affected constructed meaning after the Vancouver

Symbolic Interaction and New Social Media
Studies in Symbolic Interaction, Volume 43, 203–222

ISSN: 0163-2396/doi:10.1108/S0163-239620140000043019

sports riot, but it also contributes to the literature on how communities, in general, make early sense of and respond to destructive events.

Keywords: Riot; meaning-making; collective narrative; evocative object

INTRODUCTION

On June 15, 2011, the downtown core of Vancouver, British Columbia was heavily damaged in a massive riot after the hometown National Hockey League team, the Vancouver Canucks, lost to the Boston Bruins in the final game of the Stanley Cup playoffs. One of the most compelling aspects of this incident, however, was not the riot itself or the international attention it garnered, but the response by many residents of Vancouver in the immediate aftermath of the riot. A number of downtown store-front businesses had been looted, and had used plywood to board up their broken windows. Almost immediately, people began writing messages in response to the riot on the boards. Within days of the riot, more than 100 boards were filled with handwritten messages. These boards became collectively known as the "Apology Wall" (Orton, 2012), herein referred to as the Wall.

An analysis of these Wall inscriptions presents a unique opportunity to gain insight into how the community immediately and collectively interpreted and made meaning of the riot. Meaning making broadly refers to "the development of an understanding of an event and its implications" (Davis, Nolen-Hoeksema, & Larson, 1988, p. 561) and is a useful framework to interpret reactions to negative events such as a riot. Taken together, the collection of inscriptions on the Wall was considered to constitute a collective narrative. A narrative refers to a "communal or shared story concerning events that are commonly known or experienced by members of the group" (Mankowski & Rappaport, 2000, p. 482). Jointly, individual accounts of the same event form a community narrative representing collective knowledge and experience (Mankowski & Rappaport, 2000). In examining the Wall and its distinctive collective narrative, this study makes a number of important contributions. First, by regarding the Wall as an evocative object (Turkle, 1984), we illuminate the importance of material objects as analytical objects and meaning-making devices. Second, by studying the collective narrative, this study not only sheds light on how those affected constructed meaning after the 2011 Vancouver riot, but it also contributes to the literature on how communities, in general, make early sense of and respond to destructive events.

The Riot and Its Aftermath

Sports riots are the most common type of riot in North America; such riots are typically celebratory, involve championship stakes, occur late in the series, and take place in a natural urban gathering area teeming with young Caucasian males (Lewis, 2007). According to Lewis, Vancouver is unique in that the city has a history of rioting following the home team *losing* a championship, a phenomenon termed the "Vancouver effect" (Schwartz, 2011). In recent history, such a riot occurred in June of 1994, after the Vancouver Canucks lost to the New York Rangers during the Stanley Cup playoffs of that year, resulting in $800M in damage, the injury of 200 people, and dozens of arrests (Howard, 1995). Independent reviews of the 1994 riot produced by the City of Vancouver (Marfleet, John, Russo, & Devine, 1994), the Vancouver Police Department (1995), and the British Columbia Police Commission (1994) offered a number of recommendations, many of which were deemed to be key in avoiding similar challenges at subsequent sporting events, such as the 2010 Winter Olympics held in Vancouver (Furlong & Keefe, 2011). These recommendations included improved police planning, training, equipment, and communication. As with the 1994 riot, the 2011 riot prompted an independent inquiry, sponsored by the Provincial Solicitor General, the BC Minister of Public Safety, the Mayor of Vancouver, and the Chair of the Police Board.

On June 15, 2011, the Vancouver Canucks were to compete against the Boston Bruins in the final game of a series of seven games for the coveted Stanley Cup. Throughout the afternoon before the game, large crowds moved into the downtown area of Vancouver, which had been set up by the city as a "fan zone" for spectators to watch the game outside the stadium on a large monitor. The crowd grew larger than expected (estimated at approximately 155,000), exceeding the capacity of the zone (Furlong & Keefe, 2011). Although liquor stores had closed early and an alcohol ban was in effect, the size of the crowd made it impossible to screen for violations of the ban, and a number of fans were reportedly intoxicated (Mackin, 2011).

The Boston team took an early lead in the game. A number of altercations between Vancouver spectators in the "fan zone" occurred during the game; however, law enforcement and emergency responders had difficulty reaching the problem areas due to the large crowd. Adding to this crowding was the fact that more individuals were streaming into the downtown area both during and after the game, arriving by public transit and car, making it difficult for others to depart the area (Furlong & Keefe, 2011). By the time the game ended, with Boston winning the Stanley Cup in a score of 4–0, a full-scale riot had erupted outside the stadium. Rioters overturned and set cars on fire, smashed windows, and looted stores. Estimates place the damage to the downtown core at approximately CAN$3M ("Stanley Cup Riot", 2012), over 160 people were injured, and no fatalities reported (Dhillon, 2011).

Word of the riot quickly spread through television and other media as well as through social networking sites (Schneider & Trottier, 2013). While some individuals were posting pictures of themselves or others engaging in riotous activities in an effort to identify rioters, others were using social media to organize cleanup crews. For example, a Facebook group called "Riot Clean-up – Let's help Vancouver," created the night of the riot, quickly gained 20,000 members, and prompted individuals to go to the downtown core to clean up (Dhillon, 2011). Many volunteers assisted with the cleanup, some beginning at 11 pm, before the riot had even concluded (Furlong & Keefe, 2011). By 11 am the following day, it was reported that 90 percent of the garbage and broken glass had been cleaned up (Uechi, 2011).

The Apology Wall

A number of stores in the downtown area of Vancouver had been a target of looters during the riot and as a result had many of their windows boarded up with plywood. In the aftermath of the riot, volunteer cleaners and others began to write messages on the boards, expressing their sorrow, anger, and shame over the actions of the rioters, and also their gratitude to the Vancouver Police Department and other emergency responders (see Fig. 1). One of the first messages, posted by Vancouver citizen Ward Grant, said "On behalf of my team and my city, I'm sorry!" As the crowd watching him cheered and applauded, Grant encouraged others to write on the boards as well, and to "show your support for the good people of Vancouver" (Smith, 2011). Within a few days the boards were covered with messages. These boards became widely known as the "Apology Wall," or the "Riot Boards," but have also been referred to as "Vancouver's wall of shame, wall of

Fig. 1. Inscriptions on Vancouver's Apology Wall (Photo Credit R. Miranda, 2009–2012).

forgiveness, condolences wall, and citizen wall" (Hui, 2011). Often said to serve as a catharsis for the city, they were described in the press as "a massive bulletin board for a city's outpouring of emotion" (Hume, 2011). As the downtown businesses began fixing their broken windows, city officials, prompted by requests from residents, including a petition (Hui, 2011), sought ways to preserve the boards. The Museum of Vancouver, viewing the boards as "an open source work of art" (MOV, 2012) preserved 86 of the boards, 15 of which were displayed in the museum's "Reading the Riot Boards" exhibit in 2012.

Theoretical Approach: Meaning-Making, Collective Narrative and Disaster Narratives

We set out to understand the collective interpretation and response to the riot through the actual words of community members as inscribed on the Wall. Consistent with Nichols and Rine (2012) we approached the narratives as "claims" in the constructionist view that may conflict with one another or be part of a consistent conversation; thus the "final truth of validity of narratives is left open" (p. 123). We utilized a meaning-making lens in interpreting this collective narrative (Baumeister, 1991; Park, 2010). Discovering meaning in life events is generally studied using a constructivist approach, in which meaning is not viewed as inherent to the life event itself, but is developed over time as the person works to ascertain an understanding of the situation and its consequences (O'Connor, 2002). When encountering a stressful event such as a riot, individuals make appraisals about the implicit significance of the incident (e.g., potential harmfulness; causal attributions; future ramifications; for a review see Sweeney, 2008). According to Park (2010), individuals are motivated to engage in a search for meaning when the appraised significance of a specific event challenges a person's global beliefs (i.e., core schemas used to interpret life events including beliefs around justice, predictability), personal goals, or sense of purpose. People engage in meaning-making after negative events to restore discrepancies in world schemas (Janoff-Bulman & Frantz, 1997), re-establish personal goals (Park, 2010) and enhance self-worth (Baumeister & Newman, 1994). Meaning-making is widely viewed as an important element of coping with negative events (Gillies & Neimeyer, 2006; Park & Folkman, 1997).

One method of engaging in meaning-making is through talking about the negative event with other people. Evidence suggests that individuals exposed to a highly stressful life event often feel the need to disclose the experience to others (O'Connor, 2002). This practice, known as "social sharing," transpires through verbal conversations in which emotions and reactions to experiences are revealed (O'Connor, 2002; Rimé, Páez, Basabe, & Martínez, 2010). Sometimes social sharing takes place at a symbolic level, such as through letters, or in the present case, through inscriptions written in a public space. One function of social sharing is the regulation of negative emotions in the experience of adversity. Social sharing is a part of the meaning-making process that assists with coping with negative events.

Making meaning of lived experiences is often achieved through constructing narratives (Baumeister & Newman, 1994). Stories such as narratives are a powerful form of constructed knowledge in that they shape memory and emotion, organize experience, give meaning to events, and supply a sense of coherence (Harper et al., 2004; Mankowski & Rappaport, 2000). Moreover, stories are vital to forming, maintaining, and rebuilding individual and collective social identity (Crossley, 2000; Harper et al., 2004; Mankowski & Rappaport, 2000). This study explores a set of messages that together constitute a collective narrative capturing perceptions of and reactions to the riot. While community narratives are often expressed in written or oral forms, information about such narratives can emerge from other forms such as art, lyrics, physical structures, rituals, and public commentaries (Harper et al., 2004), such as the public inscriptions that form the subject of the present study.

Narratives are routinely useful for making sense of experiences and providing guidance on how to feel and behave in the world; however, they are of utmost importance in the midst of adversity (Rozario, 2005; Tuval-Mashiach et al., 2004). Studies examining expressive writing, which typically involves asking participants to write about a highly stressful lived experience, have found that such writing leads to enhanced physical and emotional health (for a review, see Pennebaker & Chung, 2007), likely because these activities assist in making meaning of the event (Boals & Klein, 2005). Narratives concerning the experience of disaster assist those affected in processing, negotiating, feeling, and conceptually responding to crisis. Part of the allure of disaster narratives is their ability to help survivors cope with calamity by making sense out of perceived senselessness; in this way, narratives "domesticate disasters" (Rozario, 2005, p. 33). Examinations of narratives from a number of modern cities undergoing crises uncovered that narratives were constructed to provide support and coping (Vale & Campanella, 2005). Rozario (2005) captures this notion in explaining:

> Throwing words at the chaos, spreading a narrative grid over the bewildering mayhem, was thus a therapeutic act, helping victims to cope with trauma by reassuring them that any devastation was certain to be fleeting. (p. 32)

In other words, narratives are used to help those affected cope by encapsulating damaging events into stories that soothe lingering apprehension.

How individuals narrate crises can give insight into how people interpret and respond to adverse events such as riots. Studies examining narratives of traumatic event survivors suggest that the event narrative is shaped and modified through a dynamic process over time to become more positive and coherent (Tuval-Mashiach et al., 2004). The period directly following a highly stressful event is when the most intensive processing of that event takes place (Tuval-Mashiach et al.). Because this period is a crucial time in the process of meaning-making, narratives produced in the immediate wake of an adverse event are of particular interest to study. The messages under study were physically inscribed in the immediate hours and days after the riot on boards temporarily erected to cover broken store-front windows, and thus afford a unique glimpse of claims made during this key time period.

Chemielewski (2007) discussed the importance of spatio-contextual interpretation of public inscriptions, including a consideration of the writing surface of messages in public spaces in addition to the textual content. It is significant that in a digital age where social commentary can easily be made, often anonymously, via online social media sites from the comfort of ones' home, thousands of individuals were compelled to gather at the downtown location of the Vancouver riot and physically and publicly inscribe messages on the boarded windows. It is also noteworthy that citizens worked to preserve the boards after the city was restored, emphasizing that the Wall itself was meaningful. Valuable mediums, such as Vancouver's Apology Wall embody what Turkle (1995) terms "evocative objects." Such objects can bring together, cultivate, and represent varied social and cultural meanings. For example, Leuenberger (2006) examined how others have used mediums such as the Berlin Wall and the West Bank Barrier as "evocative objects" to reveal personal and cultural traits among specific communities. According to Turkle (2007), objects are not inherently meaningful; instead, various social groups construct these mediums as being significant in diverse ways. Social groups use these objects to develop and assimilate ideas as well as catalyze changes in the perception of phenomena. Thus, we recognized the "Apology Wall" as an evocative object, an object which "can summon and embody particular meanings that can span social, symbolic and material realms" (Leuenberger, 2006, p. 18; see also, Holstein & Gubrium, 2000). As such, material objects can "...help facilitate thinking and reflecting about aspects of everyday life" (Leuenberger, 2006, p. 19).

The Wall, as an evocative object, acted as a medium for people to think and work through personal and collective concerns (Turkle, 2009, p. 159). It became a powerful means for many people to not only make sense of the Vancouver riot, but to also construct and reaffirm a positive collective identity. Perceiving the Wall as an evocative object enabled us to move beyond looking at strictly the instrumental power of the plywood (i.e., to cover the damaged windows and protect the building from the natural elements), and instead to recognize the Wall as a "companion in life experience" (Turkle, 2007, p. 5). We argue that the Wall became a powerful means for community members to establish solidarity, identity and empowerment. Thus, the Wall is an object of cultural significance that requires analytical attention and narrative analyses. The contribution to narrative analyses that this paper makes is identifying the importance of studying the objects on which the narratives are found.

Purpose of the Present Study

The aim of the study was to examine how the Wall was used as a mechanism for meaning-making by examining the collective post-riot narrative and identifying predominant themes reflected in the messages left on the Wall. These claims help to understand how community members interpreted and responded in the immediate aftermath of the 2011 Vancouver riot. Specifically, we examined how contributors perceived and made meaning of the event, as well as viewed themselves and those to blame in the wake of the riot. We conducted a narrative analysis of the messages and interpreted findings through a meaning-making framework. Our key conclusion was that positive emotional expression, solidarity, and restorative expressions were central within the collective narrative of a community in the wake of a riot. Moreover, the Wall acted as a sense-making device providing a place for the community to collectively develop and express these sentiments.

METHOD

We conducted a narrative analysis to identify and describe predominant themes and claims reflected in the written inscriptions left on the Wall. The Wall was comprised of messages written on plywood boards covering the broken windows of at least 29 stores in the downtown area ("Vancouver's Riot Wall", 2011). The central site was the Hudson's Bay Company ("The Bay"), a large department store that had many of its windows smashed. Given that the stores removed the boards when they replaced their windows shortly after the riot, we did not have access to the entire collection. We did, however, have access to a high-resolution photo mosaic of the boards covering seven adjacent windows of The Bay. These windows were located closest to the main street where the riot took place, and the boards were among the first to be written on. The photos were taken on Sunday, June 19, 2011, four days after the riot (R. Miranda, personal communication, June 17, 2013). The photo mosaic, known as a "gigapixel," consisted of 472 color photos, with a resolution of 107,271 × 8,173 pixels, or 877 megapixels (Miranda, 2012). With such high resolution, we were able to magnify the digital image of the boards to such a degree that we could clearly see and transcribe all of the comments, no matter how small.

The seven windows depicted in the photo mosaic were covered by a total of 29 plywood boards. Five of the 29 boards were transcribed and analyzed until theoretical saturation was met (Van den Hoonaard, 2012). A total of 971 individual messages (including images) were transcribed collectively by the research team and assigned a case number. Images were described in the transcripts for analysis (for example, THANK-YOU VPD [TWO SMALL HEARTS BETWEEN VPD representing periods [35]). Our analysis adopted a constructivist grounded theory approach (Charmaz, 2006), an approach that is driven by the data, but also reflexive and attentive to preexisting theories (such as meaning-making) to guide analysis. The research team met as a group to discuss dominant and recurrent themes noted in the data during transcription to develop initial codes and sensitizing concepts (Blumer, 1969; Charmaz, 2006). Following this first research meeting, the lead author coded the data. Using writing as an analytical device (Richardson, 2000), the researchers electronically shared "analytical memos" (Charmaz, 2006) that categorized and re-categorized coded sections to establish "social reliability" (Sanders & Cuneo, 2010) and identify thematically coherent interpretations of how communities make early sense of destructive events. From this analysis, we uncovered the significance of the Wall as a sense-making device providing a space for the community to collectively share positive emotional expression, construct solidarity and collective identity, and express a desire for restoration. In the following section we describe and analyze these prevailing themes.

RESULTS

Apology Wall as Evocative Object: "The Wall is the City!" [769]

As the downtown businesses began fixing their broken windows, city officials, prompted by requests from residents, including a petition (Hui, 2011), sought ways to preserve the Wall boards. The boards were at times described as the "best public art I've ever seen" [203] and are preserved and exhibited in the Museum of Vancouver. The movement to "save these boards" [189, 202] is symbolic of the importance these boards had for the people of Vancouver. As one person wrote, "This wall IS the city" [769]. The Wall became recognized as a way of "making beaut[y] out of destruction..." [185] and a space "to raise our voices" [377] and "...re-confirm how I was feeling" [419]. The way in which the people adopted and perceived the Wall reinforced the significance of the Wall as an object of cultural significance that requires analytical attention and narrative analyses.

Thus, the Wall became a socially meaningful object (Harre, 2002) for people to make visible a cohesive group who found social support and solidarity by providing an opportunity to "mend this city back together" [710]. As one person noted, "The wall provided a means for restoring my faith in Vancity" [721]. The physical wall became a means to not only demonstrate solidarity, but to also construct a positive identity – "This is true Vancouver" [797], "This is what Vancouver is really about. Way to bounce back Van..." [924], "This is the real sound of your city! And it's Vantastic" [797]. As one person wrote, "The real Vancouver is in the volunteers who helped clean up and the people on this board" [109]. The "wall shows who we're really" [257] and the Wall became used as a means to identify "...true Vancouver people" [15]. As another person sums up, "These walls represent the Vancouver I know + love" [793].

The Wall, we argue, provided a means to "catalyze self-creation" (Turkle, 2007, p. 9). It became symbolic of the "real Canuck in Vancouver" by providing a space to "think through questions about the nature of self" (Turkle, 2009, p. 159), and construct a positive collective identity. In what follows we look at the ways in which the collective narrative found on the Wall provided emotional support, a positive collective identity and a means to "rebuild our dignity today ..."[72].

Positive Emotional Expression: "Thank you for Restoring My Faith in Van City!" [721]

Overwhelmingly, messages inscribed on the Wall were characterized by expressions of appreciation and encouragement. Inscriptions commonly reflected broad positive sentiments of love and support such as "Thank you" [27, 582, 698] and "We still believe" [125, 402, 851]. Affirmative sentiments were often addressed to the city itself, with many writing "We [heart] Vancouver" [227, 592, 891] and expressing "pride" in the city [489, 829]. Another inscription captures the positivity of these communications – "I love this city. It is a beautiful place. Believe in the good and beauty" [464]. Positive sentiments were similarly directed towards city institutions, such as the hockey team, emergency services, and volunteers.

The Vancouver Canucks hockey team received a significant amount of encouragement and praise – "Congratulations Canucks on bringing the

Stanley cup playoffs to Vancouver. Job well done!" [523], "Thank you Canucks for a great season" [423, 463], and "Go CANUCKS GO!" [61, 209, 409]. Messages also contained gratitude and commendation for the Vancouver Police Department (VPD) and other emergency services, such as "Thank you VPD for keeping us safe" [194] and "Stand on guard for thee! Thanks VPD!" [438]. Another person wrote, "Thank you to all the emergency personnel – who rose above chaos and tragedy. True colours shine" [94]. Volunteers who assisted in cleaning and repairs in the aftermath of the riot were another salient group who received praise. Typically, inscribers thanked "volunteers for leading the way" [190], "cleaning up the mess" [378], and "restoring my faith in this city" [254].

The Wall provided a medium for social sharing on a collective level through the exchanging of disclosive sentiments in public wall inscriptions. This notion is captured in the message: "... Thanx to the people who have come down here and re-confirmed how I was feeling! Stay strong! Stay faithful! Stay canucks." [419]. The Wall appeared to function as an important mechanism for public emotional discharge, most notably affirmative emotional expression. The social sharing phenomenon accounts for the construction of the Wall itself, as well as the vast amount of positive sentiment and encouragement evidenced on the boards. This collective narrative provided direction on how others should interpret the significance of the riot and impact on the community. In this way, the Wall served as a place to seek and provide positive supportive interpretations from fellow community members. As discussed, seeking such solace is common in the wake of adverse events and serves as one explanation for the significant amounts of messages of encouragement. To the extent that creating a narrative facilitates meaning-making, the construction of the Wall can be viewed as a mechanism to cope with the riot, particularly through guiding interpretations to be positive and reassuring.

Solidarity and Positive Collective Identity: "These are the Real Fans" [779]

While the Wall provided a space where residents could assert positive sentiments about their "beautiful city" [678] and express their appreciation regarding "the way everyone helped" [678], it also provided a space to establish solidarity and construct a positive collective identity As described below, solidarity and identity was conveyed primarily through the use of group-based pronouns; the denotation of who is, and who is not, a "True Vancouverite" or "True Canuck"; "othering" the rioters; and casting blame. The Wall was replete with statements of unity and solidarity expressing Vancouver as "...the city we all love. The proud city that comes together" [157]. Solidarity was further identified in statements of healing (e.g., "Together we shall heal ..." [524]) and "rebuild[ing] together as one" [827]. Further, solidarity was expressed implicitly, through the notable use of group-based pronouns such as "we," "our," and "us." The following inscriptions capture this sense of unity: "We are Canucks. We are Vancouver and we love our city" [159], "Van WE Love" [660]; "Rioters – we forgive you. Thanks for teaching us how much we care" [25]. Although the contributors to the Wall may not have known each other personally, through the use of "we" rather than "I" these inscriptions are illustrative of a collective identity (Brewer & Gardner, 1996; Dovidio, Piliavin, Gaertner, Schroeder, & Clark, 1991). Given previous observations that emergency situations enhance the sense of shared identity and bonding among crowds in crises (e.g., Drury, Cocking, & Reicher, 2009), the sense of solidarity apparent in the Wall inscriptions suggest that the writers perceived themselves and other victimized citizens as a cohesive group, bound by their shared distress at the actions of the rioters.

Unity and solidarity were most notably evident in statements delineating "real Vancouverites" [617] and "true fans" [801]. Collective identity was constructed in a number of ways. First, collective identity was established through focusing gaze on specific positive deeds such as repairing the city as illustrated in the following inscriptions, "The real Vancouver is in the volunteers who helped clean up and the people on this board" [108] and "Thanx Clean-up volunteers for showing the face of the REAL Vancouver" [937]. Second, community identity was established through appeals to true fandom, including references to expected attributes and behaviors of genuine fans, such as "True Canucks wouldn't hurt our city" [852], "The true fans are cleaning our city up" [221], and "True fans live through losses" [801]. Third, by constructing the rioters as villains, Wall inscribers were able to reaffirm a positive collective identity relative to "the others." As one person notes, "Wow brutal! Real fans are proud of our canucks. These r not fans ... ppl with some serious issues ... love and peace is what Vancouver is supposed to be about!" [492]. Conversely, those who participated in the riot became vilified. For example, a significant number of messages condemned those perceived to be responsible for the riot as being fundamentally flawed, such as "lacking emotional intelligence" [523], or referred to rioters as "stupid" [67]. One inscriber wrote, "Shame on what those crazy and heartless people did to this beautiful city..." [350]. Thus, by vilifying and shaming the rioters, a positive collective identity became constructed in contrast that established blame for the physical, emotional and cultural damage caused by the riot as belonging to "the other." The need to ascribe responsibility and blame are clearly illustrated in the following two inscriptions:

> Canucks Fans aren't responsible for this. Hockey Fans aren't responsible for this. Drunk Losers + pathetic morons who never got over being picked last in gym class did this. [heart] ... [160].

> What happened? You who did this are not Canuck Fans, Shame on you. I hope this stays with you including 1994 [317].

Narratives of blame and responsibility were bolstered by some who called for justice. For example, one person noted that "every fool coward that participated in the riots should be prosecuted to the fullest extent of the law!!! Make a strong example of them. This is unacceptable!!!!!!!!" [932]. Others argued that "the death penalty would be too soft" [405]. These ardent claims indicated the strong negative impact the rioter's actions had on the community, and strengthened "us versus them" delineations.

Through the Wall, people were able to not only identify themselves as victims ("I'm sorry they did this to us & you! [heart]" [139]), but clearly identify the rioters as "...not true Canuck fans" [416]. This collective othering may have served to displace responsibility and related backlash from the community to outsiders. This finding is consistent with reports of media labeling of dissidents in the UK summer riots of the same year (i.e., 2011) as being external, or alien to the community (Briggs, 2012). Claims constructed to other those involved in the disturbances worked to "suggest that somehow they [the rioters] were not part of the 'real community' " (Briggs, 2012, p. 98), thereby attempting to deflect responsibility and damaging depictions away from the community. In sum, solidarity and collective identity were demonstrated through the use of group-based pronouns, delineating genuine Vancouverites/fans, the use of othering the rioters and casting blame.

Restoration and "Rebuilding" [73]

While the Wall became a sense-making medium and a tool for healing through the expression of positive sentiments, solidarity and collective identity; it also became a display of strength and rebuilding. For example, themes centering on the idea of restoration and rebuilding were a common component of the riot narrative demonstrated in the Wall inscriptions. Inscriptions illustrating this theme include, "we'll rise again" [608]; "...we will rebound & rise above the ashes" [602]; and "Proud to build it once. Proud to build it for those here on the wall again!" [611].

Many messages focused on restoring hope, faith, and dignity: "Last night I watched with shame. Today I feel a new hope for the city I [heart]. This is my Vancouver" [627], "Thank you for restoring my faith in Van city!" [721], and "Rebuilding our dignity today - we are sorry [heart]" [73]. In this context were also references of strength - "[heart] you Vancouver. Stay strong." [491], "I am proud of our team and the fans... This will make us stronger next year" [32], and "[heart] you Van! - Strongest city in the world" [4].

The disaster and community resilience literature can be useful in understanding elements of the collective riot narrative uncovered during the study. Themes of restoration and healing of the city and community revealed here are common in previously published disaster narratives of those recovering from city-wide crisis (see Vale & Campanella, 2005). For example, in examining disaster narratives of three significant catastrophes in American history (i.e., The 1871 Great Fire of Chicago, the 1906 San Francisco Earthquake, and the 9/11 terrorist attacks in New York City), Rozario (2005) found that common themes of progress and optimism were prominent elements of disaster stories. Specifically, narratives promoted the expectation of a favorable outcome that fortune was imminent, and a brighter future was on the horizon. Similarly, Walsh (2007) discussed that in times of adversity, hope and a positive attitude is vital for recovery because these approaches help to galvanize commitment to rally, rebuild and re-vision. To meet challenges, a community that is resilient builds unity, seizes opportunities, and anticipates positive growth (Brenton, 2001). Thus, broad themes of restoration as well as solidarity and encouragement exhibited in the riot narrative may serve to bolster a community in the difficult days after a crisis to carry on.

DISCUSSION AND CONCLUSION

This study investigated how a community responded in the immediate aftermath of a sports riot by examining a collective narrative. In exploring the Apology Wall as an evocative object, we emphasize the significance of material objects, such as these plywood boards, as embodying investigative value. The methodological contribution this paper offers to narrative analysis lies in drawing attention to the materiality on which community narratives are inscribed as objects of analysis in their own right, above and beyond the words and symbols etched therein. By taking such a position, our investigation solidified the importance of the Wall, not only as a cultural artifact, but as a communication tool that facilitated sense-making in the immediate wake of the riot.

Using a meaning-making framework, the purpose of the study was to identify emergent themes in the post-riot community narrative. We conducted a narrative analysis of messages inscribed on Vancouver's Apology Wall. Three prevailing themes emerged from the Wall inscriptions: (i) positive emotional expression, (ii) solidarity and collective identity, and (iii) restoration. Interpretations of these themes through a meaning-making framework suggested that the creation of the Wall may have been a mechanism for emotional expression and receiving of positive support, through social sharing. Themes of solidarity and bonding emphasized an enhanced sense of shared identity, likely brought about through mutual involvement in an adverse experience, but also bolstered by joining in collective writing on the Wall. Affirmative aspects of the post-riot narrative, such as appreciation, encouragement and focus on positive attributes were interpreted as efforts in constructing a positive, collective identity. Finally, collective themes centering on anticipation of restoration are common in disaster narratives, and are believed to assist in motivating communities to initiate and continue the difficult work of rebuilding. Taken together, these three themes underscore a main finding of the significance of maintaining positive community identity and affirmative emotional expression in the immediate aftermath of adversity.

This study was not without limitations. The first is that the event and community reactions under study may not be generalizable to other communities that experience more severe catastrophes where devastation is greater and trauma more severe or, in fact, to other communities that experience less severe negative events. Further, adaptive capacities appeared to be high in Vancouver. A city with economic resources and social capital may be able to overcome adverse events more effectively than communities whose resilience is reduced. Thus, communities of varying resilience may respond to adversity in different ways than reported here. A second limitation is that we did not have access to the entire collection of boards that constituted the Wall. While we utilized a substantially large subsection of the Wall, it is not possible to ascertain the representativeness of boards chosen for inclusion in the photo mosaic examined in the study. A third limitation is that the boards appeared to be dynamic, where some messages were censored by other inscribers (e.g., crossing out messages that were offensive to the winning hockey team, the Boston Bruins). That the messages were directed to a public audience, and were not, strictly speaking, anonymous, may have influenced what people revealed and how they chose to be portrayed. It can be argued, however, that this editing is an expected aspect of constructed narrative.

To conclude, evocative material objects, such as the Apology Wall, are a powerful sense-making apparatus that facilitate the construction of collective narratives, and therefore warrant their own investigation. Post adversity, collective narratives are useful for negotiating meaning-making and identity, as well as expressing positivity and hope. As such, collective narratives are important vehicles to assist the community in coping with negative events. To the extent that crises are experienced and felt at the community level, insight into how communities initially respond to adverse events may assist in rendering recovery-oriented services. Our study captures a shared narrative in the immediate aftermath of the riot, and thus provides a glimpse of early collective sense-making during a crucial period in the coping process. Our findings highlight the initial importance of positive emotional expression, solidarity and collectivity, as well as restoration in the community's response to this destructive event. Such sentiments may be significant in the coping and recovery among other communities experiencing large scale adverse events.

ACKNOWLEDGMENTS

We extend our gratitude to Wilfird Laurier University student researchers Jennie Rideout and Jessica Lalonde for their assistance in transcribing messages and developing the coding scheme. We are thankful to Changfei Wang of Wilfrid Laurier University for translating selected Apology Wall messages.

REFERENCES

Baumeister, R. F. (1991). *Meanings in life*. New York, NY: Guilford.

Baumeister, R. F., & Newman, L. S. (1994). How stories make sense of personal experiences: Motives that shape autobiographical narratives. *Personality and Social Psychology Bulletin*, *20*, 676–690. doi:10.1177/0146167294206006.

Blumer, H. (1969). *Symbolic interactionism*. Englewood Cliffs, NJ: Prentice-Hall.

Boals, A., & Klein, K. (2005). Word use in emotional narratives about failed romantic relationships and subsequent mental health. *Journal of Language and Social Psychology, 24*, 252–268. doi:10.1177/0261927X05278386.

Brenton, M. (2001). Neighborhood resiliency. *Journal of Community Practice, 9*, 21–36. doi:10.1300/J125v09n01_02

Brewer, M. B., & Gardner, W. (1996). Who is this "we"? Levels of collective identity and self representations. *Journal of Personality and Social Psychology, 71*, 83–93.

Briggs, D. (2012). *The English riots of 2011: A summer of discontent.* Sherfield Gables, UK: Waterside Press.

British Columbia Police Commission. (1994, October). *Report on the riot that occurred in Vancouver on June 14–15, 1994.* Retrieved from http://beta.images.theglobeandmail.com/archive/01289/Report_on_the_1994_1289365a.pdf

Charmaz, K. (2006). *Constructing grounded theory: A practical guide through qualitative analysis.* Thousand Oaks, CA: Sage.

Chemielewski, E. (2007). Framing [con]text: Graffiti and place. *Space and Culture, 10*(2), 145–169. doi:10.117712063331206298545.

Crossley, M. L. (2000). Narrative psychology, trauma and the study of self/identity. *Theory & Psychology, 10*, 527–546. doi:10.1177/0959354300104005

Davis, C. G., Nolen-Hoeksema, S., & Larson, J. (1988). Making sense of loss and benefitting from the experience. Two construals of meaning. *Journal of Personality and Social Psychology, 75*, 561–573.

Dhillon, S. (2011, December 20). When rioters trashed Vancouver, Twitter fanned the flames – and gathered the evidence. *The Globe and Mail.* Retrieved from http://www.theglobeandmail.com/news/british-columbia/when-rioters-trashed-vancouver-twitter-fanned-the-flames—and-gathered-the-evidence/article4182089/

Dovidio, J. F., Piliavin, J. A., Gaertner, S., Schroeder, D. A., & Clark, III, R. D. (1991). The arousal: Cost-reward model and the process of intervention: A review of the evidence. In M. Clark (Ed.), *Prosocial behaviour: Review of personality and social psychology* (Vol. 12, pp. 86–118). Newbury Park, CA: Sage.

Drury, J., Cocking, C., & Reicher, S. (2009). Everyone for themselves? A comparative study of crowd solidarity among emergency survivors. *British Journal of Social Psychology, 48*, 487–506. doi:10.1348/14466608X357893

Furlong, J., & Keefe, D. J. (2011, August 31). *The night the city became a stadium.* Report of the independent review of the 2011 Vancouver Stanley Cup playoffs riot. Retrieved from http://www.pssg.gov.bc.ca/vancouverriotreview/docs/riot-review-report.pdf

Gillies, J., & Neimeyer, R. A. (2006). Loss, grief, and the search for significance: Toward a model of meaning reconstruction in bereavement. *Journal of Constructivist Psychology, 19*, 31–65. doi:10.1080/10720530500311182.

Harper, G. W., Lardon, C., Rappapor, J., Bang, A. K., Contreras, R., & Pedraza, A. (2004). Community narratives: The use of narrative ethnography in participatory community research. In L. A. Jason, C. B. Keys, Y. Suarez-Balcazar, R. R. Taylor, & M. I. Davi (Eds.), *Participatory community research: Theories and methods in action* (pp. 199–218). Washington, DC: American Psychological Association.

Harre, R. (2002). Material objects in social worlds. *Theory, Culture & Society, 19*, 23–33.

Holstein, J. A., & Gubrium, J. F. (2000). *The self we live by: Narrative identity in a postmodern world.* New York, NY: Oxford University Press.

Howard, R. (1995, February 4). No mistakes made in riot, Vancouver police review says Chief faults technical problem; in Stanley Cup fracas. *Globe and Mail.*

Hui, S. (2011, June 19). Vancouverites cover wall of shame with messages after Stanley Cup Riot. *Vancouver Straight.* Retrieved from http://www.straight.com/blogra/vancouverites-cover-wall-shame-messages-after-stanley-cup-riot

Hume, M. (2011, June 20). Museum finds a home for Vancouver's post-riot graffiti. *The Globe and Mail.* Retrieved from http://www.theglobeandmail.com/news/british-columbia/museum-finds-a-home-for-vancouvers-post-riot-graffiti/article2068411/

Janoff-Bulman, R., & Frantz, C. M. (1997). The impact of trauma on meaning: From meaningless world to meaningful life. In M. J. Power & C. R. Brewin (Eds.), *The transformation of meaning in psychological therapies: Integrating theory and practice* (pp. 91–106). Hoboken, NJ: Wiley.

Leuenberger, C. (2006). Constructions of the Berlin Wall: How material culture is used in psychological theory. *Social Problems, 53,* 18–37.

Lewis, J. M. (2007). *Sports fan violence in North America.* Lanham, MD: Rowman & Littlefield Publishers.

Mackin, B. (2011, June 15). BC liquor board boss feared a Stanley Cup Riot. *The Tyee.* Retrieved from http://thetyee.ca/News/2011/09/21/Liquor-Board-Boss-Feared-Van-Riot/

Mankowski, E., & Rappaport, J. (2000). Narrative concepts and analysis in spiritually-based communities. *Journal of Community Psychology, 28,* 479–493. doi:10.1002/1520-6629(200009)28:5<479

Marfleet, P., John, C., Russo, K., & Devine, J. (1994). *Riots: A background paper. City of Vancouver review of major events, September, 1994.* Vancouver, BC: City of Vancouver.

Miranda, R. (2012). Ronnie Miranda (2009–2012). Gigapixel Retrieved from http://www.gigapixel.com/image/gigapan-canucks-apology.html

MOV. (2012). Exhibitions: Reading the riot boards. *Museum of Vancouver.* Retrieved from http://www.museumofvancouver.ca/exhibitions/exhibit/reading-riot-boards

Nichols, L. T., & Rine, J. (2012). Collective identity narratives: Historical and emergent stories of selfhood in a deindustrializing community. In Norman K. Denzin (Ed.), *Studies in symbolic interaction* (Vol. 39, pp. 121–149). Bingley, UK: Emerald Group Publishing Limited.

O'Connor, M. (2002). Making meaning of life events: Theory, evidence, and research directions for an alternative model. *OMEGA, 46,* 51–75. doi:10.2190/0CKD-PVQ0-T260-NTXU

Orton, T. (2012, June 12). Riot apology wall reflects Vancouver city spirit. *24 Hours,* Vancouver. Retrieved from http://vancouver.24hrs.ca/News/local/2012/06/12/19870226.html

Park, C. L. (2010). Making sense of the meaning literature: An integrative review of meaning making and its effects on adjustment to stressful life events. *Psychological Bulletin, 136,* 257–301.

Park, C. L., & Folkman, S. (1997). Meaning in the context of stress and coping. *Review of General Psychology, 1,* 115–144.

Pennebaker, J. W., & Chung, C. K. (2007). Expressive writing, emotional upheavals, and health. In H. S. Friedman & R. C. Silver (Eds.), *Foundations of health psychology* (pp. 263–284). New York, NY: Oxford University Press.

Richardson, L. (2000). Writing: A method of inquiry. In N. K. Denzin & Y. S. Lincoln (Eds.), *Handbook of qualitative research* (2nd ed., pp. 923–948). Thousand Oaks, CA: Sage.

Rimé, B., Páez, D., Basabe, N., & Martínez, F. (2010). Social sharing of emotion, post-traumatic growth, and emotional climate: Follow-up of Spanish citizen's response to the collective trauma of March 11th terrorist attacks in Madrid. *European Journal of Social Psychology*, *40*, 1029–1045. doi:10.1002/ejsp.700.

Rozario, K. (2005). Making progress: Disaster narratives and the art of optimism in modern America. In L. J. Vale & T. J. Campanella (Eds.), *The resilient city* (pp. 1–27). Toronto, ON: Oxford University Press.

Sanders, C. B., & Cuneo, C. (2010). Social reliability in qualitative team research. *Sociology*, 44, 1–19.

Schneider, C. J., & Trottier, D. (2013). Social media and the 2011 Vancouver riot. In Norman K. Denzin (Ed.), *40th anniversary of studies in symbolic interaction* (Vol. 40, pp. 335–362). Studies in Symbolic Interaction. Bingley, UK: Emerald Group Publishing Limited.

Schwartz, D. (2011, June 16). Analysis: Vancouver not typical sports riot, sociologist says. *CBC News*. Retrieved from http://www.cbc.ca/news/canada/vancouver-not-typical-sports-riot-sociologist-says-1.1087616

Smith, C. (2011, June 16). Canucks fans take to the streets to clean up downtown Vancouver after Stanley Cup Riot. *Straight.com*. Retrieved from http://www.straight.com/news/canucks-fans-take-streets-clean-downtown-vancouver-after-stanley-cup-riot

Stanley Cup Riot cost at least $2 million to investigate. (2012, April 18). *Canadian Broadcasting Corporation (CBC) News, British Columbia*. Retrieved from http://www.cbc.ca/news/canada/british-columbia/stanley-cup-riot-cost-at-least-2m-to-investigate-1.1188307

Sweeney, K. (2008). Crisis decision theory: Decisions in the face of negative events. *Psychological Bulletin*, *134*, 61–76.

Turkle, S. (1984). *The second self: Computers and the human spirit*. New York, NY: Simon and Schuster.

Turkle, S. (1995). *Life on the screen: Identity in the age of the internet*. New York, NY: Simon and Schuster.

Turkle, S. (2007). *Evocative objects: Things we think with*. Cambridge, MA: MIT Press.

Turkle, S. (2009). Constructions and reconstructions of self in virtual reality: Playing in the MUDs. *Mind, Culture, and Activity*, *1*, 158–167.

Tuval-Mashiach, R., Freedman, S., Bargai, N., Boker, R., Hadar, H., & Shalev, A. Y. (2004). Coping with trauma: Narrative and cognitive perspectives. *Psychiatry*, *67*, 280–293. doi:10.1521/psyc.67.3.280.48977

Uechi, J. (2011, June 16). Vancouver riot clean up brings city back together. *Vancouver Observer*. Retrieved from http://www.vancouverobserver.com/city/canucks/2011/06/16/vancouver-riot-clean-brings-city-back-together

Vale, L. J. & Campanella, T. J. (Eds.). (2005). *The resilient city*. Toronto, ON: Oxford University Press.

Vancouver Police Department. (1995, January). *Review of the Stanley Cup Riot June 14, 1994*.

Vancouver's Riot Wall to come down. (2011, June 20). *Canadian Broadcasting Corporation (CBC) News, British Columbia*. Retrieved from http://www.cbc.ca/news/canada/british-columbia/vancouver-s-riot-wall-to-come-down-1.1053281

Van den Hoonaard, D. (2012). *Qualitative research in action: A Canadian primer*. Toronto, ON: Oxford University Press.

Walsh, F. (2007). Traumatic loss and major disasters: Strengthening family and community resilience. *Family Process*, *46*, 207–227.

AUTHOR BIOGRAPHIES

Shing-Ling S. Chen is an Associate Professor in the Department of Communication Studies at University of Northern Iowa. Her research centers on information technologies, the self and the community. Currently, she has contributed to studies that key on the presentation of self in cyberspace and the notion of cyberspace as a public sphere involving varieties of groups and group interests.

Jeffrey Coons is a student at the University of Northern Iowa, majoring in Communication Studies with a minor in Graphic Technologies. He plans to work in the printing industry, preferably in a pre-press department.

Judy Eaton is an Associate Professor of Psychology at Wilfrid Laurier University. Her areas of research include social cognition, interpersonal relationships, conflict resolution, and restorative justice. Much of her research focuses on the use of apology and forgiveness in the resolution of interpersonal conflict.

Mark D. Johns is an Associate Professor of Communication Studies at Luther College in Decorah, Iowa. His research interests include religious expressions on the internet, uses of social networking applications by groups and organizations, and internet research ethics.

Michael A. Katovich is a Professor of Sociology in the Department of Sociology and Anthropology at Texas Christian University. He has written a variety of articles on various subjects from a symbolic interactionist perspective.

David Kirschner earned his Ph.D. in Sociology at Nanyang Technological University in Singapore in 2014. His dissertation focused on how players make meaning in virtual environments and showed how players experience socialization into digital games. Leveraging his background in social science education, David's work brings together human-computer interaction, learning, literacy and new media.

Jennifer A. A. Lavoie is an Assistant Professor of Criminology at Wilfrid Laurier University. Her areas of research include stress and coping, mental health and justice, forensic psychology, and mixed methods designs. Her current program of research focuses on mental health issues within corrections and policing contexts.

Lara Lengel is a Professor in the Department of Communication at Bowling Green State University. She researches international and intercultural communication and new media. She is co-author of *Computer Mediated Communication: Social Interaction on the Internet* (with Thurlow & Tomic, Sage, 2004) and co-editor of *Casting Gender: Women and Performance in Global Contexts* (with John T. Warren, Eds., Peter Lang, 2005).

Simon Lindgren is a Professor in the Department of Culture and Media Studies at Umeå University, Sweden. He researches patterns of social organization, participation and conflict through discourse studies of digital culture.

Annette N. Markham is Associate Professor of Information Studies at Aarhus University, Denmark and Affiliate Professor of Communication at Loyola University, Chicago. Her current research explores innovative and cross-disciplinary methodologies for studying contexts of complexity. She also studies ethics of internet research and identity practices in digitally-saturated culture. She is author of the book *Life Online: Researching Real Experience in Virtual Space* (Alta Mira, 1998), and co-editor of *Internet Inquiry: Dialogue Among Scholars* (with Nancy Baym, Sage, 2009).

Justin A. Martin is a Ph.D. student at Southern Illinois University, Carbondale where he is specializing in the sociology of education. His research interests lay in social inequalities and social justice, specifically in the areas of education and human sexualities. A version of his master's thesis, "Simulating the Orgy: Commodification, Consumption and Paid Sex Work in *Second Life*" was chosen for the 2010 Carl Couch Internet Research Award.

Victoria Ann Newsom is a Professor of Communication Studies at Olympic College in Bremerton, Washington. Her research centers on the negotiation of power, gender, and identity in performative and communication contexts. Her current projects include work in media activism, peace studies, postcolonial feminism(s), performative pedagogies, and cultural studies-grounded analyses of transnational policy making.

Carrie B. Sanders is an Associate Professor of Criminology at Wilfrid Laurier University. Her theoretical areas of interest are social construction of technology, symbolic interactionism, and critical criminology. Her research interests include qualitative methodologies, technology and organizational change and policing. Her ethnographic research on police information technologies is funded by the Social Sciences and Humanities Research Councils of Canada through an Insight Development Grant.

Avi Shoshana is a Senior Lecturer at the Faculty of Education, University of Haifa, Israel. His research interests have focused on social psychology, ethnographies of the self, emotions, ethnicity; culture, subjectivities and education. His current research looks at ethnographies of self transformations in Israel; self, education and social classes; Technology, sexuality and alternative cultures.

Matthew Smith is a graduate student in the Criminology Master's program at Wilfrid Laurier University. His research interests include physical health and perceptions of self among youth in custody. His current research focuses on the role of physical strength, nutrition and self-perception of strength competence in protecting against victimization among incarcerated youth.

Zahirah Suhaimi-Broder is a Sociology graduate from Nanyang Technological University, where she assisted in research studying the role of new media technologies in shaping social experience. Her research interests include studying the relationship between new media discourse and political-economic contexts and transnational political ecology.

Laura A. Terlip (Ph.D., University of Oklahoma; M.Sc., London School of Economics) is an Associate Professor in the Department of Communication Studies at the University of Northern Iowa where she teaches courses in organizational communication, communication ethics, and research methods. She has a wide range of research interests in applied communication and currently is working on several projects focused on the influence of visual communication at work, the need to include communication ethics in STEM education, and the development of better understanding of how popular culture images of work affect the personal meanings we make of our work.

J. Patrick Williams is an Associate Professor of Sociology at Nanyang Technological University, where he teaches courses on culture, social psychology, and media. His research interests revolve around the roles that new media technologies play in mediated personal and cultural experiences.

Printed and bound by CPI Group (UK) Ltd, Croydon, CR0 4YY
17/09/2026
14964145-0001